LIKABILITY FACTOR

THE BOOK OF
INFLUENCE

BASED ON THE WORK BY
DALE CARNEGIE

CREATED BY MULTI #1 INTERNATIONAL BEST-SELLING AUTHOR & AWARD WINNING SPEAKER ON HABITS

ERIK "MR AWESOME" SWANSON

LIKABILITY FACTOR

THE BOOK OF INFLUENCE

LIKABILITY FACTOR

FEATURING

ERIK SWANSON

BOB DONNELL ~ JESSICA RADETSKY ~ JON KOVACH JR.

FOREWORD BY ERIC LOFHOLM

#1 BESTSELLER

Orders by U.S. trade bookstores and wholesalers.

Email: Info@BeyondPublishing.net and Team@IntegrityPub.com

Manufactured and printed in the United States of America and distributed globally by Beyond Publishing and Integrity Publishing.

Library of Congress Control Number:
Hardback ISBN: 978-0-9894136-8-8
Paperback ISBN: 978-0-9894136-6-4

THE BOOK OF INFLUENCE TESTIMONIALS

"Classics are here for a reason. This is exactly the case when it comes to the books and trainings by Dale Carnegie. What an honor to join Erik Swanson and so many other leaders in a modern-day book series bringing the principles into today's era."

Brian Tracy ~ Author, Speaker, Motivator ~ BrianTracy.com

"If you want the best information from the top influencers from around the world - look to International #1 Bestseller Erik Swanson and the team of influencing authors. I am honored to be among those collaborating to give the most important steps in how to influence in today's world. This book series must be in your library and among your top reads! It's important for today's world of connectivity and trust to be filled with rich information you can implement right now for your success!"

Jill Lublin ~ International Speaker, Master Publicity Expert and Bestselling Author ~ JillLublin.com

"What an honor to join such leaders from around the world in sharing our secrets, techniques, and principles of success in building relationships based on like and trust. Dale Carnegie has had either a direct or indirect influence on everyone throughout the world. Allow these 4 books, in this soon to be a future classic series, to change your life and your relationships forever."

Erik "Mr. Awesome" Swanson ~ Multi Time #1 International Bestselling Author, Award Winning Speaker, Featured on Ted Talks and Amazon Prime TV, Founder & Creator of Speaker Hearts International ~ SpeakerHearts.com

"What a classic book Dale Carnegie wrote in 1936. *How to Win Friends and Influence People* has changed so many lives in business and in personal relationships throughout the world. It definitely changed my life. Grab this book series and hold on tight, as it will take you from so-so to hero in your relationships if you put the techniques into practice."

Alec Stern ~ America's Startup Success Expert, Entrepreneur, Keynote Speaker, Business Startup Mentor, Investor ~ AlecSpeaks.com

"Having been a student of life-long learning and self-development and following the teachings of the late, great Dale Carnegie, it is my honor to be included in this profound body of work of Erik Swanson's *The Book of Influence*. The messaging in this series will impact people from all walks of life because of it's simplicity and applicable principles."

Bob Donnell ~ Founder of Everything Next Level, Human Behaviorist Author of *Mastering Your Inner Game, Connectology, The Art Of Intervention, 30 Days To Your Next Level, The 13 Steps to Riches* ~ EverythingNextLevel.com

"What an honor to be included in this beautiful series produced by my ever-inspiring friend Erik Swanson! These books offer a fresh view on influence and the work of Dale Carnegie, who's subjects are as relevant today as when they were first published back in 1936. Every book in this series is a must read!"

Jessica Radetsky ~ Founder of Broadway Hearts, 17 Year Broadway Performer on Phantom of the Opera, Breathwork Trainer ~ BroadwayHearts.org

"As a big believer and implementer of the principles of Dale Carnegie's work in *How To Win Friends And Influence People*, I highly recommend diving into this book series so that you can deepen your knowledge and understanding of the power of influence. Erik Swanson has created a masterpiece in highlighting modern-day examples of true influence."

Jon Kovach Jr. ~ International Motivational Speaker, Founder of Champion Circle, Habitude Warrior Mastermind Team Lead, #1 Bestselling Author ~ SpeakerJonKovachJr.com

"Becoming fully self-authentically expressed leads to a peaceful sense of gratitude, that leads to clarity, that is the bridge to untold riches. What you are is conscious of being! "

Sir James Dentley ~ Entrepreneur, Bestselling Author, Speaker, Business Strategist, Philanthropist ~ JamesDentley.com

"This is a collaboration of greatness! If you are ready to become an asset to every room you enter this book series is for you. Strategy, truth and principles that will endure for ages fill these pages. Dive in and get ready to rise!"

Danelle Delgado ~ Millionaire Maker, Business Strategist, Co-Founder of Engage Corporate Training ~ DanelleDelgado.com

"The definition of friendship, influence, leadership, and selling is the 'Transference of Trust.' Learning why and how to positively persuade others to redefine what's possible and to think, feel, act, follow, and buy is the most significant and valuable tool we can acquire in life. What an honor to join such influential leaders and honor the late, great Dale Carnegie."

Dan Clark ~ Speaker Hall of Fame & NY Times Bestselling Author ~ DanClark.com

"Bravo, Bravo, Bravo! Growing up in Italy with our family values and traditions was so important to learn and to bring into my adult years. We need to continue to teach these principles to our youth of today."

Sir Bruno Serato ~ Philanthropist, Founder of Caterina's Club, CNN Man of the Year, Bestselling Author, Owner and Chef of the Anaheim White House ~ AnaheimWhitehouse.com

"A MUST-READ for anyone looking to build long-lasting relationships and becoming an influence to the world."

Greg S. Reid ~ Award Winning Bestselling Author, Filmmaker, Speaker ~ GregReid.com

"The privilege of being alive and able to learn and grow is one of the most profound gifts we've been given. What an honor to write a chapter in this series and share in this profound conversation about how we expand what we do and become more kind, skilled, and effective communicators."

Jason W. Freeman ~ Author, Impediment Busting Speaker, Imperfect Best Mentor ~ JasonWFreeman.com

Global Speakers Mastermind &
Habitude Warrior Masterminds

Join us and become a member of our tribe! Our Global Speakers Mastermind is a virtual group of amazing thinkers and leaders who meet twice a month. Sessions are designed to be 'to the point' and focused while sharing fantastic techniques to grow your mindset as well as your pocketbooks. We also include famous guest speaker spots for our private Masterclasses. We also designate certain sessions for our members to mastermind with each other & and counsel on the topics discussed in our previous Masterclasses. It's time for you to join a tribe who truly cares about *YOU* and your future and start surrounding yourself with the famous leaders and mentors of our time. It is time for you to up-level your life, businesses, and relationships.

For more information to check out our Masterminds:
Team@HabitudeWarrior.com
www.DecideTobeAwesome.com

BECOME AN INTERNATIONAL
#1 BESTSELLING AUTHOR & SPEAKER

Habitude Warrior International has been highlighting award-winning Speakers and #1 Bestselling Authors for over 25 years. They know what it takes to become #1 in your field and how to get the best exposure around the world. If you have ever considered giving yourself the GIFT of becoming a well-known Speaker and a fantastically well known #1 Best-Selling Author, then you should email their team right away to find out more information in how you can become involved. They have the best of the best when it comes to resources in achieving the bestselling status in your particular field. Start surrounding yourself with the N.Y. Times Bestsellers of our time and start seeing your dreams become reality!

For more information to become a #1 Bestselling Author & Speaker on our Habitude Warrior Conferences
Please text the word AUTHORS to 619-304-6268
And also go to:
www.DecideToBeAwesome.com

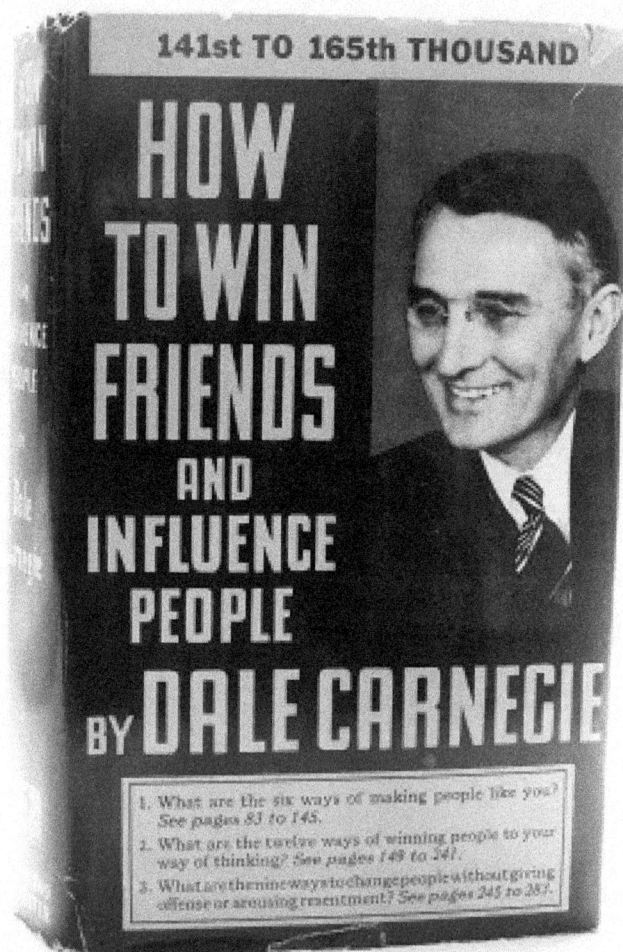

Acknowledgement to Dale Carnegie

I am honored and would like to acknowledge and thank Mr. Dale Carnegie for his dedication and influence to millions throughout the world. From his mentorship, leadership, philanthropy, and commitment to worldwide learning and education, Carnegie's legacy is unmatched.

We would like to pay tribute to his ongoing and continuous training, including his 1936 classic in self-improvement and interpersonal communication, *How to Win Friends and Influence People*, as well as the other legendary books and training programs he had created throughout the years. His influence reaches beyond the millions upon millions of students who have all taken part in his training around the world.

For this, I thank you Mr. Carnegie, from the bottom of my heart and the top of all our connections and relationships. Thank you for inspiring us all to build stronger connections, better trust, and genuine experiences with those who we serve. Let us all use our power of influence for the betterment and service toward others and make this world an amazing place to live!

~ Erik "Mr Awesome" Swanson & The Awesome Team of Authors
Multi #1 International Bestselling Author & Award Winning Speaker

CONTENTS

LIKABILITY FACTOR

INTRODUCTION TO THE BOOK OF INFLUENCE

BASED ON THE WORK BY DALE CARNEGIE

For the first time ever in history, 33+ professionals, celebrities, mentors, and authors are brought together by Multi #1 International Bestselling Author and Award Winning Speaker, Erik "Mr. Awesome" Swanson, to share modern-day examples, stories and applications in this book series based on the work by Dale Carnegie. The Book of Influence series consists of four books in which all of the book volumes dive deep into four vitally important classic areas.

In this National Bestselling series of The Book of Influence, each of the four volumes in the series will cover the following topics:

Book Volume #1 - AUTHENTIC COMMUNICATION

In the training by Dale Carnegie and in his classic NY Times Bestseller, How to Win Friends and Influence People, Carnegie focuses on the fundamental techniques in connecting with people. Volume #1 of The Book of Influence discusses and shares many principles and strategies in connecting with others in such an authentic way through modern core values.

Book Volume #2 - LIKABILITY FACTOR

In How To Win Friends and Influence People, Carnegie addresses the importance of building like and trust. Being likable and utilizing our modern-day techniques are paramount in building long-lasting relationships and foundations with others. Learn the secrets to becoming 'likable' so that the world finds you irresistible, magnetic and people seem to be drawn to you.

Book Volume #3 - CREATING ALIGNMENT

A big part of Dale Carnegie's training is on influence. He taught how to influence others and gain their cooperation: avoid arguments, show respect for others' opinions, never say "you're wrong," admit your mistakes, begin in a friendly way, get the other person saying "yes," and let the other person do most of the talking. This volume in the series will highlight lessons, stories, and teachings from our authors in this universal law with counsel on creating alignment for success.

Book Volume #4 - WIN-WIN THEORY

Dale Carnegie's trainings always consisted of lessons in how to become a leader. In volume #4 of The Book of Influence - Win-Win Theory, our readers are taught to create Win-Win relationships through various theories and philosophies of professionals who have use time-tested techniques that always begin with praise and honest appreciation.

The Book of Influence emphasizes the importance of treating people with respect and dignity, building positive relationships, and creating win-win outcomes in an authentic way. This National Bestselling book series provides practical advice and counsel derived by experience to improving one's communication and social skills. It can be used by anyone looking to improve their personal and professional relationships for success.

FOREWORD BY ERIC LOFHOLM

The Powerful Benefits of Likability

Being likable matters in every aspect of our lives! Being likable matters in every relationship we have. The reason is because being likable increases the likelihood that other people say yes to us.

When I was a teenager and into my early twenties, I didn't have a clue how to get what I wanted. As a young man, I wanted what many young men want. Here are some of the things I wanted: I wanted to get into a good college. I wanted to get a good job. I wanted to have a girlfriend. I wanted to have more money. I had no idea what to do to create what I wanted.

At age twenty-two, I got my first sales job. In sales, being likable is required if you want to get good at making sales. My first year I struggled. I was the bottom producer out of a team of about fifteen sales reps. I was introduced to the sales of ideas of sales training genius, Dr. Donald Moine. Dr. Moine had spent a career learning the science of persuasion. With his ideas, I quickly became the top producer!

From Dr. Moine, I learned that I could predictably get people to like me if I followed certain principles. One of those principles is sincere flattery. Another is active listening. I became hooked on learning how I could get people to like me!

I continued to study the top sales and influence minds in the world including Tony Robbins, Robert Cialdini, Brian Tracy, Tom Hopkins, Zig

Ziglar, Jay Abraham and many others. With my new knowledge I began to create what I wanted.

Likability is a learned skill. This book provides instruction on how you can instantly become more likable. Here are some ideas to consider as you are getting ready to read this book:

If you work for someone, does your boss like you?
If you have people who work for you, does your team like you?
If you have kids, do your kids like you?
If you are married, does your spouse like you?
If you have business partners, do your business partners like you?
Do your neighbors like you?
If you have customers or clients, do they like you?

If, after reflecting on these questions, you discover that there are key people in our like who may not like you, then set the intention that you will become more likable! Study this book and implement the best ideas and watch your life transform!

The man who asked me to write the forward is Erik Swanson. Erik is one of the most positive people I have ever met! I like being around positive people. Erik is someone who is always looking to add value! Erik thinks of other people! Erik is friendly! Eric posts positive things on social media! Erik is likable because he is BEING likable—as in his state of being. Because Erik is so likable, he has developed a global network of friends and clients all over the world!

The last thing I would like to share with you before you start reading the book is to explore in your own mind what are the characteristics of a likable person. In my experience, being likable is a choice. It is my choice to BE likable. It is my choice to be friendly or not. It is my choice to offer to help someone who needs help or not. It is my choice to be kind or not. It is my choice to be my word or not. It is my choice to encourage others or not.

These choices have a direct impact on whether people like me or not. If they like me, they will likely help me, buy from me, say yes to me, and support me. If they don't like me, they will likely do none of these things and they may even try to block my progress or success.

If I want someone to like me, if I look at their experience with me from there viewpoint, I can gain insight into how to be likable with them.

Enjoy the book. Soak in the ideas! Most importantly, take action on the ideas you learn!

Success,

Eric Lofholm
CEO – Eric Lofholm International
CEO – Being Movement, LLC

ERIC LOFHOLM

Eric Lofholm is a Master Sales Trainer who has taught his proven sales systems to thousands of professionals around the world. He is President and CEO of Eric Lofholm International, Inc., an organization he founded to train people on the art and science of selling professionally.

Eric began his career as a sales failure. At his first sales job, he was put on quota probation after failing to meet the minimum quota two months in a row. It was at this point that Eric met his sales mentor. After being professionally trained, Eric achieved his quota and eventually became the top producer at that company. Eric went on to become the top producer at two more companies before starting Eric Lofholm International.

Eric is a naturally gifted teacher. For over 14 years, Eric has been sharing his proven sales-increasing ideas with people worldwide.

Eric believes that selling equals service. He also believes in mastering the fundamentals of lead generation, appointment setting, and delivering a high-quality presentation.

Eric has delivered over 1,500 public and private presentations in companies such as:

Microsoft, Smith Barney, Primerica, State Prison, Bell South, Norwest Mortgage, Bank of New York, GTE, Lexus, World Financial Group, Citicorp, MCI, ERA, Sega, Chamber of Commerce, Toastmasters Century 21, RE/MAX, Bell Atlantic, Texas Instruments, Ford Motor Company, Mary Kay, Excel Communications, Chrysler, Pritchett and Associates, Ikon, Sheraton, Nabisco, Time Warner, Silicon Graphics, Toyota Prudential, Acordia, Phillips, The U.S. Army, Fortis, Olde Discount Brokers, Merrill Lynch, Coldwell Banker, Sebastiani Vineyards, Hilton, Danka, Sun Microsystems, Pitney Bowes, Acura, and Honda.

He is also an instructor for CEOSpace and Networking University.

Eric is the author of *How to Sell in the New Economy*, *How to Master the Science of Goal Setting*, and *21 Ways to Close More Sales*.

Eric and his two children, Brandon and Sarah, live in Rocklin, California.

www.EricLofholm.com

LIKABILITY FACTOR

ERIK SWANSON

TO LIKE OR BE LIKED... THAT IS THE QUESTION!

....

"Happiness doesn't depend on any external conditions, it is governed by our mental attitude."
~ **Dale Carnegie**

Early in my career in the self-development space, I learned how important it truly is to become a person who is likable. I saw the need to learn this all-important skillset and make it a daily habit of mine.

It is so true that people around the world want to surround themselves with like-minded and positive people. They want to see that there is hope in the world. They want to see that other people are living lives of abundance and happiness and that they, too, can live this way.

I decided to set a goal to become a person who others would want to surround themselves with. I wanted to become a magnet for success. One way to become a magnet is to simply appeal to other people's senses. Harness a magnetism in you that other see and want to spend more time with. So, my journey started to develop these skills.

Become a Magnet

Why should we strive to become a magnet in the world? Well, magnets draw things towards them. It is a universal law that with a strong enough magnet, you can draw even the strongest of forces.

As too, with people, you can become magnetic. Have you ever heard people say the phrase, "They are so magnetic"? That is a good thing. In fact, that is a great thing!

To have a magnetic personality is to bring in those around you to look at you in such a way to be drawn to you. They can't help it. They literally don't know why they are drawn so much to you, but they are.

You can use this to your advantage. Notice I said, "to your advantage," rather than "take advantage of." I will share amazing techniques and principles in this chapter for you to build upon, but only if you use it for good, not evil. I'll be watching you!

In *How to Win Friends and Influence People*, Dale Carnegie addresses the importance of building like and trust. Being likable and utilizing our modern-day techniques are paramount in building long-lasting relationships and foundations with others. Learn the secrets to becoming 'likable' so that the world finds you irresistible, magnetic, and people seem to be drawn to you.

Major Key Techniques to Live By

Be genuinely interested: It is far better to be interested rather than interesting. Show a sincere interest in the people you're communicating with. Ask open-ended questions and listen actively to their responses.

Be a good listener: Stress the value of being an attentive listener. Encourage people to ask questions and engage in meaningful conversations to understand others better.

Give honest appreciation: Acknowledge the value and contributions of others. Be specific in your compliments and praises. Seek out opportunities to praise them, rather than looking for opportunities to correct them.

Speak in terms of the other person's interests: Tailor your communication to address the interests and needs of your audience. Show that you understand their perspective. I do this by paraphrasing or repeating what they just shared with me. This shows you are paying attention and that you understand.

Smile: Smiling opens up positive communication. Smiling can also be heard in your voice and it helps create a positive impression and response.

Tonality in your voice: I always strive to match the tonality of the other person. This allows the other person to feel more comfortable and open · up more.

Use dynamic and positive language: Frame your messages in a positive and empowering way. Avoid negative or discouraging language. Not only will this help the other person feel more comfortable and at ease, but it will also leave a positive impression even long after the actual conversation. Infuse your communication with enthusiasm and energy. Vary your tone and pace to keep your audience engaged.

Share compelling stories: Share personal anecdotes and stories that illustrate your points and make your messages more relatable to the person you are in a conversation with.

Use good eye contact: Train yourself to actually make good eye contact while in conversation with others. This is vitally important. It promotes listening skills and allows the other person to subconsciously appreciate your attention. Note: In today's world where we have many conversations virtually, rather than in-person, I always promote the use of Zoom on video. Seeing the other person's eyes and expressions is so important these days.

Empower and inspire: Focus on inspiring and motivating your audience. Encourage them to take action and believe in their potential.

When you are uplifting to them, they will open up more and share more with you.

Have an Action-Oriented Approach: Encourage individuals to take awesome action towards their goals. Promote the idea that success is a result of consistent effort and resilience in the face of challenges. The more successful they become, the more likable you become in their eyes.

Mindset and beliefs: Emphasize the power of a positive mindset and the role of belief in achieving success. Encourage individuals to overcome limiting beliefs and adopt a growth mindset.

Connect emotionally: Build a strong emotional connection with your audience by expressing empathy and understanding their challenges and aspirations. When you open up to them, they will in turn feel more comfortable opening up to you.

Remember that developing likability in your communication style takes practice and self-awareness. It's important to adapt these principles to your own personality and voice while staying true to the essence of each of these influential speakers. Additionally, keep in mind your specific audience and their needs, as effective communication often requires tailoring your approach to the situation and the people you are addressing.

Honoring Others

One of the best ways to create a likable personality is to appeal to others within their interests. Uplift them by asking great questions that open up the conversation. Strive to have them do most of the talking. This will allow them to talk more about themselves, rather than having us do most of the talking. My personal rule of thumb is the ratio: 2 to 1. I'm sure all of us have heard of the saying that we have 2 ears and 1 mouth, therefore we should listen twice as much. So, my 2 to 1 ratio is simply where I ask them 2 questions to any one of my answers or stories.

What's Your Name Again?

This is a question you never want to ask. Studies tell us that everyone's favorite word in the world is their own name. They love to hear it. It makes them feel super comfortable. If you think about it, it's one of the first words we constantly hear as a child.

I used to be terrible at recalling people's names. I used to go up to them and try to fake that I remembered it. I would say things like, "How do you spell your name again?" They would reply: "B-O-B—how do *you* spell Bob?" It would make me so embarrassed.

Then, I decided to develop this awesome strategy. Saying something like, "I'm sorry, I am terrible at recalling names" emphasizes the fact that I'm terrible at it and I would never actually get better, either. So, instead, I now use this statement: "That's not like me; I'm usually really great at recalling people's names. Can you share it with me again, please?" They would always feel more comfortable sharing their name with me and it would also support my new habit of remembering names.

3 Step Process in Recalling Names

1) Place their name in the beginning of your first sentence.
2) Place their name towards the end of the next sentence.
3) Repeat their name 3 to 5 times… NOT out loud!

Let me give you a quick example of this. Let's say you just met someone and they just shared their name with you. Let's say their name is Morgan. You want to implement the 3 steps above. So, it would sound like this: *"Morgan, great to meet you today. Hey, let me ask you a quick question, Morgan."*

Then you want to say the name "Morgan" 3 to 5 times in your mind. Trust me, they next time you run in to Morgan, you will most likely recall her name and impress her with your interest in her, which in turn makes you a likable person.

Give all of these techniques a try and implement them in to your every day habits and you will soon see yourself turn into a magnetic personality and soon master the art of of the likability factor.

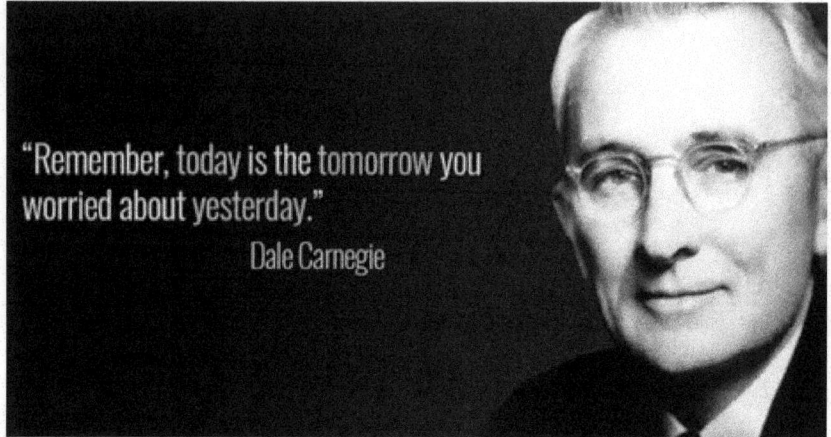

"Remember, today is the tomorrow you worried about yesterday."
Dale Carnegie

ERIK SWANSON

As an Award-Winning International Keynote Speaker and Multi Time #1 International Bestselling Author, Erik "Mr. Awesome" Swanson is in great demand around the world! He speaks to an average of more than one million people per year. Mr. Swanson has the honor to have been invited to speak to many schools around the world including the prestigious Harvard University. He is also a recurring Faculty Member of CEO Space International as well as an Alumni Keynoter at Vistage Executive Coaching. Erik's speeches can be found on Amazon Prime TV as well as joining the Ted Talk Family with his latest speech called, "A Dose of Awesome."

Erik got his start in the self-development world by mentoring directly under Brian Tracy. Quickly climbing to become the top trainer around the world from a group of over 250 handpicked coaches, Erik started to surround himself with the best of the best and very quickly started to be invited to speak on stages alongside such greats as Jim Rohn, Bob

Proctor, Les Brown, Sharon Lechter, Jack Canfield, Lisa Nichols, and Joe Dispenza—just to name a few. Erik has created and developed the super-popular Habitude Warrior Conference, which has a two-year waiting list and includes 33 top-named speakers from around the world. It is a 'Ted Talk' style event which has quickly climbed to one of the top 10 events not to miss in the United States! He is the creator, founder, and CEO of the Habitude Warrior Mastermind and Global Speakers Mastermind. He is also the creator and publisher of *The 13 Steps To Riches* book series as well as *The Principles of David & Goliath* book series. His motto is clear: "NDSO!": No Drama – Serve Others!

www.SpeakerErikSwanson.com

BOB DONNELL

LIKABILITY THROUGH GENUINE LISTENING & CONVERSATIONS

**"Speak in such a way that others enjoy hearing
what you have to say; listen with an openness that
makes others open up more freely."
~ Bob Donnell**

Likability is often the key ingredient in success. Decisions drive our actions, yet their foundation often rests upon how well we connect and communicate with others. Dale Carnegie once underscored the significance of making people like you; now that communication spans continents within seconds, these principles have become more essential.

Over my two decades of studying human behavior and working with respected figures like Garth Brooks, Evander Holyfield, and Will Smith, I've come to appreciate that meaningful conversation can be the cornerstone of influence. To influence effectively means mastering genuine listening and conversation.

Help People Feel Valued

I want to share one lesson from my personal journey: When faced with heart-wrenching experiences such as the death of my 3-year-old daughter in an accident, I learned the hard way that sharing our vulnerabilities is what truly makes us relatable; by sharing pieces of ourselves—our true selves—with others, you make them feel valued—not always about business but often about human connection and connection!

Listen Intently

Imagine being in the presence of Wayne Gretzky or Reba McIntyre; their presence can be absolutely astounding, yet what I noticed from them during backstage Grammy's and Academy Awards shows was their power of listening—when they listened, they focused entirely on who was speaking—making sure each individual felt heard, seen, and valued; thus adhering to one of Dale Carnegie's principles with flair: being genuinely interested in other people is an artform that transforms lives!

An Easy Way to Be an Engaging Conversationalist

Real conversations don't depend on flashy words or the showoff of knowledge: they rely on mutual sharing between participants. By listening attentively, asking relevant questions, and showing genuine interest, you can lay the foundation for memorable dialogues that build lasting bonds between individuals. "It's all about who you are, not what you do" is something I often say when speaking with colleagues about my job as an interviewer.

At Arbonne International and for other clients alike, I always emphasize the principle of interest over introduction. Conversations often progress more naturally by showing genuine curiosity for people you meet; when introduced instead, interactions become transactional.

How to Interest People

Take the Next Level by Association (NLBA) approach as an example: What was distinctive was the emphasis placed on genuine relationship currency, on building rapport and trust with one another rather than pushing business cards or making sales pitches; instead, it focused on making authentic human connections that resonated with our desire for genuine human connection—no doubt why Dale Carnegie emphasized genuine interest as the keystone of likability!

THE BOOK OF INFLUENCE

How To Win People Over

Remember when I said likability was the secret ingredient? Here's my recipe for success:

Genuine Interest: Being genuinely interested in knowing, understanding, and supporting another individual doesn't involve pretending. Instead, it involves truly seeking to know, understand, and assist that person.

Active Listening: Listening actively means considering the emotions behind words heard rather than just hearing words spoken out loud.

Sharing Vulnerabilities: Your vulnerabilities, stories, and life experiences should not be seen as weaknesses; instead, they serve as gateways to deeper relationships.

Being Present: With so much noise around today, being fully present during conversations is the greatest compliment you can pay someone.

Authenticity: Be genuine in all interactions; people can quickly differentiate between genuine interest and faked courtesy.

Boundaries

Alignment is necessary when communicating with others and creating mutual likability. That can enhance your connection and relationship when you decide to align yourself with someone, even if you completely disagree with them on a belief system, such as hot topics like politics or opinions. Also, aligning with them in something you can agree on accelerates likability, even if you disagree on many other concepts. When I look at likability, one of the most incredible things we can do to create likability is to know and reaffirm our boundaries.

Boundaries are essential for likability because people love knowing where they can and can't go. People love to know what they can and can't say. People love to know what your beliefs are and how you're going to affirm those. Unfortunately, we occasionally acquiesce, leaving people guessing whether they like us based on how we respond when they disagree.

I think boundaries are probably one of the best things we can do for people, even though at first they're like, "I don't like that boundary." But guess what? They know what they can and can't do now and begin to love you for it because now they know.

For anyone aspiring to reach the next level in their personal or professional lives, mastering conversation and genuine listening are two indispensable skills that will take them there. They form the basis of influence and are essential steps toward unparalleled success. From my journey through life's highs and lows, I have discovered that every interaction offers opportunities to learn, share knowledge, grow personally, and influence others.

As Dale Carnegie rightly observed, we can make more friends in two months by becoming interested in others than by trying to gain their interest. Let's embark on this journey of genuine relationships and create a life filled with meaningful conversations!

~ Bob Donnell, founder of Everything Next Level.

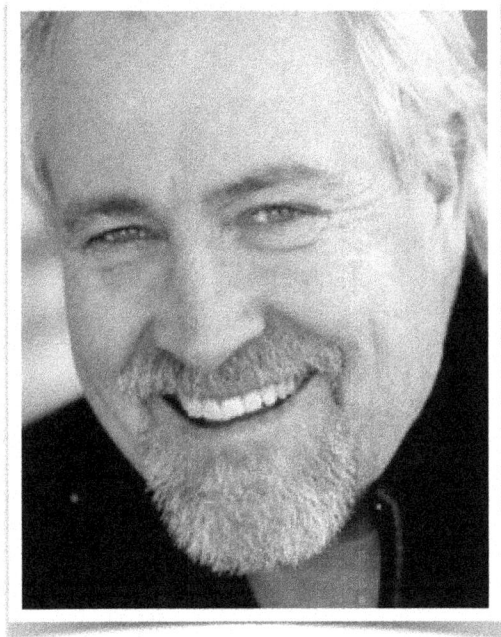

BOB DONNELL

In the growing world of personal development and strategic coaching, few people are as well respected and adored as Bob Donnell. Combining a heart-centered authenticity with winning strategies for business and life, Bob has separated himself as a true leader in the industry.

Having cultivated an entrepreneurial spirit at an early age, he started his first non-profit organization at 19, focused on helping at-risk families in crisis. From there, Bob made an impact in the world of sales and management until he decided to devote the entirety of his life to helping others in transformation. That road, however, wasn't arrived at easily.

From growing up in poverty to never knowing his father, from the untimely loss of his mother during his teen years to tragically losing his 3-year-old daughter in a freakish car accident, Bob decided that life is too short to continue struggling. He has since devoted his life and business to helping others design their life by getting the results they've been wanting to see. Now, as a Human Behaviorist, Bob continues to work with entrepreneurs, sales professionals, celebrities, professional athletes, as well as any who desires to take their life and business to the next level. He focuses on aligning your behavior with your desired results in order to help you achieve outrageous results in every area of your life.

Bob's body of work includes authoring several Books, recording audio programs, hosting radio programs, and currently hosts a weekly live video-streaming, interactive program with members worldwide. Bob has worked with a distinguished list of clients, including Coldwell Banker, Long Beach Grand Prix, Arbonne International, ReMax, World Ventures, Oakley Inc., and Pre-Paid Legal. In addition, Bob has loved working within the entertainment industry; the Academy Awards, the WB Music Awards, Victor Awards, The Grammy's and, as a result, has been able to interact with and study some of the great artists in the world including Garth Brooks, Wayne Gretzky, Evander Holyfield, The Backstreet Boys, Eddie George, Reba McIntyre, and Will Smith, and a host of others.

The culmination of Bob's 20+years of studying human behavior has led him to create Everything Next Level over a decade ago, which continues to stand as a beacon for those desperately looking to take their lives to the next level. His expertise in knowing the human condition and the keys to getting stronger, faster results sets him apart from his peers.

Simply put, Bob Donnell gets results. If you're looking to take your life or business to the Next Level, there's no better time than the present to start getting results that speak for themselves.

www.EverythingNextLevel.com

JESSICA RADETSKY

CURTAIN CALL: INFLUENCE & LIKABILITY THROUGH THE LENS OF A BROADWAY PERFORMER

When my dear friend of 30+ years, Erik Swanson, asked me to contribute a chapter to this book, I was thrilled. Then I began to think in earnest about the concept of being liked. What does it mean to be liked? Am I liked? What makes one person more likable than another? And how might my experiences on a Broadway stage relate to those on the other side of the footlights.

When people think of Broadway, they picture a vast world of lights, music, dance and excitement. The theaters where this magic happens are a tourist destination for the entire planet. Years ago, when I first started performing in *The Phantom of the Opera*, I had the same landscape in my mind. I quickly realized that life in a Broadway show can often feel like a little snow globe of a world, utterly unique and all consuming to those inside. In truth, 'Broadway' consists of merely 18 blocks of real estate. There are 41 Broadway theaters packed into less than a mile. Within this little rectangle, — actors, dancers, musicians, stage managers, stagehands, ushers, dressers, etc, gather eight times a week (six evening, and two matinee performances), to tell stories. There are upwards of a hundred people under one roof, all finding a way to work along side each other in harmony. Many thousands of hopeful performers audition every year for a handful of roles in Broadway productions. I remember vividly a director once telling me that, in a climate where talent is abundant, sometimes the final choice in an audition will come down to who might be a better fit, personality-wise, for the company.

When I thought about this chapter, the excitement of what to share started building, but how to begin? Should I focus solely on mindset highlighting the differences of what's needed, mentally, in an audition room vs working within a Broadway show? Should I focus on the dynamics of the Broadway community, which like any community, can be lovely and supportive, but also at times can be quite competitive and unkind. Perhaps I should focus on how to handle the excitement and/or stress of live theater where anything can happen? There were so many avenues to take, I could have written a chapter on each. Ultimately, I returned to the book from which this book is inspired.

When I first read Dale Carnegie's 'How to Win Friends and Influence People', it struck me that I'd been witnessing his principles in action for most of my life, in the day to day behavior of my parents.

My mother, Nancy, is an extremely generous, appreciative person. She always has been. She's the kind of person who will stop a stranger on the street to tell them she likes a garment they're wearing. She's the kind of person who changes the course of another person's day. She makes others feel valued and important no matter who they are. People have always wanted to be around her and have asked after her. She will notice and take delight in things which aren't obvious, and with a sincerity that often brings tears to my eyes. She's also funny, and the combination of these facets are like a magical elixir to be around.

Live theater, which is about as collaborative a space as one can find themselves, requires utilizing these qualities which my enchanting mom came by so gracefully. Being likable is essential in a backstage environment. The tiny 8x8 area where I used to warm up for the show at Phantom was shared with several colleagues. I'd do my ballet warmup at a makeshift barre located directly under the stage. The barre was actually the railing of a bridge where we'd cross from one side of the theater to the other. The bridge was suspended over a deep cavern which housed, among other scenery, automated candelabras, which rose and fell through little trap doors in the stage all throughout the show. To my right were two stagehands getting into their period 'stagehand' costumes and across from me sat a trumpet player warming up with a silencer on the bell of his horn. The wall which he leaned against was the wall of the orchestra pit and if we peeked through the sliver of door next to him, we could see the audience arriving for the show. To my left were two fellow dancers warming up.

Warming up was crucial. Our stage was made from a steel material which could withstand pyrotechnics, heavy scenery and trap doors. Rumor was that it was the same material that WWII submarines were made from. It was fantastic for the show, however it was exceptionally hard to dance on, especially in pointe shoes, and we felt the residual effects on our muscles and joints each night at the end of a performance. In addition, our dressing room was on the 7th floor of the theater, making our count of stairs soar around 800 for each performance. Double that for a two show day. Our own daily Stairmaster! Our individual warmups varied from night to night, but we always came together right before the 'places' call for a timed, group plank. Our little area looked a bit like a clown car except with much more delicate shoes.

During a Broadway show, there is intricate backstage choreography, with large set pieces and heavy costumes, mostly performed in the dark and if something isn't done correctly, it could result in serious harm. In my own backstage choreography or 'track' as we call it, I had five exits where I left the stage, ran down a flight of stairs, crossed the basement bridge, ran up another flight of stairs, changed into a different costume and entered the stage on the opposite side. All in under 5 minutes. I had dressers, wig personnel and crew members to help me with these quick changes. It was imperative that we all had a deep appreciation for each other's contributions to the production so that our show could succeed at it's highest level. Having my mother's magical combination of generosity and humor in mind, always set me on the right path.

Then there was my father, Peter. He was the best listener I've ever known. Most everyone who knew him had the same observation. He made you feel as if the conversation and the words you were saying were absolutely riveting. It was because he was actually interested in what you had to say. He never lost that curiosity. It was as if he truly saw you. That feeling of being 'seen' is unlike any other. My father, in so many ways, has shaped who I am. However it wasn't until I was an adult that I realized that listening, being genuinely present for another person, was one of the greatest gifts you could give.

Active listening in the professional world, means everything. In dance, it's inherent to the art form. On an artistic level, listening to the point of feeling the music in your body while dancing, can create a musicality and depth in performance that's magnetic to watch. Experiencing that feeling as a dancer can be quite profound. In an audition or rehearsal room where the responsibility is to learn choreography quickly or be able to apply a correction immediately, time is such that if you're not completely present in the moment, you might lose your opportunity. This could be devastating to a career. As an actor, listening is paramount to being a good scene partner. It is especially important in a long running show when one has performed the same scene hundreds of times. Our job is to make the audience believe it's the first time we're saying these words or having these thoughts on stage, that's not an easy task in a scene you might perform over 400 times in a year. Listening to your onstage partners, allowing for spontaneity within a scene, creates a space that allows a deeper connection, and that's malleable and fun to be a part of each night. It also makes the show compelling and unique for the audience.

Performing can be joyous, therapeutic and intoxicating. It can also be exceedingly tough on a person's psyche. Putting yourself out there to be judged and criticized is it's own exquisite type of torture. For the majority of performers, the audition/job ratio is heavily skewed towards auditioning, meaning, dealing with rejection might be a weekly occurrence. That's impossibly tough to handle. Time and time again, I've gone back to another of Carnegie's teachings, be your authentic self. It's all you have. In the performing arts world on a whole, the more authentic you are, the better chance you have of succeeding. The more 'you' you are, the better. Gone are the days of directors wanting everyone to look the same. Now is the time for your uniqueness to shine. Broadway is currently enjoying a renaissance of diversity and individualism where all are celebrated. The snow globe has never been more vibrant.

These days, the word 'Influencer' has become a much sought after moniker. Carnegie was way before his time with this concept. In today's world, I'd imagine he would've had 10M Instagram followers. In my experience, influence has always gone hand in hand with passion. When the thing I've been passionate about has felt infinite in its possibilities. Earlier in my life, I had a fear of public speaking. My heart would race, my legs would feel unsteady, and I'd want to run from the room. That changed when I founded my children's hospital outreach Foundation, Broadway Hearts. Broadway Hearts brings Broadway performers, music and joy to kids in treatment at children's hospitals across the country. The exuberance which I felt (feel) when I spoke about Broadway Hearts was such that time would fly by and I'd find myself still excitedly talking. My passion for what I was creating was invigorating, and therefore influenced others to become involved. Broadway Hearts was a melding of all of my worlds — my family (Broadway Hearts is dedicated to my father), the Broadway community, giving back, music, laughter. It was all of the things that I loved (still love!), and it has become one of the very best parts of my life. I've also found this idea of passion and influence to be true with teaching. It's been such a thrill and an honor to help young performers chase after their own dreams. I've found that the enthusiasm with which I'm able to share my hard earned knowledge, acts as a sort of buoy, that elevates the level upon which my students and I are able to connect.

So the question, I suppose, is…. How does one truly harness something as intangible as being likable? Dale Carnegie gives us very clear principles which we can follow, but once applied, what makes a person more or less likable than another? Is it humility? Is it passion? The right balance of the two? It might be hard to define, but we sure know it when we see it.

My husband, Bradley, is shy and introverted. I think he's ridiculously charming, though he would disagree. In fact, socially, he has a tough time fitting in. He's also an extraordinary performer. He's been in 12 (twelve!) Broadway shows, numerous Broadway tours, Off-Broadway shows and regional productions. I could write an entire book on his career. However, it's his second passion as a voice teacher that I'm going to spotlight. He teaches a beautiful technique which only a few people in the world teach, and much of his time and energy is spent thinking of new ways to help his students improve. He delights in it. His support, knowledge and love for teaching allows his students to excel to levels they didn't dream were possible. When I listen to him teach or speak about his students and vocal technique, energetically he becomes radiant, and outwardly, it's mesmerizing. In these moments he is far from introverted, he is pure charisma.

Perhaps, rather than focusing on how likable we are, we might focus on being as skilled and driven about the things which give our lives meaning. Maybe the answer is to clearly define what you love inside your own little snow globe.

I've been very fortunate to have the most significant role models in life as my parents, I certainly haven't had to look far to find those to emulate. Through the daily actions of my parents, which also happen to mirror many of the core principles of Dale Carnegie, I've learned how to cultivate a genuine connection with loved ones, colleagues, students, a theater audience, and industry collaborators. With the authentic qualities of my parents in mind, I've not only been able to enhance the level of my performing ability, but also enrich my personal life and aspire for continued growth as a person.

As Phantom was nearing its final performance in April 2023, after 35 years occupying the northeast corner of 44th Street, my Production Stage Manager did a little math...

* I was a dancer in the Broadway company of *The Phantom of the Opera* for almost 21 years.

* My estimated number of shows performed in *The Phantom of the Opera*, on the Majestic Theater stage was 6,391!

* If "Jessica Radetsky" were a Broadway show, it would be the 6th longest running show of all time ... Just shy of *Cats*, tying *Les Miserables*, and surpassing *A Chorus Line*!

These statistics are somewhat difficult to wrap my brain around. My husband often reminds me that I have had, 'more Broadway work weeks in pointe shoes than any other pointe shoe wearer in the history of pointe shoe wearers on Broadway.' That's his phrasing, and it always makes me laugh. For my time spent in the theater and on the Broadway stage, it feels at once as though it went in slow motion and also as fast as a bullet train. These statistics also delight and profoundly move me.

However, it's the experiences I've had along the way that mean the most to me. Meeting my husband and the friends who now feel like family. Having the inspiration and time to create Broadway Hearts, and having the opportunity to teach and help younger performers achieve their dreams. And of course, the thousands of beautiful, diverse Broadway fans, I've met at stage doors who've honored me with their stories and shared love of live theater. It's these extraordinary elements of my life, in part, which I attribute to possessing the spirit of gratitude. Gratitude for my little snow globe of a world. If I am indeed a likable person, perhaps, it's a happy side effect of learning to be a thoughtful human being. I am so lucky.

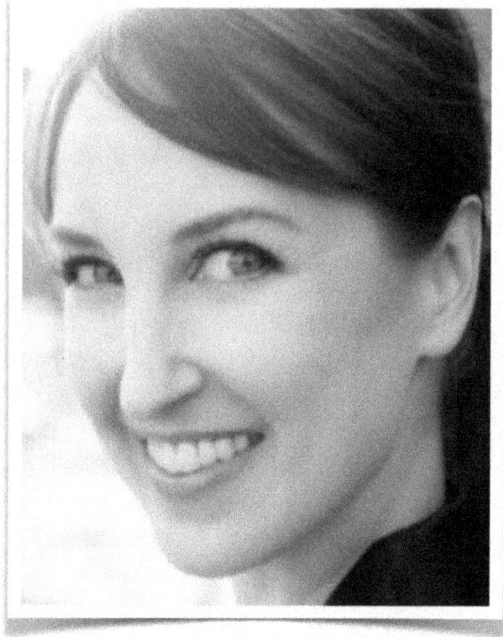

JESSICA RADETSKY

Jessica Radetsky is an artist and an entrepreneur. She began studying classical ballet at the age of 5, and has been dancing professionally since the age of 17. Her career has taken her all over the world. Some of the highlights include dancing with the Kirov Opera Ballet, in the Phantom of the Opera on Broadway, and in the Jazz Age dance group The Canarsie Wobblers.

In 2017, Jessica founded the children's hospital outreach nonprofit Broadway Hearts. Inspired by experiences with Make-A-Wish recipients, she focused on the idea of bringing a Broadway experience to children in treatment. Now a thriving foundation, her volunteers, all professional performers in and around Broadway, visit with, and bring music to kids in children's hospitals around the country.

www.JessicaRadetsky.com & www.BroadwayHearts.org

JON KOVACH JR.

THE LAWS OF MAGNETISM

. . . .

Likability in its own sense and meaning is magnetic or something I call the law of magnetism.

I have been a very likable person for as long as I can remember. My sister and I are very alike: charismatic, enthusiastic, positive, and optimistic. These positive qualities make up who we are and what we're recognized for. It is true for many that they are attracted to positive people because negative people create toxicity and negative emotions. Although my sister and I are very alike, I believe I inherited my qualities and skills from my mother. She always had a way of making sunshine from darkness. If her life were described as a lemonade stand, she would have made the world's best and most approachable lemonade business.

It's not hard to be likable, as many of these qualities are innate to humanity. But there's a difference between being likable and being a people pleaser. Too many people cannot see the difference, and when they see others who emit the qualities of a likable, magnetic person, they immediately think people pleaser. Likability is equal to attractiveness, magnetism, contagiousness, and stickiness. People pleasing is comparable to caring about what others think, adjusting actions for others, and disingenuously sharing positivity. Both are very effective ways of influencing people, but ultimately, one has the power to create the most significant relationships, solutions, and outcomes.

"You can make more friends in two months by becoming interested in other people than you can in two years by trying to get other people interested in you." ~ Dale Carnegie

At the Public Relations Student Society of America national assembly in Austin, Texas, I arrived to run for the office of the Vice President of Customer Relations/Member Services. I knew that I couldn't just win people over with a speech. I needed to get my hands dirty and meet as many people as possible, share a smile, learn people's names, build relationships, and earn the trust and respect of the national society leaders.

This was not an easy task, as there were over 200 student leaders, young professionals, and attendees to meet. Instead of stressing out about making a good impression, I constantly reminded myself and be interested in others. As I went about the assembly and conference meetings and sessions, I often would share in exchange, introduce myself, and ask about other people. Rather than campaigning and telling people who I was and what I was running for, I shared a genuine interest in learning about as many people as possible.

Two days into the assembly, it was time for me to give my speech and to ask the national leaders for their votes. The speaker before me, who I was running up against, was overly qualified for the position. If we compared resumes, she was the most qualified person for the job. But the difference between my speech and hers was when I got up there, I looked out across the sea of leaders and saw nothing but smiles and new friends. People had already learned my name, had a great conversation with me, and knew I was interested in them.

The leaders of the society cast their votes, and I won by a landslide. I heard my name over the pulpit when the results were announced: "Your new Vice President of Member Services on the National Committee for the Public Relations Student Society of America is Jon Kovach Jr." So many people stood up; you could say it was a standing ovation. I walked over and shook my competitor's hand, who looked disappointed. It seemed she had prepared for this position her entire college career.

As I shook hands with her, I told her that I was nearly as qualified for this position as she was and that I was more than willing to learn from somebody who knew what this society needed. I shared with her that I would build a committee and would like to invite her to be a part of it, as

I had a lot of learning to do. But mostly, I encouraged her to run for any unfulfilled positions on the committee.

She was shocked at my invitation and how I expressed genuine interest in having her on my committee. She was a true team player and was grateful. She did apply for an unfulfilled position and won with a resounding landslide. Ultimately, I was able to work with this individual, and we had the opportunity to sit on the board together.

I have a knack for swooping in and taking the win by a landslide. Compared to people with greater résumé and experience, it's like comparing apples to another foreign fruit. I may not have much experience, but likability is created through a genuine interest in others. Carnegie emphasized the importance of genuine interest in others as a way to be likable and build meaningful relationships.

At a public speaking competition in Salt Lake City, Utah, where I met Erik Swanson for the first time, I was registered as one of the candidate speakers. Still, I missed the entire first day of coaching, consultation, and speech practice. I was busy working and coaching a high school football team, which kept me away from the benefit of the event. I was told that all I needed to do was attend the second day and compete in the competition.

I was returning from coaching a football game when I received a text from the event organizer saying, "You're up next." I walked into the ballroom, somebody handed me a microphone, and I heard my name called as I stepped onto the stage: "Jon, Kovach Jr." I had no idea who was in the audience. I didn't even know who the judges were.

All I knew was I was supposed to give a three-minute speech, sharing a story and winning the judges' hearts. It seemed easy enough, but this time, I did not have a day of connecting and, relationships must be built to win the votes. Nonetheless, I did what I always do: tell incredible, exciting, enthusiastic stories. I talked about being an eight-year-old and going backpacking for the first time. It drew in the audience as if they were hiking with me. I focused on relating the story to everyday problems, which resonated with the audience, who were enthused with a speaker who finally spoke to them as if I had a magnetic interest in helping them overcome their challenges.

The speech created a standing ovation—again. Each of the judges asked, "Who are you? Where have you been? Why haven't we met you yet?" I smiled and said, "I'm Jon, and I'm delighted to meet you." I think I also won them over during the feedback and Q&A session, as I stood there, politely nodding while I received and expressed gratitude for each piece of advice. I was grateful to get feedback and was excited to improve my speaking skills. Overall, the judges favored me and gave me a high score. I was ranked number one in the competition going into the final round.

Erik Swanson approached me after the event and said, "I see a lot of myself in you. I completely resonate with your speaking style and stories. I think you're a great speaker." To have a celebrity like Erik Swanson say those things and share those qualities was like winning the jackpot. Although I went on to take second place in the competition, I felt like I had already won. Again, likability is less about pleasing people and more about being inquisitive and learning more about others.

"To be interesting, be interested."
~ Dale Carnegie

Carnegie encouraged individuals to show curiosity and engage with others in a way that makes them feel valued and important, ultimately making them more magnetic in social interactions.

Growing up in grade school, I had a lot of talents. To name a few, I was one of the fastest kids in the school; I was also an excellent dancer and could make up dance moves on the spot. I was a great communicator, and I could give presentations and talk all day. At recess, I would get that upbeat and energetic inspiration when I saw my crush on the playground. I would do funny, silly, and adventurous things in her sight to grab her attention. I thought it was a primal move to show her my talents so she would be impressed and want to be my girlfriend.

However, this couldn't be further from the truth. I can't tell you how often I did not learn my lesson by showing off my talents and then approaching my crush to ask her more about what she thought, only to find out that she felt I was a super show off—showing off? Yes, but I was showing her so that she would know how talented I was and how lucky she would be to be with me.

This is the wrong approach, and as a youngster, I took a while to learn this lesson. Again, it's not about showing off; it should be about others. When I thought I learned my lesson, I changed my strategies around. Instead of showing off my talents, I would find an appropriate opportunity to connect with my crush and learn about their dreams and goals. The more I listened, asked questions, and learned about them, the less work I had to do.

Not only did I win by taking an interest in others, but most people love to be heard, validated, and respected. If those are the qualities of likability, repeat them out loud every day. Here are three incredible affirmations to help you become more likable:

1) People love me because I'm a great listener.
2) People love me because I help validate others' truths and give life to their dreams.
3) I am a conduit of respect, and people feel respected around me.

These affirmations have incredible characteristics, and I highly recommend you repeat them aloud daily. Carnegie's believed that people love to talk about themselves and their interests, giving them a platform to share makes you more likable and magnetic in their eyes.

"Talk to someone about themselves, and they'll listen for hours."
~ Dale Carnegie

There is another angle to likability that one must know. Likability isn't just being likable but also about attracting and magnetizing people to you. I've met plenty of mean people, arrogant jerks, and more, yet many still like them. This anomaly has made me wonder and question what my belief is in likability.

How can someone so negative be so liked? People resonate with truth, and following these simple principles mentioned earlier, they create likability even when they are not likable at all. Again, they've mastered the art of magnetism by genuinely hearing the people's voices, seeking, expressing, validating, and commanding respect. People resonate with people who speak truth and knowledge and grind against normality and commonalities.

When you observe and listen to what people want and you talk to that, your name could be Winston Churchill or Adolf Hitler, yet people will still follow you. People also like you if you validate people's concerns, interests, and desires. And last, if you come in with respect and stand up for the people, you become incredibly likable. I can't tell you if one has a more significant influence over the other. Still, I can confidently say I've seen both examples, influencing millions in the United States and worldwide.

> *"The rare individual who unselfishly tries to serve others has an enormous advantage."*
> ~ Dale Carnegie

Carnegie stressed that being of service and helping others is a crucial aspect of likability and personal magnetism.

In Dale Carnegie's book, *How to Win Friends and Influence People*, he did not title the book, "How to be Liked and Influence People." I believe there's a reason for this, and the purpose behind his original title is less critical about manipulation, showing off, and having people follow you. Instead, the focus and mission are to create intentional communicators who influence the world through leadership, guidance, direction, and relationships. Otherwise, you might as well title that book or seminar on how to trick people into liking you. I know that sounds sinister, but I can't see it any other way. Likability is earned, but it doesn't have to be complicated. It can be a very natural process.

In the realm of social magnetism and the art of being likable, it's essential to cultivate an aura of magnetic energy that draws people towards you. This energy is rooted in authenticity and a genuine interest in others. One of the most potent techniques to harness this magnetism is active listening. When you engage in a conversation, focus entirely on the person speaking. Ask open-ended questions that invite them to share their thoughts, feelings, and experiences. Show empathy and understanding by validating their emotions. This makes the other person feel heard and valued and establishes a connection built on trust and mutual respect.

Charisma plays a significant role in this equation as well. While some individuals are naturally charismatic, it's a skill that can be developed and refined over time. Charisma is not about being the loudest voice in the room but rather about exuding confidence, warmth, and positivity. Smile genuinely, maintain eye contact, and use open body language. Share your own stories and experiences in a relatable manner, and don't be afraid to inject humor when appropriate. Charisma is infectious; when you radiate positivity and enthusiasm, others are more likely to be drawn to your magnetic energy.

Furthermore, to be a positive influence in others' lives, it's crucial to cultivate an attitude of kindness and generosity. Small acts of kindness, such as offering a helping hand, providing encouragement, or simply lending a listening ear, can profoundly impact how people perceive you. Remember that being likable isn't about manipulating others but building genuine connections based on trust and goodwill.

The power of social magnetism lies in your ability to authentically connect with others, using techniques like active listening and charisma to make a lasting positive impression. By being genuinely likable and fostering an environment of kindness and generosity, you can positively influence those around you, creating lasting bonds and enriching your own life.

When building a tribe, following, or influencer of others, I encourage you to quit focusing on the number of followers or social media statistics. I can promise you that the true reward is knowing that you've influenced somebody's life to some extent by serving them and creating that likability within each other.

Too many people are trying to attract followers that they don't like. I believe likability is a two-way highway. It's not just being liked; it's enjoying who likes you. You've probably heard the phrase, "Who is your ideal client?" And your answer should be, "Somebody I love working with." Then, go on to define what that is. Who do you love to serve, who gives you light and inspiration when you help them, and who tells you how great it was to work with you? Likability is earned. And it shouldn't be a guess as to who likes you because you create the likability by those you seek out and like yourself.

The Laws of Magnetism: Unlocking the Attractive Power of Genuine Connections

The Laws of Magnetism represent a set of principles that govern the art of being likable and fostering meaningful connections with others. Much like the laws of physics, these principles are fundamental and timeless, guiding us in our quest to become individuals who attract positivity and radiate it into the world.

Law 1: The Magnetic Aura of Authenticity

At the core of likability lies authenticity. Authenticity is the magnetic energy that draws people towards you. It's about being your true self, unapologetically and confidently. When you embrace your authentic self, you not only become more likable, but you also create a genuine connection with others. Authenticity transcends superficial interactions and allows you to form bonds built on trust, respect, and understanding. To learn more about Authenticity, you can read the first volume in this series, *The Book of Influence ~ Authentic Communication*.

Law 2: The Resonance of Active Listening

Active listening is one of the most potent techniques within the Laws of Magnetism. When you engage in a conversation, make a conscious effort to listen attentively and empathetically. Ask questions that invite others to share their thoughts and emotions. By validating their experiences, you create a resonance that makes people feel valued and appreciated. In turn, this strengthens the magnetic pull of your likable presence. Like a muscle, you can practice and exercise active listening every day.

Law 3: The Charismatic Glow

Charisma, another essential facet of magnetism, isn't reserved for a select few; anyone can develop and hone it. Charisma is the art of exuding confidence, warmth, and positivity. It involves maintaining eye contact, using open and inviting body language, and sharing relatable stories. Charismatic individuals have a natural magnetism that attracts others like a moth to a flame.

Law 4: The Kindness Ripple Effect

Kindness and generosity are the cornerstones of likability. Small acts of kindness, such as lending a helping hand or offering words of encouragement, create a ripple effect of positivity. Likable individuals consistently express gratitude and respect for others, fostering an environment where people are naturally drawn to their magnetic energy.

Law 5: Mutual Enjoyment of Connection

Likability isn't a one-way street; it's a mutual exchange. The Laws of Magnetism emphasize the importance of enjoying the company of those you connect with. Aim to appreciate those around you just as you seek to be liked. Define your ideal connections by identifying those who inspire and resonate with you. Building relationships with people who align with your values and aspirations ensures that the likability factor flows effortlessly in both directions.

These Laws of Magnetism provide a blueprint for unlocking the power of genuine connections and likability. By embracing authenticity, mastering the art of active listening, cultivating charisma, practicing kindness, and seeking mutually enjoyable relationships, you can become a magnetic force in the lives of others and draw positivity and fulfillment into your own. Likability becomes a natural, enriching, and empowering journey when approached with these principles.

LIKABILITY FACTOR

A great example of this is how I like to work with business owners who know the importance of accountability and personal development. I work with people who are motivated and effectively communicate. I love working with people who admit when they're wrong, are open to feedback, and express gratitude when they achieve success. I work with people who inspire me through their actions. I love to work with people who lean in, double down, and trust in themselves and the plan led before them so that they may acquire and attain the success they desire.

This definition ultimately describes who I am and what many people see in me. These qualities are why people and I get along. That constant expression of gratitude and appreciation to one another creates an environment for accelerated success. Stop working with people you don't like. Start working with people you like because they resonate with you.

To this day, I work with Erik Swanson and Habitude Warrior Mastermind, somebody who shares genuine interest and likability with me. It was reciprocal when I realized that Erik was the person I wanted to model and pattern my speaking career after. Likability attracts likability.

JON KOVACH JR.

Jon is an award-winning international motivational speaker and global mastermind leader. Jon has helped multi-billion-dollar corporations exceed their annual sales goals, including Coldwell Banker Commercial, Outdoor Retailer Cotopaxi, and the Public Relations Student Society of America.

In addition, in his work as an accountability coach and mastermind facilitator, Jon has helped thousands of professionals overcome their challenges and achieve their goals by implementing his accountability strategies and Irrefutable Laws of High Performance.

Jon is the Founder and Chairman of Champion Circle, a networking association that combines high-performance-based networking activities and recreational fun to create connection capital and increase prosperity for professionals.

Jon is the Mastermind Facilitator and Team Lead of the Habitude Warrior Mastermind and the Global Speakers Mastermind & Masterclass founded by Speaker Erik "Mr. Awesome" Swanson.

Jon speaks on topics including accountability, The Irrefutable Laws of High Performance, and The Power of Mastermind Methodologies. He is a #1 Bestselling Author and a featured keynote on SpeakUp TV, an Amazon Prime TV series, with his keynote speech titled, Getting Unstuck. In addition, he stars in over 100 speaking stages, podcasts, and live international summits each year.

Jon's motivational messages have been viewed by over 500,000 people online. His positive messages have trended and been used by global brands on TikTok and Instagram, such as: Red Bull, Michael Bublé, NHL, Powell Books, GoDaddy Studio, Canada's Wonderland Amusement Park, and the LSU Cheer Team.

www.SpeakerJonKovachJr.com

ALEXANDER BALL
LIKABILITY IS DETERMINED BY AUTHENTICITY

The intriguing concept of likability—Throughout my journey, I've realized that likability goes deeper than charisma or charm; it requires authenticity, honesty, and sincere commitment to helping others, and being honest while empathic can dramatically affect personal and professional relationships.

Discover Your True Self Now

An essential step toward being likable is discovering your strengths and passions. My awakening was gradual; over time, I understood that corporate finance and operations management were my strong suit. Acknowledging genuine skills and talents is central to authentic likability —when people see that you feel confident about yourself and know your abilities, they tend to gravitate toward you more readily; personally, this realization proved transformative.

Integrity and Honesty in Business

My approach to likability centers around integrity and honesty—both are vital in creating lasting business relationships. People quickly pick up on any hint of insincerity, so being transparent and sincere throughout all your interactions is essential for making people likable.

Take my experience as an example from financial advisory: During a challenging period for one of my clients, I made her a promise and assured her I'd be there to guide and support her during such difficult times. By fulfilling that commitment and offering unwavering support throughout, not only did I earn her trust, but I also demonstrated its power.

Successful First Impressions Depend on Matching Personalities

First impressions matter, and I understand the significance of matching my demeanor and attire with those I meet. Let me show this through two examples. When meeting formal individuals, dressing appropriately while maintaining an authoritative tone can create a great first impression; conversely, when conversing with more relaxed individuals, adapting your approach to make them comfortable is often more successful.

My point is that adaptability and empathy are crucial in forging connections with others. Being attentive to social cues and adapting your behavior accordingly can help establish rapport and likability quickly after meeting someone for the first time.

Listening and Empathy in Fostering Relationships

One of my pillars of likability philosophy is active listening. People love talking about themselves, and by actively listening, you not only make them feel valued but gain invaluable insights into their lives, goals, and dreams, as well as valuable information that helps you understand — which builds trust and fosters connection between individuals.

My goal in approaching people is for them to talk about themselves 90 percent of the time while I listen attentively; this encourages likability while helping me uncover what truly matters to them.

Helping Others Achieve Their Goals

My approach to building likability centers around my desire to help others succeed. My philosophy emphasizes the value of being of service to others and adding value in every interaction—which I consider my duty and goal as part of building my likability.

Service orientalism means prioritizing others' needs and aspirations above your own in all your interactions with them. Rather than seeking personal gain through self-promotion, service orientation emphasizes commitment to helping others realize their dreams.

Authenticity Is Key

My journey towards likability exemplifies the power of authenticity, integrity, and empathy in creating meaningful relationships. Overcoming personal struggles while accepting myself for who I am and using my experiences to assist others is proof of authenticity's effect on personal and professional success.

Consider that being likable doesn't involve creating an artificial persona or pretending to be something you aren't instead, it consists of being genuine, empathetic, and committed to positively contributing to others' lives. My approach to likability serves as a shining example of how genuineness can lead to meaningful connections that endure over time.

ALEXANDER BALL

About Alexander Ball: Alexander J. Ball loves helping business owners reach their real estate investment goals within 1-2 years and tax free through life insurance investment strategies. Whether you are seeking to buy properties within 1-2 years, take advantage of tax free accounts, or keep money liquid while still outpacing inflation and having your money work for you, Alex specializes in helping people from all walks of life.

Alex has work for World Financial Group (WFG) for over 7 years and is currently Marketing Director helping successful business owners and high performers in business take control of their financial futures. Alex loves to give free 30-minute consultations on how to use cash flow and leverage success to build a financial empire, whether that is real estate investments, buying companies, or expanding your own.

Alex's skills include Real Estate Investment, Investment Properties, Life Insurance, Indexed Universal Life Insurance, and Capital Gains Tax. Alex can help people seriously reduce or eliminate capital gains tax on sale of real estate or other large assets.

Author's Website: *www.linkedin.com/in/Alexander-J-Ball-888201137*

Book Series Website: *www.TheBookOfInfluence.com*

AMY MINGIN

BECOMING LIKABLE REQUIRES INTEREST IN OTHERS

My daughter found a video online that showed her "how to get a boyfriend." She was a 6-year-old at the time and shared it with our adult friends one night at a party. My sister-in-law was in a courting stage with a new guy, so whilst it was a seemingly inappropriate video for my daughter to be watching (to some people), I was amazed and humored that she found a way to relate the video she had watched with the context of my sister-in-law and dating.

She found a way to express her external environment via role play and therefore made sense of her world around her.

The adults at the party loved her rendition of the way to dance and interact with others to "be liked" by someone new. It's so easy for a child to make new friends and I wonder if you've considered how you've made friends as an adult compared to how you used to do it as a child?

I am often asked for parenting advice once people meet me and see how my kids interact with the world around them.

Henry Ford said, "Whether you think you can or if you think you can't, you're right." The same goes with parenting. I've always said to my kids, "If you want to climb, go for it." So, they climb to the tops of the trees and figure to how to get down. "If you want to create, go for it." So, they imagine up wild stories, funny plays, and incredible curious questions about the meaning of existence.

I wonder how often you realize you're doing this, too? How wild are the stories you tell yourself?

Many people wish they were more likable. Perhaps there's an inner people pleaser in you that just wants to be seen, heard, and loved. So, you stop at nothing in order to create situations and people in your life that "teach" you that.

I write "teach" in quotation marks because when we desire something or ask for something, we are often sent the lesson so we can learn how, cognitively, and experience the lesson in our body.

I remember a time when I felt liked, and equally a time when I felt disliked. What's the difference? My perception.

We might often think we are likable, and yet we are having conversations in our own heads about what we think the other person means, what could their opinion be, and then making assumptions before even hearing the person's voice.

I wonder if cave people used to care about other's opinion that much?

Likability gets you places. It creates rapport, it helps you move through life more smoothly, and it is also more pleasant for people around you.

So, what constitutes likability?

According to Tony Robbins, communication is made up of 7% content, 38% tone of voice and 55% body language. Yet 95% of people are so focused on what they will say next that they miss out on the important cues from someone's body language and voice tonality.

Each person will process their world through a particular lens. Therefore, how can you easily meet people where they are and communicate in a likable way?

1. Take care of your physical appearance. It's not just first impressions that count. When you're well groomed, it's obvious that you take care of yourself, and others unconsciously will feel safer around you. There's an assumption you'd take care of them, also.

2. Find relatedness. Without talking about yourself too much, finding commonality between the information the other person is sharing and something you can offer or you've experienced is a key in being likable. There's a great saying that goes, "Like people like people." When there's relatedness, there's often a sense of "They are just like me," so therefore you're more likable.

3. Create a shared experience. Have you ever had a time in your life with a person you've just met, or a person you know only at a shallow level, then you shared something intimate or personal and your relationship blossomed? Relationships can be built fast when we are transparent with who we are, what we believe in, and express how we feel.

4. People tend to be drawn to those who are optimistic, cheerful, and generally positive. A positive attitude can be infectious and can make others feel fabulous in your presence.

5. People who are good listeners and can understand and relate to the feelings and experiences of others are highly likable. This can make people feel heard and validated and can create a strong bond of trust.

6. People who are genuine and true to themselves tend to be more likable than those who are trying to be someone they're not. When people sense that you're being authentic, they're more likely to feel comfortable and at ease around you.

7. People who are self-assured and confident tend to be more likable than those who are unsure of themselves. Confidence can be attractive and can give others a sense of security and stability.

8. People who have a good sense of humor and can make others laugh tend to be more likable. Humor can break down barriers and help people feel more comfortable around each other.

LIKABILITY FACTOR

Dale Carnegie, who wrote *How to Win Friends and Influence People*, said: "You can make more friends in two months by becoming interested in other people than you can in two years by trying to get other people interested in you." This quote highlights the importance of focusing on others and showing genuine interest in them if you want to build positive relationships and be liked.

Being likable is not about being perfect or trying to please everyone. Rather, it's about cultivating positive traits and behaviors that allow you to connect with others on a deeper level. By being genuine, empathetic, confident, and positive, you can create strong bonds of trust and respect with the people around you.

Remember that likability is not something that can be achieved overnight, but rather it is a journey of self-discovery and personal growth. With practice and perseverance, you can develop the qualities that make you likable and build meaningful relationships that last a lifetime.

AMY MINGIN

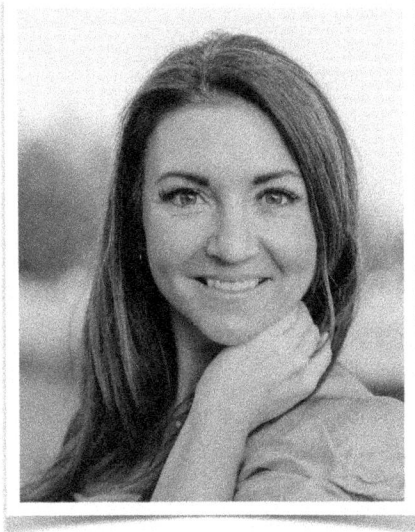

About Amy Mingin: Amy Mingin is a business coach for influencers, best-selling author, speaker, naturopath, yoga & meditation teacher, wife and mum of two, residing on the Gold Coast in Australia.

She has helped thousands of people find their inner spark, access their version of perfect health & scale sustainable businesses over the last 15 years.

She facilitates personal development events, retreats, and quantum healing training for people in Australia and worldwide.

Author's Website: *www.AmyMingin.com*

Book Series Website: *www.TheBookOfInfluence.com*

ANGELA HARDEN-MACK

PLEASING, NOT PEOPLE PLEASER

Women in the workplace and marketplace may find themselves experiencing the likability penalty. The penalty is defined by two opposing states: When a woman is seen as competent, she is seen as less likable; and the opposite state is that when a woman has more likability, she is seen as being incompetent.

What are ambitious, accomplished, successful women to do? How does likability impact self-esteem, quality of life, and professional and business fulfillment? The answer to this conundrum isn't people pleasing —it's authenticity and a pleasing personality.

By focusing on self-worth, building a support network, being a self-advocate, and taking risks with confidence, it's possible to achieve personal and professional fulfillment and be an impactful leader while nurturing likability.

The likability penalty is the result of the likability bias, which is rooted in outdated expectations. Men are expected to be assertive, which is considered a positive trait for me. Women are expected to be quiet and demure. Assertiveness expressed by women is not desirable and assertive women are often described as pushy and aggressive and their leadership styles as undesirable, intimidating, and domineering.

While bias of any type is often unconscious, it's crucial to become aware of the bias, identify strategies to eliminate the bias, and implement the strategy. Ambitious, accomplished, successful women must not only be aware of the likability bias, but empower themselves with the necessary strategies and techniques to nurture self-worth and authenticity to increase likability that can lead to personal and professional fulfillment.

The likability factor has been on my radar for quite some time. My education in the matter of likability began during high school in leadership development activities. Leadership development training included education on the association of likability, personal achievement, and success. Leadership training emphasized that leadership involved leading others, but began with leading self. Self-leadership foundations included emotional mastery, self-esteem and self-confidence.

Mentors also provided tips on how to develop likability. My initial likability plan started with an emphasis on self-advocacy and building a strong support network. The adult mentors would often say, "Don't be afraid to speak up for yourself. It matters. It's important."

I teach and empower others to be their best advocate and loudest cheerleader. If you can cheer for yourself, you like yourself. If you like yourself, you can like others. If you like others, you develop a pleasing personality. If you have a pleasing personality, you can become highly likable and blossom to be the best you and live your best life!

I get excited just thinking about likability and the personal evolution in becoming the best you. Additional components of my likability plan included giving attention and appreciation to others, and growing in confidence to take appropriate risks for growth and development, while avoiding the tendency to become a people-pleaser or lack authenticity.

Likability is defined as personality traits that correspond to being agreeable, favored, or liked by others. Habits exhibited by highly likable people include being attentive, being an active listener, smiling, being generous with compliments, employing positivity and positive body language, taking the time to know individuals by name, and being genuine.

The traits described above focus on relating to others and are optimized by starting with self-worth. Understand your worth and other components of likability will follow.

With pressing life responsibilities and demands, so often it can be easy to forget your own value and not realize how much potential lies within. If it's been a while since you encouraged yourself, pause now and speak words of love, joy, and encouragement to yourself. Be intentional about setting aside time for yourself and really get to know yourself more and in deeper ways. If you have embraced change, you are growing, evolving. You are not the same person you were last year. Knowing you and your value help build up your self-worth and set the stage for greater confidence.

Self-worth is the foundation for everything else that follows when it comes to cultivating likability. When we focus on our strengths rather than our weaknesses and recognize our worthiness for success and recognition, we will naturally exude confidence which attracts others to us. This does not mean we should overlook areas of improvement or shy away from difficult conversations—it means understanding that mistakes are part of growth and embracing our imperfections along with our successes.

Networks composed of strong relationships with mentors or colleagues who have been successful in their field can be incredibly beneficial for ambitious women looking to nurture likability. Mentors, sponsors, and colleagues can provide advice from their own experience, help build personal, social, and professional connections and provide valuable feedback on career decisions or projects you're working on—all of which will help build your credibility and trustworthiness over time.

It is important to remember that success doesn't happen overnight—it takes commitment, hard work, perseverance, and resilience to achieve greatness in any field.

Women experiencing imposter syndrome—elevated levels of self-doubt or fear of being perceived as aggressive—often have difficulty advocating for themselves in the workplace or business environment.

Instead of worrying about how you may come across when asking for what you want (or deserve), try focusing on why it matters—not just for yourself but also those around you who benefit from your success: When women are honest about what they need from others, everyone wins.

By speaking up confidently and respectfully sharing your opinions without hesitation or apology—even if they don't line up with others—you will begin to gain respect for not only what you say but how you say it. Assertiveness is speaking up with confidence and empathy; assertiveness is not aggression. Developing competence in assertiveness is a skill needed to thrive in life and business. Showing assertiveness rather than aggression will go a long way toward leadership development, career advancement, and helping foster good relationships with colleagues or clients alike.

Likability is about social interactions. Every interaction is an opportunity to make someone feel appreciated or respected by expressing genuine interest in them through active listening skills. Women are often the caregivers for multiple individuals, and it can be easy to forget how powerful appreciation can be—when done right it has the potential to forge relationships stronger than ever before. Compliments to coworkers, subordinates, and colleagues can do wonders to foster relationships and increase likability.

Appropriate risk-taking results in rewards. It takes courage and boldness to take risks and step out of comfort zones. Having faith in yourself is essential when stepping outside of your comfort zone; showing courage instead of fear will result in greater accomplishments down the road.

And finally, authenticity as a factor of likability. Authenticity is consistency in words, behaviors, and beliefs. Authenticity is showing up as your unique self. Authenticity produces consistency, and consistency results in building relationships based on trust.

My message to ambitious women is that you are amazing and successful and can be viewed as likable and competent. Build your support network and be thankful for the network. I'm thankful for the good people in my life—positive influences in my life, those who appreciate me for me and help me soar. Look for opportunities to support others.

I'm thankful for the opportunity to give attention and show appreciation. I believe showing appreciation is a privilege and enhances relationships with others. On any given day, my appreciation may involve a smile, a thank you, a compliment, and telling someone I appreciate them. All acts of appreciation produce results far greater and lasting beyond the initial encounter.

Don't be silent; your voice matters. Speak up for yourself and for others. I celebrate the opportunities to speak up and be heard. Standing in my power gives me the confidence to share my voice. My contributions to the world matter. My service to the world matters and adds value to those I'm called to serve in life, love, work, and business. Who are, and have been, your cheerleaders? My parents were my first cheerleaders and taught me to cheer for myself. I'm thankful for my parent's love and encouraging words. Their words empower me to trust myself so I am able to take risks, and to continue to aim for higher levels of personal achievement in life, work, and business.

Likability isn't just about being liked by those around us; it's also about connecting with people who respect us and appreciate us for who we are. When likability is developed through self-confidence, it translates into giving attention as well as support—the keys for unlocking one's best self. Likability is about a pleasing personality, not becoming a people-pleaser.

With these tips in mind—knowing your worth, surrounding yourself with good people, speaking up and being heard, giving attention and showing appreciation, and believing in yourself and taking risks—you can unlock greater wellbeing, fulfillment, happiness and joy by unlocking your best self through likability!

DR. ANGELA HARDEN-MACK, MD

About Dr. Angela Harden-Mack, MD: Dr. Angela Harden-Mack is recognized as one of the most prominent voices for wellness and women's empowerment. She is a #1 best-selling author and a leading expert in creating wellness in women. A holistic approach to wellness is at the heart of her work as founder and CEO of Live Great Lives, LLC, a company that helps professional women embrace wellness and Live Great Lives. Drawing on more than 25 years of experience as a physician and teacher, Dr. Angela uses her keynote and books to motivate women to take action to release the stressful and pressured Superwoman lifestyle. Women are then able to embrace a healthy Well-woman lifestyle to live great lives. She has a simple but powerful formula that helps women achieve wellness and success in all areas of their lives.

As a motivational speaker, Dr. Harden-Mack shares stories that stir souls and ignites listeners' imaginations. Dr. Angela's energy is evident as she captures the audience's attention. Her captivating style and powerful message have made her a favorite keynote for virtual and live audiences alike.

Dr. Harden-Mack is the founder of the Live Great Lives Academy, host of transformational coaching programs, a mastermind, and Live Great Lives Network community and membership for women. Live Great Lives Network is THE community of Well-women who show up for life as authentic, confident, whole, and powerful women. Dr. Harden-Mack is a graduate of Johns Hopkins University and a graduate of Wayne State University Medical School.

Author's Website: www.LiveGreatLives.com
Book Series Website: www.TheBookOfInfluence.com

ANGÈLE LAMOTHE

PERSONAL MAGNETISM

We are highly energetic beings, and we dictate what we attract into our lives and into our fields by our thoughts, actions, and emotions. Our likability factor is our personal magnetism, also known as our superpower as humans! You choose what you want, desire, and attract into your field, based on your likability factor. Like attracts Like.

We are magnetic and create our realities; what we focus on grows and what we think, we become. Your likability factor and your environment will forge your reality and what you will choose to manifest into your life!

We have control over our thoughts, actions and patterns and can deepen our likability factor by showing love, generosity, compassion, and joy. Love is our natural state as humans and the universe is always working for us in attracting the highest possible outcome, and in the most practical and abundant ways.

By continuously choosing love, compassion, empathy, understanding, gratitude, and joy, over and over, it shifts your inner reality so that you attract more of what you want into your life, and into your outer reality.

The likability factor is born from within and is optimized and is a catalyst of change when your inside matches your outside reality!

Your likability factor is also influenced by compassion, understanding, and your ability to communicate openly and to connect with another person's interests, wants, and needs from an authentic and loving space of unconditional acceptance.

When you improve these areas in your life and boost your likability factor, you bring out the best in others and within yourself; you handle life's challenges with ease and grace, enjoy better health, better relationships, and lead your most abundant life.

When your inner being, your likability factor and energetic field is filled with love, gratitude, joy and compassion, it returns back to you exponentially. The universe has no choice but to match those high vibrations and to bring it into your physical existence.

I had been conditioned at a young age to believe that girls were naturally quiet and didn't speak their minds openly and freely; they listened, played it safe, and certainly did not ruffle anyone's feathers or step on any toes. My likability factor relied on external forces, and as a wife and mother, I had fallen into the trap of pleasing everyone else and was beginning to pay serious prices in my life.

I was selling myself short on my personal goals, dreams, and aspirations and came to understand that my feelings of anger, resentment and overwhelm were self-imposed. They were based on paradigms, a belief system, and my environment and frankly I did not know any other reality.

I recognized that my deepest desires had nothing to do with pleasing others at the dispense of my aspirations. I had the inner wisdom to recognize that I could free myself from the beliefs that I did not control my reality. One of the most pivotal moments in my life is when I discovered that my likability factor meant authenticity—yes, being authentically me, no matter what! It meant living my most authentic and abundant life, regardless of what others might think or expect of me!

Healthy boundaries are simply opportunities to determine if a certain reality aligns with your values, and if not, how you can align or let them go without feelings of guilt. We have the freedom and choice to give and receive love and it's a universal energy of the highest power and currency; it represents the true meaning of life and fuels humanity at its core.

At that moment, I made a committed to myself, to my children, and to humanity and chose to operate based on the likability factors of joy, love, generosity, harmony, and gratitude. It became my soul mission and my life purpose to help transform the world so that these likability factors, these energies would prevail, and everyone would live their best life possible.

We can spread the likability factor—it starts from within ourselves, with small changes, such as transforming our thoughts, our inner dialogue, our actions, and our universe. By choosing to focus outwardly with unconditional love, understanding and compassion, we can truly come from a space of understanding and openness by seeing the other person for who they truly are.

Significant shifts occurred in my life when I recognized that love, abundance, and joy were natural states of humanity. The Universe provides more than enough for everyone, and it always delivers more than we could possibly imagine when we are open to receiving and giving and develop our likability factor.

I discovered the keys to allow the flow of abundance into my life and extended my reality to receive what I desired and deserved to live my best life.

We are responsible for creating our likability factor; we are responsible for our happiness and every single thing that shows up into our lives. When you live in the highest possibility and in love, you align all of your dreams and desires. When decisions are made from that space, things happen naturally, people flow into our lives, and we naturally attract our deepest desires.

Before I realized that I had the ability and freedom to create my reality, I was suffering because I had the illusion of being separated from my power and the control of my environment.

We possess the power to shift the consciousness of the world, to shift out of toxicity and fear and create the dream and visions that we desire for ourselves and humanity.

We have so much freedom and power to choose and can rapidly manifest our dreams when we have the courage to work on our likability factor. You will shift from worried to abundant and unlock your inner magnet to attract your desires, unlock your dreams, and lead your best life.

In what vibrations are most of your thoughts? When you spend more time in joy love, abundance, and gratitude you will become a magnet to those frequencies.

You can be the creator of your life—just decide to commit and change your likability factor. Where your energy goes, your life flows! Your life is created by design and you always have a choice; you are the creator of your life and your likability factor will directly influence the flow of abundance into your life.

There are two distinct ways to approach change. I spent most of my early adult life thinking that there was something wrong with me, that I needed to be fixed. I had negative self-talk, judgement and believed that I wasn't enough. I felt like I needed to fix everything and started doing whatever offered a temporary fix, until I realized that my inside reality was simply a mirror of my outside world.

At the time, I didn't realize that I was approaching change from the lens of needing to be fixed. I shifted my journey of exhaustion into conscious ways of living; I mastered my mind and recognized that I had full control of my likability factor! I was in charge of attracting my desired reality and my soul knew that I required change, but I didn't know how to proceed.

It was a game changing moment for me when I realized that there was nothing wrong with me—it shifted my journey of exhaustion to mastering my mind and reconnecting, and to realizing that *I* was the likability factor. I was in charge of attracting that desired reality and aligning my passion and my purpose in everythingI attracted into my life.

LIKABILITY FACTOR

I became the creator of my life; I harnessed the power of my mind, body, and soul and achieved potentials in all areas as I took inventory of how I spent my energy. We really do have the power to choose and change our realities; through our intuition, our soul, and our power, we act from that space to create our deepest dreams.

We can attract more abundance into our field by vibrating at the same frequency; the more we vibrate in the higher frequencies of love, peace, compassion, abundance, and gratitude, the faster we can align our desires —also known as your likability factor.

If you want to connect with people, they need to get to know you on a deeper level with authenticity and have trust in you. The likability factor is the bridge between the two. It's a prerequisite to trusting. Being genuine and honest is essential to being likable. People gravitate toward those who are genuine and authentic because they know they can trust them.

By making a mindful effort to be genuine and likable, you'll find that more people are willing to engage with you. Individuals will confide in you, and you will be perceived positively by your friends, family, and surroundings. You will cause others to feel inspired and positive around you and have the ability to magnetize their deepest desires as well! That's the true meaning and purpose of life and the groundwork to the likability factor.

ANGÈLE LAMOTHE

About Angèle Lamothe: Angèle Lamothe is a high-vibrational leader who lives a heart-centered life and whose mission is to help raise our planet's consciousness so that everyone lives their most abundant life. She is a mom of three, a triathlete, and a soul transformational coach who works with high-performing leaders who are feeling overwhelmed and helps them create abundance, unlock their purpose and develop their intuition to live their richest life.

She also has a degree in psychology, a Master's in Health Sciences, training in energy medicine, and has completed leadership trainings. Angèle has worked for 20 years in an acute care hospital. She is obsessed with people's transformational journeys and how the power of the mind creates miracles when aligned with purpose and action. She continues to be inspired by highly motivated individuals who seek opportunities to make changes in their lives, grow through challenges and accelerate transformation.

Angèle leads a high-performance lifestyle and has more joy, energy, and time to do things she deeply enjoys. She can support you in developing tools and strategies to help you connect to your intuition and unleash your full power so that you can lead a balanced and abundant life!

You can find out more about Angèle by visiting:
linktr.ee/AngèleLamothecoaching

Author's website: *www.AngèleLamotheCoaching.squarespace.com/*
Book Series Website: *www.TheBookOfInfluence.com*

BONNIE LIERSE

RELATIONSHIPS & TRUST LEAD TO LIKABILITY

What do you think of when it comes to likability relationships?

To be a major—and I mean major—INFLUENCER, the key is to have likability relationships. So. where does that start?

I am now on a new path that will serve many people across the WORLD. I know Erik Swanson and Jon Kovach Jr, and also Erin Ley, as they introduced me to the Habitude Warriors Mastermind over a year ago. They helped me find my passion about being an author, as well as a writer. It is important you understand that I don't take anything for granted!

When I look back on my many journeys, of both success and failures, the key truly was to be real, authentic, genuine, loving, caring of others' feelings and emotions, and putting someone else first. My main focus is to always serve others on that path. It did not matter, whether it was in elementary school, secondary school or even high school—relationships are key!

As I look back at my days in school, I see the pattern of not only of others, but of my own self. One of the blessings I was gifted was that I made friends easily. I was not into the drugs and drinking, nor was I focused on others that were into peer pressure. I didn't always hang out with the more popular students, but those that were likeminded and put others first.

I loved the outgoing individuals, so one of my passions was to be a twirler in High School. Yes, I went to all the games, and people came to me for a stable friendship. They truly remember me today on social media and I am blessed, humbled, and honored they still love me and I them.

It did not matter how different our personalities were then. I was still their Florence Nightingale or Clara Barton. That was completely hilarious, by the way. When I would go to the parties and I was the only one not stoned, IT WAS STRANGE FOR ME. It was definitely challenging for me to always be sober, but it was worth it.

I was a part of a House Plan in college, which was similar to a Sorority. Our House Plan did not want to party with substance, so we were the clean House Plan. It was NOT easy to be different, but no matter what, I was liked by the students in other house plans, and humbled by that. I was not into drugs ever, I still had a life with many friends that I still see today.

In high school, a riot broke out at a football game. Everyone was told to leave and I was the first one that helped others get out. During Senior Day, another major riot broke out and instruments were thrown from the stage. All I could think of was *who* I had to get out. We did get out safely, thank God. It was not the safest high school in New York, to say the least.

Later, I was able to rescue a friend from her detective husband who was abusive; another time, I rescued a friend in a snowstorm. To be likable, you have to go the extra mile, so you need to rethink your journey and make sure you're humble and honest at all times.

Moving forward, I was part of a large leadership group, and there were many teams; I did not care about the teams that people were on, I just cared about supporting each individual in order to help them through their journeys. I personally helped individuals that I knew because I understood that they needed some extra maternal loving-type person in their life. There were a multitude of situations where others saw me as more LIKABLE and TRUSTING, NON-COMPETITIVE and NON-THREATENING, and they would seek me out. I still hear from many of them to this day. I did not know how I affected others or understood it back then, but I guess I do know now because these relationships can be CRITICAL!

There were numerous instances where I had the opportunity to not only heal friendships, but to rescue others from a dangerous situation with their spouses or someone else. In the years since, they usually forgot I existed, but one person still adores me and still keeps in touch. You serve others NOT to RECEIVE. I know in my heart that people are only put on our path for a certain time and then they are gone. NO EXPLANATION.

I once had a manager who knew that someone in my life had an alcohol addiction. This manager was in alcohol addiction recovery herself. One day, she loaned me some money due to a personal situation and then said, "Please, no returning it. My gift!" I NEVER SAW HER AGAIN, BUT NEVER FORGOT. If others treasure you, they will support you if they are truly genuine; if not, they will not.

Please, always stay refreshing, honest, humble, and lovable—it will serve you in this lifetime.

Sometimes, we serve others, and they will take advantage of the moment, but we learn from the error in judgement and create new boundaries, like I have recently, with others. It has changed my life and self-esteem and I am beginning to LOVE MY HIGHEST SELF!

When I shop in retail stores, I always connect with those that work there. They will go out of their way to assist me in anything I need. For example, I was with some friends that were behind the scenes and they saw a manager come up to me. The manager lit up because of my gentle demeanor and said, "How can I help you?" He could not stop assisting me, and loved chatting with me; I was so humbled. So, I graciously thanked him for his help and eventually left after shopping. When I went back, he surprised me and truly remembered me. I was humbled by the attention of a caring manager that actually remembered me. He still would say hello if he saw me in the store.

Relationships are a key factor to success or failure. One of my main teachings is to find a genuine compliment to express to someone you do not know. They will be touched and flattered. I know just that person who did it to me a long time ago and still loves me today!

I am now so passionate about the changes that are coming to my life that I will be a part of changing the world, including yours. We will know, when it is your time to know the truth, of my miraculous journey.

I live in a place that has a rental division and we know that the ladies and gents are salary. However, I personally know that I am extremely ecstatic about them, and they adore me, as well. We cannot get enough of each other. The women absolutely love me and I them, but the maintenance partners, I also caringly connect with and they are so likable and supportive—it is all professional and considerate.

From my handsome husband, Tommy, though my Mediumship readings to me personally: "You MY LOVE, you are the reason I am changed because you taught me LIKABILITY years ago, when we my wife, BONNIE BONFIRE, first met. You, Bonnie (my Gamine), are my universe and I am SMITTEN—we will be together for eternity. ARE YOU READY?"

BONNIE LIERSE

About Bonnie Lierse: Bonnie Zaruches Lierse is extremely artistic and creative, with an entrepreneurial bent. Besides that, she is a seasoned agent with more than twenty years' experience in real estate in the New York/Long Island area. She relocated to Northern Virginia in 2012 and continued her real estate career there.

Another passion is creating leaders by working in business leadership development with *Leadership Team Development (LTD)*, marketing products supplied by *Amway*. She was also a member of *The Screen Cartoonist Guild of Motion Pictures* for many years. Also, she did freelance for *Sesame Street* in New York City. In addition, she was a District Director for an interior accessory design company, as her own business.

Bonnie is blessed with five beautiful grandchildren and is very close with her children and family, some of whom are also in Virginia. Her missions are leadership, mentorship, paying it forward, and changing lives one at a time. Her motto is "You be the difference!"

Author's website: *www.amway.com/myshop/SplashFXEnterprises*

Book Series Website: *www.TheBookOfInfluence.com*

CHARLOTTE DELON

KNOW, LIKE, TRUST

Do I like you?

When thinking of "likability," what comes to mind is KLT: Know, Like, and Trust.

When considering the "likability factor," you want to be intentional about spending less time in your space and more time in the space of others. Now, I don't mean physical space, but really considering the other person you are engaging with.

You might be saying, "I still don't get it." Don't worry; in the beginning I didn't, either. Years ago, I was working in direct sales. This meant I had to meet lots of people. I couldn't understand why others in the same business were able to meet a lot of people and I struggled meeting one. It was the "likability factor." I assumed, because I was tall, that people were naturally intimidated by me and that was the issue. In the midst of exploring what could it be, someone suggested that I may not be creating a space for clients to feel welcome.

What does making someone feel welcome look like? When I'm out and about, there are random strangers all around me. How do I make them "feel welcome?" I tested a theory and I went out and chose to let my guard down—to my amazement, people from all walks of life began talking to me randomly. In that moment, it became less about me and more about them.

People make a decision on whether they like you within seconds of meeting you. If they don't like you, you don't stand a chance in gaining their trust. It's KLT: Know, Like, Trust—they get to know you and decide if they like you. In choosing to like you, they determine if they want to extend trust. The "likability factor" can make or break you.

Some key steps to the likability factor:

Speak first. Remember, decisions are being made in the first few seconds. Because you're are on a mission to be liked, you must go first. Choosing not to speak can cause a person to make a judgement about you that you are not approachable.

Years ago, I had taken on an assignment. I walked into the meeting where I was the most junior with layers of executives. I sat down, took my notes, and went on to my next meeting. One of the executives didn't know who I was began exclaiming after I left. "Who was she? Was she brought in to see how we are doing so that she can report up to leadership?"

There was major panic. It wasn't my intent to intimidate. It was my intent to simply get what I needed in that hour. Truthfully, I was intimidated to some degree. This was a high profile piece of work where all of the other efforts had executives leading, and I was the only director doing the same job. In hindsight, I could have taken a second to introduce myself and build rapport. I could have made a friend and an ally that day and I missed an opportunity. When possible, always speak first.

Be approachable. Being approachable helps people feel psychologically safe. Having psychological safety causes a person to feel like they can say anything and be okay. Having a sense of feeling safe causes individuals to like and trust you. It causes them to put their guard down because you put yours down first. Invest in getting to know people. Think about the day someone made you feel important.

Remember the Theodore Roosevelt quote: "People don't care how much you know until they know how much you care."

Make eye contact, smile, and acknowledge the person. No one wants to feel invisible. Everyone in some capacity wants to feel seen. Have you ever experienced feeling invisible? It's the worst feeling ever. All of these years later, I still remember when I was walking down a hallway at work and I noticed a coworker walking toward me. As I began to say hello, they turned from me to look at the wall to avoid speaking. Imagine a wall being more important than you.

From then on, I was on a mission to make sure people felt valued by me. You want to make sure the person knows you see them. This small gesture will cause the person to feel like the most important person to you.

Demonstrate empathy even when no one is watching—because, guess what, people are always watching. Imagine having an employee who lost their mother and father back to back to Covid. I will never forget the day I received a call from an employee hysterically crying. I could barely make out what she was saying. She called at six in the morning to share her parent had fallen ill to Covid. This was when the doctors didn't know exactly what to do. I sat and listened to her cry, not knowing what to do. Honestly, I cried with her.

After completing the call, I contacted our team and told them that she was going to need us to wrap our arms around her during this time. We created food schedules. Other people delivered water. We took over her work--anything we could do to help her. I didn't realize other teams were watching. They were amazed at what we did. The empathy was contagious. People who were not on our team signed up to help as well. Learn how to be present and demonstrate empathy.

Serve others. Even if you are the leader, serve. Years ago, when I was a developer, I had a leader who took me under his wing. I had to transition to a new programming language and I was struggling to pick it up. The pressure of feeling like I'm at risk of losing my job didn't help. This leader invested in me and within months I was thriving. After this experience, there was nothing I wouldn't do for him. I followed his lead and began training and building up others. Within months, we had the strongest and most progressive organization. He served me and, in return, I served others.

This leader could have done like the others and judge without extending a hand, but he chose to serve me and provide me with skills I did not have. This one experience has impacted hundreds, if not thousands, of lives. Any organization I lead, I lead with a heart of service. Any leader (executive, director, manager) I coach, the first thing they learn is leading with a heart of service. They must understand that they are at the bottom of the pyramid and their people are on the top.

Provide legitimate compliments. If you see something or experience something worth complimenting, say so. Don't keep the compliment in your head. People love to be around people who make them feel good. When you give a compliment, be specific. Don't just say someone is amazing--express why. For example: "You are amazing. I can trust that when you provide me details X, Y, and Z it will provide what I need to make decisions on A, B, and C. Your work is thorough and organized and I truly appreciate it." This is a legitimate compliment. This is showing that you truly see them.

Be consistent and demonstrate integrity. If a person can't trust you, they will most certainly not like you. On this journey of the "likability factor," your words and actions are everything. There's a saying, "Your actions speak so loudly I can't hear a word you are saying." If your actions are inconsistent with your words, people will pick up on that. This will cause them to not trust you and will erode the respect they may have had for you.

I worked with someone who was charming and charismatic. This person was instantly given trust and he wasn't a good steward of it. It got to a point where no one trusted his words nor his actions and he damaged a lot of relationships before they could be established. Likewise, I recently had a discussion with someone where I was being tested. We had a meeting and there was a misunderstanding. He said, "I think I heard you say X, but I don't believe that's what you meant." I cleared up the communication and said thanked him for having the courage to have this discussion with me.

Later, he shared that it was a test to see how I would respond. Had I blown up, became argumentative or started labeling him as being negative, I would have failed the test. Words plus action matters.

CHARLOTTE DELON

About Charlotte DeLon: Charlotte is a motivational speaker and coach with over 16 years of transformational leadership experience. She helps organizations transform culture for optimal output defining operational tenants and assessing behavioral gaps that can impede or accelerate change.

Charlotte is a Maxwell Leadership Certified Team Member and Certified Advance Behavioral Analysis DISC coach. Through the discovery of DISC results, Charlotte helps individuals define their superpowers and also what can be holding them back from being all that is possible.

Some key highlights: Speaking: Keynote speaker, panel discussions for women in IT providing strategies on how to manage work, family and life, launched leader to leader series discussing Leadership Philosophy's and benefits.

Coaching: Executive leadership coaching to improve organizational health. Career and life coach helping people succeed in career and managing life challenges like fear.

Teaching: Facilitate Leadership Acumen Mastermind series. Train on leadership styles (situational, transformational and servant). Teach how to build Leadership Philosophy's to deliver and drive inner and outer accountability.

Favorite quote: "No one cares how much you know until they know how much you care." - Theodore Roosevelt.

Author's Website: *www.LeadershipByCharlotteDelon.com*

Book Series Website: *www.TheBookOfInfluence.com*

CHE BROWN

INFLUENCE DURING EXTRAORDINARY TIMES

Life often presents us with unexpected obstacles and disruptions. The COVID-19 pandemic provided a reminder that even well-planned events could become chaotic instantly. But amid all this unpredictability lies an invaluable opportunity to gain valuable lessons about influence—these can be applied personally, professionally, and interpersonally.

Acing Your Wedding Amid Imperfection

My oldest son, Che Brown, and Brittanee Brooks embarked on a journey that would test their love and resilience nearly three years ago when they decided to marry during the COVID-19 pandemic. While initially they planned a grand venue wedding with family and friends gathered around, changes had to be made due to ever-evolving circumstances.

Teaching Point #1: Everyone Has an Important Role To Play

Influence, at its core, involves uniting people around a common purpose. Influence is essential when planning any event like this one—to ensure everyone involved stays safe from COVID-19 infection at every event venue selected, influence must play an integral part in any plan to make sure COVID does not spread further than planned.

At every turn, we implemented stringent safety measures—mandatory testing, temperature checks at the door, mask wearers, and safe distance measures were all implemented—to create an environment in which no one's health was ever at risk; each person played an essential part in creating such an atmosphere; influence wasn't just about convincing but about protecting those we cared for most.

Uniting for Safety

Coordination was of vital importance in making this wedding event successful, prioritizing safety measures while making all participants feel their role was significant—showing just how influential leadership can bring people together for one common cause.

Compassion and Patience Are Always Necessary

At times of uncertainty, like a pandemic, effective communication was paramount. Our communication with our community had to be thoughtful and considerate, as misinterpreted words or tones could cause unnecessary strain.

Arranging seating at the venue required tact and patience as COVID-19 distancing regulations meant some guests needed to be placed further from the altar than they anticipated; to minimize any discomfort for those affected, we positioned these guests closer to the bride and groom during the reception; it was an act that required empathy and understanding on both parts.

Navigating Complicated Situations

We carefully considered our words and their potential emotional impacts and ensured a drama-free evening for all involved. This underscores the significance of patience in managing emotions and maintaining harmony.

Finding Solutions Is Always Possible

After experiencing constant changes and uncertainties leading up to our wedding, we discovered there is always an answer. Influencing is about adapting and pivoting in response to unexpected situations.

We always asked ourselves one simple question: What's a doable solution that will still make this memorable moment? Being able to pivot quickly and find solutions on the fly is an invaluable aspect of influence.

Adaptability in Action

Our adaptability and creative problem-solving helped ensure an unforgettable wedding celebration, emphasizing the value of being adaptable and accommodating when dealing with influence. This illustrates why being flexible and solution-driven are such essential traits in leadership roles.

Life and Business Lessons Learned from China

My family's extensive wedding experience has provided invaluable lessons that transcend special occasions; these experiences have far-reaching ramifications for various aspects of our lives and careers.

Influence is more than persuasion; it's about uniting people together, understanding their needs and concerns, and finding solutions that benefit all parties involved. No matter if it's dealing with global crises or daily business challenges, these principles of influence remain timeless and invaluable.

As we travel on our respective paths, remember that even during times of great adversity, we still possess the power to unite, show kindness, and find solutions. These three components form the cornerstones of influence—when used wisely, they can lead us toward extraordinary achievements even during unexpectedly trying circumstances.

CHE BROWN

About Che Brown: Che Brown is a globally renowned giant in the sales world. He has cracked the once elusive code of entrepreneurial success with a game-changing model that unlocks unlimited financial potential, power, and wealth. In just six short years, he has dominated the sales space, coaching thousands of rising business leaders to achieve exponential growth and success in their industries, to the tune of over $400 million and counting. His acclaimed 7-Figure Sales Team concept has forever erased the outdated notion that generating revenue in business is a sole-source game—instead illustrating it is indeed a team sport.

Che lives, breathes, and sleeps his craft. He has his fingers on the pulse of profit generation and an instinctual insight into why the heart of a flailing business has stopped. Most importantly, he can resuscitate the flow of revenue in any company with just a whiteboard and a conversation. Che Brown is the CEO of EasySalesHub (www.EasySalesHub.com), scaling businesses to six and seven figures. This all-in-one solution generates leads, qualifies prospects, books appointments, closes deals and frees entrepreneurs to focus on other business needs. Che was named one of the Top 15 entrepreneurs to keep an eye out for across North America in 2021 by USA Today News.

Che is the Executive Producer of *www.TheMakingOfAnEntrepreneur.com* DocuSeries, Host of the #1 Business Development and Late Night Show *In The Country: The Happy Entrepreneur Show* (*www.HappyEntrepreneurShow.com*), and Founder of Comeback Champion (*www.ComebackChampionSummit.com*).
Author's Website: *www.CheBrown.com*

Book Series Website*: www.TheBookOfInfluence.com*

CYNTHIA GALLARDO

LEGACY & LIKABILITY: THE DYNAMIC DUO

According to the Merriam-Webster Dictionary, likability is defined as having qualities that bring about a favorable regard; pleasant, and agreeable.

Legacy is a term that can be used in many different ways. For our purposes, we will define legacy as the tangible gifts you can leave others, such as material assets and lessons learned. Lessons learned are tangible because they can be written down. I encourage you to write down your lessons learned so that they can be shared now and in the future to leave a positive impact.

We each have a responsibility to lead and pave the way for others, just as others have paved the way for us. The intangible part of a legacy is a person's reputation, character, and values.

Legacy and likability go hand in hand. They are like BFFs (best friends forever), two peas in a pod, and a dynamic duo. In the late 1970s, there was a popular superhero duo called the Wonder Twins. They were a brother (Zan) and sister (Jayna) duo that activated their superpowers by touching the rings on their hands and saying, "Wonders Twin powers— activate!" They had to work together, creating a synergy, to activate their powers.

LIKABILITY FACTOR

Once their "Wonder Twin powers" were activated, Jayna could transform into any animal and Zan could transform into any state of water. Legacy and likability work in the same way. In order to be effective, legacy and likability have to work together.

Your legacy includes your past, present, and future. Your legacy starts with you. It's the power of one. You are the catalyst. Yet, you can accomplish so much more and impact more lives positively by combining your energy with the energy of those around you to create a synergy.

Synergy is defined as "the whole is greater than the individual parts." In order to effectively create synergistic relationships that will drive a powerful legacy, the likability factor is imperative. Think about it this way: If you don't have "qualities that bring a favorable regard, pleasant, and agreeable," then you will not be able to live and leave a lasting legacy, because most individuals do not want to be around someone that is unfavorable, unpleasant, and disagreeable. A legacy is about leaving a positive impact, mark, and footprint.

Likability plays a key role in each of the 5 steps of the Legacypreneur™ Blueprint, which consists of five instrumental steps that build upon each other to allow you to live and leave a lasting legacy.
The Legacypreneur™ Blueprint steps are:

1. Save Yourself (SY)
2. Next Everyone Else (NE)
3. Reevaluate, Readjust, Repeat (R)
4. Give (G)
5. Yes! Yes! Yes! (Y).

The last step is where you celebrate your successes, large and small. The small successes lead to the large successes. The momentum created allows you to continue forward. Placing each of the steps together spells out SY-NE-R-G-Y™.

Likability is a subjective term because, ultimately, we cannot control how others feel about us; yet, we can control how we perceive ourselves.

As individuals, it is important to first be pleasant and agreeable with ourselves, and we can then transfer this quality of likability to others.

We can take a holistic approach to likability. It starts from within; therefore, you must save yourself (SY) first in order to focus on others—next everyone else (NE). This reminds me of my son, Elijah, who is five years old at the moment. He has a strong sense of self. He doesn't question himself as many of us do when we reach adulthood. We can be our own worst enemy. We must learn from all those strong willed and confident five-year-olds out there and get out of our own way.

When you've done that, you can continue developing into the best version of yourself by consistently implementing the Rs: Reevaluate, Readjust, and Repeat. It's a process. You can then give (G) to others in ways you never imagined as part of your legacy. You can share your lessons learned and material assets during any part of your journey.

There are steps that individuals, entrepreneurs, and intrapreneurs can take to protect and preserve their legacy. For example, legacypreneurs™ can create a will or trust for individuals and businesses. In addition, a business legacy can be protected and preserved with a trademark.

Likability also involves applying the platinum rule: Treat others as they want to be treated. We must get to know those around us—those we interact with at school, work, home, community, and the world—to know how they want to be treated. With social media today, we can travel and impact the world with the technology at our fingertips.

Since we have such a large reach and potential to impact so many, synergy is an important part of our legacy. Synergy is the catalyst that creates a legacypreneur™. In order to create the biggest footprint, it is important for a legacypreneur™ to have the likability factor.

Legacypreneur™ combines legacy plus entrepreneur and legacy plus intrapreneur. An entrepreneur is defined as one who organizes, manages, and assumes the risks of a business or enterprise. An intrapreneur is defined as an employee of a large corporation who is given freedom and financial support to create new products, services, systems, etc., and does not have to follow the corporation's usual routines or protocols.

A fusion of the two words creates a synergy and final product of legacypreneur™. It is powerful equation: legacy + entrepreneur = legacypreneur™ and legacy + intrapreneur = legacypreneur™. As individuals, entrepreneurs, or intrapreneurs, we have the potential to live and leave a lasting legacy utilizing the likability factor.

Life, business, and legacy are about making connections and building relationships. People naturally gravitate to those they like and trust. Communication is at the core of the following components of a legacy— making connections, building relationships, the likability factor, and gaining trust. Communication is the transmission of information and can be verbal or nonverbal or a combination of both.

Our body language plays a major role in effective communication. Think about it: Two people can have a power struggle without even speaking; a conversation can be had without even speaking. In addition, active listening is critical to have effective communication. I distinctly remember a Mentor sharing that we have two ears and a mouth so that we can listen more than we speak. Active listening is a powerful tool that can be utilized to increase the likability factor and develop a positive legacy.

When I moved to Louisiana, I learned a lot about Southern hospitality and about making connections. I learned a word that continues to make a lasting impact on me and my legacy. The word is "lagniappe." It means giving that "little extra." I'd love to give you some lagniappe and share a special gift. You can go to *www.cynthiagfreegift.com* to receive the gift. Enjoy!

Remember, likability and legacy are a dynamic duo. They must work together to be most effective. You have the superpower to make a positive and lasting impact on those around you while you live and leave a lasting legacy by implementing the Legacypreneur™ Blueprint. You can make a difference one action at a time and one letter at a time through SY-NE-R-G-Y.

CYNTHIA GALLARDO

About Cynthia Gallardo: Cynthia Gallardo, your Leading Legacy Lawyer™, keynote speaker, author, business strategist, legacypreneur™, and lawyer. Cynthia is passionate about providing a positive interaction with every person she meets on a daily basis, whether in a personal, professional, or academic setting. Cynthia's creed is "Results. Not excuses."

Cynthia is a catalyst that empowers and inspires entrepreneurs struggling to transform a business idea into a vision, and from a vision into the reality of a profitable business by discovering their unique business DNA to launch, build, and protect their legacy.

Cynthia graduated with honors earning her MBA and law degree. Cynthia is a proud graduate of Southern University Law Center. Cynthia is CEO and founder of Cynthia Gallardo Law, LLC and Synergy Solutions PRO, LLC which houses Launch to Legacy Academy™. Cynthia practices immigration law, transactional law, and estate planning. Cynthia takes a holistic approach to business and shares her 5 Step Launch to Legacy™ Blueprint outlining the framework to live and leave a lasting legacy. Cynthia worked in the corporate environment for nearly fifteen years transitioning from front line representative to management roles to a leadership role. Cynthia is a lifelong learner and strives to guide others to become the best versions of themselves personally and professionally.

Cynthia lives in Louisiana with her husband and son where they enjoy spending time together in spiritual activities. In addition, the Gallardo family has four fur babies—three Doberman pinschers and a cat. The Gallardo family is a strong advocate of the foster to adopt program as they have personally taken the foster to adoption journey.

Author's Website: *www.CynthiaGallardo.com*

Book Series Website: *www.TheBookOfInfluence.com*

DANIEL KILBURN

THE POWER OF POPULARITY: HOW LIKABILITY SHAPES OUR LIVES

. . . .

People are more likely to respond positively to someone they like, so it is essential to cultivate a charming and amiable personality. But how easy is it to cultivate a charming and amiable personality? The need to be liked starts at a very early age. I remember my daughters and granddaughter coming home at one point in time from elementary school, bemoaning the fact that nobody liked them.

People want to be liked at an early age for a variety of reasons. It could be a desire for acceptance, the need to fit in with their peers, or simply the natural human inclination to want to be appreciated and respected.

Whatever the reason, getting approval from others can give young people a strong sense of security, belonging, and validation. In addition, being well-liked can open doors that would otherwise remain closed and could provide access to opportunities that they might not have had if those around them hadn't accepted them.

They were certainly unaware that to become likable, one needs to do something with others, not just sit down in the corner waiting for them to come to you. It is very clear that we as individuals are certainly the most special people in the world, and we all want to know what's in it for us.

Therefore, it is very important to find opportunities to reach out to other people and do something for them that will be special for them. You did something for them they will eventually do something for you, but will it also raise your likability factor?

Waah, Nobody Likes Me!

My granddaughter, Aliza, often came home from school despondent because nobody liked her. Although she often overlooked it, I had to remind her how remarkable she was. She was smart and captivating—traits many couldn't understand or appreciate.

There came a time when she stopped trying to get people to like her, and suddenly people started liking her a lot more. It also helped that she became supportive of her schoolmates and took charge of things in her school and the surrounding community. The key is to be genuine and let others appreciate who you are. By doing so, you'll attract more authentic relationships and have better success at forming meaningful connections with those around you.

We are naturally attracted to people who can offer us support or status, whether it be through their actions and successes, physical stature, societal standing or simply by virtue of being in the right place at the right time. In essence, likability is often a product of what someone has to give.

Positioning

Many years ago, in my younger days, I was a bouncer in a prominent nightclub on Cannery Row. One Thursday, my night off at the nightclub promised to be an exciting one. I was supposed to meet someone there for a date. I walked in the front door, and there she was on the other side of the room. Our eyes met immediately—it felt like minutes rather than seconds before we both smiled knowingly at each other.

It seemed nothing could ruin this moment until reality set in. Despite this perfect scenario, I was anxious—dreading the potential catastrophe should any of the three other women in the room catch wind! If I spoke to any one of them first, the others might hit me over my head with their purse. It would spell disaster.

Thinking fast, I realized I knew everybody in the nightclub. All the tables were packed, and every seat was taken. Everyone there seemed to be someone I knew, and it felt like a reunion! Energized by the atmosphere, without hesitating for even one second, my feet carried me around everyone's table in the club while I exchanged warm greetings, from compliments about how awesome the band would soon sound—they played at my wedding reception later down the line—to wishing everyone an enjoyable night ahead despite knowing right then and there that none could come close to mine.

As I moved through the club that night, making sure to connect with each person at their table, there was a particularly important one, my girl. I let her know something had come up and reassured her that our standing date would happen later in half an hour across the street at The Sardine Factory.

With a hop in my step, I greeted the other club-goers, including the three women, and made sure they knew that even though tonight would not be our night together this time, we would still meet up later in the week. I said goodbye with just enough charm to walk away unscathed—phew! I left the club and crossed the street into what promised a wonderful evening of adventure.

Knowing and being liked by people can be a powerful asset, and I'm living proof! Being strategically at the door of important events, I made an impression on everyone. And because my friendly attitude and fairness created goodwill with those same individuals, they ended up viewing me as someone worth knowing—allowing all kinds of exciting opportunities down the line!

Likability Factors

There are many ways to achieve this: being a good listener, showing genuine interest in others, avoiding criticism, and being kind and understanding. I can also stress the significance of making the other person feel important by complimenting them on their achievements.

Becoming likable requires a combination of social skills, emotional intelligence, and positive character traits. Here are some skills and techniques that can help you become more likable:

- Active listening: When someone is speaking to you, make sure you are fully present and engaged in the conversation. Listen actively and show that you are interested in what they are saying.

- Empathy: Try to put yourself in other people's shoes and understand their perspective. Show empathy and offer support when needed.

- Authenticity: Be yourself, and don't try to be someone you're not. People can tell when someone is genuine, and they tend to appreciate honesty and authenticity.

- Positive attitude: Maintain a positive attitude and outlook on life. People are naturally drawn to those who radiate positivity and optimism.

- Sense of humor: A good sense of humor can go a long way in making you more likable. People enjoy being around those who can make them laugh.

- Confidence: Be confident in yourself and your abilities. This can be a magnet for attracting people to you.

- Kindness: Show kindness and consideration to others. Small acts of kindness can make a big difference in how people perceive you.

- Gratitude: Express gratitude for the good things in your life. People are drawn to those who have a sense of appreciation and gratitude.

- Non-judgmental attitude: Avoid making snap judgments or being overly critical of others. Adopt a non-judgmental attitude and be accepting of others.

- Politeness: Use polite language, show good manners, and be respectful of others. These small courtesies can make a big difference in how people perceive you.

You Are A Mirror

There is more to being likable than being able to follow a checklist of things to do. Becoming likable is becoming someone people want to like, associate with, and call a friend. There are several ways to do that. Go places where people go that you want to be associated with. Do things that people you want to be like do. Assist them whenever possible.

Additionally, being cooperative and compromising instead of being confrontational or argumentative can build strong and positive relationships with others and, in turn, increase influence and the ability to achieve goals. But I will say there may be some places where these four attributes must be evaluated.

Being argumentative is one always to avoid. People who like to argue only want to be right and prove the other person wrong. Choosing to discuss, not argue, is always beneficial.

Respectful dialogue allows for different points of view and ultimately a better outcome than trying aimlessly to prove one's superiority—it cultivates an atmosphere that encourages exploration and understanding without hurt feelings! If a dialogue is impossible, take the high ground and walk away from an impending argument.

Cooperation and compromise are often essential components of healthy relationships and successful collaborations. However, there are some situations where these approaches should be avoided. For instance, cooperation and compromise can be detrimental in cases where one's values, ethics, or integrity are at risk.

Similarly, when faced with individuals or groups who are intentionally deceitful, manipulative, or harmful, attempting to cooperate or compromise may only serve to enable their negative behavior further. In these situations, it is important to stand firm in one's convictions and prioritize protecting one's well-being and that of others.

Closing Remarks

Overall, likability is a crucial factor in human relationships. It is essential to cultivate it to be successful in both your personal life and your professional life. The ability to be liked is an invaluable asset in any setting. Whether you're trying to make a sale or build lasting relationships with customers and colleagues, likability can give you an edge that will help propel your success.

With these tips on how to increase your likability, you should now have the tools necessary for building meaningful connections with people who matter most. What strategies will you use to ensure others find you likable?

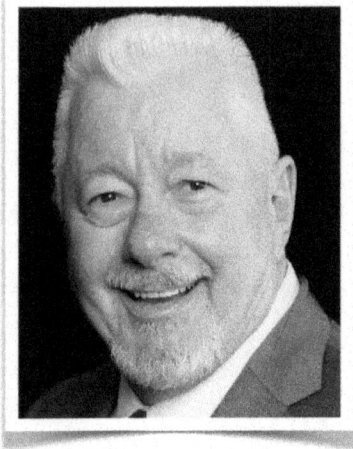

DANIEL KILBURN

About Daniel Kilburn: Improve your leadership skills with Daniel Kilburn, America's renowned "5-Star Leadership Coach". Learn to communicate effectively, adapt to challenges, and develop strong leadership qualities. Gain the necessary skills to handle difficult conversations, emergencies, and natural disasters confidently. Protect your loved ones and create a secure environment for your family and organization.

His passion for disaster management can be traced back to the Loma Prieta earthquake in 1989. It became his mission to learn disaster management so that he could protect his children. As a single father, Daniel raised two beautiful daughters while serving in the U.S. Army.

Daniel is a retired U.S. Army Senior Infantry Drill Sergeant and has instructed at the U.S. Army Sergeants Major Academy. Daniel has trained over 15,000 young men and women, foreign nationals, and Department of Defense Civilians to survive on the modern Battlefield.

Pairing his instructional background and education in disaster management, He specializes in the All-Hazards Disaster Planning approach and acceptable risk aversion.

Daniel has been featured in the following: *Authority Magazine.*, *Lifestyles Over 50*, Tan Talk Radio Network, WFLA News Channel 8, and *Carewell*. Daniel will successfully help 1,000,000 Urban families communicate and prepare for natural and man-made disasters by 2027.

Author's Website: *www.DanielKilburn.com*

Book Series Website: *www.TheBookOfInfluence.com*

DAPHENE BOOKER-HARRIS & TODD HARRIS

BUILDING RELATIONSHIPS THROUGH BUILDING RESPECT

R-E-S-P-E-C-T

Aretha was on to something when she belted to the world, "All I'm asking is for a little RESPECT"! In business, it's not always getting respect, but giving respect. For nearly 20 years, my husband, Todd, and I have had to learn and create strategies to enable us to maintain healthy business and personal relationships. Building positive relationships has been vitally important as we have developed enterprises within our business, the community we serve, and our friends and family.

So, what is respect? Webster gives us the definition of respect as "a feeling of deep admiration for someone or something elicited by their abilities, qualities, or achievements." The importance of showing respect and building positive relationships in your life is exhibited by the ways in which your employees, friends, and customers are treated.

In business, showing respect shows up in the way you engage with those with whom you work and do business and also the personal relationships you have. The relationships you build will grow naturally and bear fruit in the form of loyalty from customers and staff members, the growth of your business, and success in your endeavors. Respect is about honoring and understanding where the person you are dealing with is coming from and what their motivation is.

In turn, it is the same honor and admiration you've earned from those relationships that are reciprocated. To be honest, that did not always come easy for me.

Success

Success has been very sweet for Todd and me. For nearly 15 years, we have developed a group of enterprises in a variety of industries. Our success did not happen overnight, and it did not happen by chance. Todd and I have built an empire through consistent hard work, sweat, and tears.

At times, however, few and far between times, we have felt the brunt of misunderstandings. As a husband and wife entrepreneurial team effort for nearly 15 years, we have accomplished many things—all while juggling family, friendships, and the everyday ups and downs of life. The success has come, though not void of stressful experiences.

The obstacles to our success were often those closest to us who did not believe we were deserving of the accessories that accompanied our success. The cars we drove, the house we lived in, the way we raise our children, and when and where we vacationed, were all under a microscope.

Attitude Matters

Early in our childcare business, I did not always handle challenging interactions between myself, the staff, and customers in appropriate ways. At times, the way I handled situations caused those that I interacted with to become distant and withdrawn. My first response would be, "I don't care, I'm the boss!"

However, I soon learned that that way of thinking stagnated my ability to grow in business. I couldn't keep employees and I was wearing myself thin trying to wear so many hats as the owner. I became the driver, the director, the cook, and the teacher. It was impossible to scale my business if I continued with that mindset. I had to come to terms with the fact that perhaps my tone and my reactions in certain instances did not always lead to the best outcomes.

Communication

In the book, "Crucial Conversations," Patterson, Grenny, et. al, talks about having potentially dangerous but important conversations on a corporate level to maintain respect and healthy workplace boundaries that help your business and/or organization in the long run. The knowledge they shared was not anything that I hadn't heard before, but it was a great reminder. Those lessons from kindergarten, the same lessons we teach our preschool students, are the same lessons I had to return to in order for my business to be successful.

The key takeaways that helped me in my business:

1. **Listen** to someone until they are finished speaking.
2. **Engage** with the person by repeating what the person said back to them. This ensures that you heard them correctly, and it makes the person feel respected.
3. **Appreciate** the person you are speaking to, whether they are at a higher or lower level, but above all, as a human being.

I had to learn that a good leader listens to, engages with, and appreciates those with whom they are in a relationship. Knowing that when someone is angry or reacting negatively, 80% of the time it is a reaction to an experience and only 10-20% of the time truly reacting to the present circumstances. Bearing this in mind, Todd and I have learned to listen to and appreciate the members of our team.

Putting in the Work

We learned early on that we had to focus on the people we were in a relationship with. Our process changed, and we began to focus on building strong relationships. As we developed strategies to scale our business, we saw a turnaround. With just a few children under my care, we began an in-home childcare business.

Over time, as word of mouth spread about my nurturing style of caregiving, more families sought me out for their children's needs. Within a few years, the business had grown enough to expand into three full-service childcare centers across town that offered several after-school programs as well.

Through perseverance and hard work, parents saw the impact of the quality mentorship and guidance provided by our team of educators and caregivers at each center. Our services were something they couldn't find elsewhere in our community. This made us stand out from other similar services available nearby.

We also invested in our employees heavily through training materials for staff members so that everyone involved fully understood how best to serve those we cared for most—the kids!

We had to learn to develop systems that would help safeguard miscommunication and misunderstandings in the way we foster community. Even through misunderstandings, we have made our principal value to treat everyone with kindness and respect. Those are values that we both learned from our grandparents: "Kill'em with kindness."

The Likability Factor

Likability is a crucial aspect of building trust in relationships. When we feel likable to others or find someone likable, we are more likely to open up to them, share more personal information, and feel comfortable around them. This, in turn, builds trust as we start to believe that they have our best interests at heart and will not betray us.

Building trusting relationships requires honesty, integrity, and consistency in behavior. When these elements are presented, it becomes easier to develop strong, long-lasting relationships built on mutual respect and understanding.

In "The Likability Factor," Tim Sanders explains the four personality characteristics that help us all bring out the best in ourselves and others. Tim says that likability is made up of four elements: friendliness, relevance, empathy, and realness.

In any relationship, business and personal, those are all important facets we look for in others and try to emulate in ourselves. This is where we have found success: in our relationships.

What We Know for Sure

Oprah Winfrey ends each of her monthly magazines with a reflection, "What I know for sure." Much like Oprah, Todd and I can reflect on our successes, challenges, and absolute failures and the invaluable lessons we have learned along the way. Our success story has not stopped. It is a continually evolving story of growth.

Over the years, our business and sphere of influence have expanded beyond where we first began. This expansion is in great part to the relationships we have been able to build and maintain throughout our city.

These partnerships were not always in place—so we remain humbled and grateful for them. Partnerships with local businesses who supported our cause such as special events like family fun days have been essential.

The result has been a profound sense of belonging among all those who were part of this journey—both within our organization but also amongst those within the greater community whose lives were positively impacted by what we were doing day in and day out together! All with great RESPECT!

DAPHENE BOOKER-HARRIS & TODD HARRIS

About ToDario A. Harris: ToDario A. "Todd" Harris, NAREB, NAR, ABR, CCIM, is the founder and principal broker for Metropolis Real Estate Services. Todd Harris has brokered both commercial and residential real estate sells and lease transactions throughout his career.

As a preschool purchase and lease specialist, Todd Harris has provided clients with insight on how to evaluate a programs value, feasibility of acquisition, and facilities assessments. From start-up to business with real estate purchases, Todd Harris has the experience, skill, and expertise to get you to a desired end.

Mr. Harris has held two offices with the National Association of Real Estate Brokers (NAREB), local board President and Commercial Investment Division's National Treasurer. As the largest minority trade organization in the US, NAREB is an advocate for minority participation in the Nation's Housing Policies.

Mr. Harris attained the prestigious CCIM Designation in 2021. Todd is a graduate of the Fogelman College of Business located on the campus of the University of Memphis. Todd currently holds real estate brokerage licenses in Tennessee and Mississippi. He also consults clients and brokers throughout the United States.

About Daphene Booker-Harris: Daphene Booker-Harris, the Preschool Icon®, is changing the trajectory of children and families throughout the city of Memphis and beyond. As a much sought-after childcare consultant, she launched Global Preschool Consulting, designed to teach new and expanding childcare providers with proven blueprints and principles for building profitable childcare empires. When asked about the foundation of her work, she summed it up by saying, "We are creating achievers who will become leaders," which encapsulates her core philosophy about investing in the value and uniqueness of children, nurturing their intellectual genius, developing their overall health and wellness.

Through her GPS blueprint, Daphene's mission is to transform the childcare industry by empowering new and expanding owners through increased visibility, brand recognition, and profitability. Through any fallacy, Daphene's challenges have helped her become the success story she is today. Daphene Booker-Harris, the Preschool Icon®, is indeed a trustworthy GPS for a childcare business owner.

Authors' Websites: www.MetropolisRealEstateServices.com & www.GlobalPreschoolConsulting.com

Book Series Website: *www.TheBookOfInfluence.com*

DAWNESE OPENSHAW

LISTENING IS ESSENTIAL IN LIKABILITY

God gave us two ears and one mouth for a reason, so that we may listen twice as much as we speak. While initially this adage annoyed me, as time passed, I came to appreciate its profound wisdom in cultivating genuine communication. Authentic dialogue is at the core of effective leadership as it facilitates colleague relationships. This chapter will look into becoming authentic communicators with Dale Carnegie's timeless principles as our guide.

As a teenager, I first encountered the "two ears, one mouth" concept and wondered whether my "social butterfly" persona may have caused too much of my talking to occur; indeed, I became the runner-up for Homecoming Queen during high school!

Curiously, when I was 14, my father gave me Dale Carnegie's "How to Win Friends and Influence People." What had an immense effect was learning the importance of calling people by their names while listening attentively.

As I began high school, I aimed to form meaningful relationships with as many students as possible. By learning their names and engaging them through active listening techniques, I made friends and attempted to understand each person as a unique individual with unique qualities.

At an early age, I saw my peers sharing their experiences: in the parking lot crowd discussing their desire for understanding, among band kids who felt isolated by peers, among cheerleaders and student council members, among nerds/geeks who sought recognition of who they truly were; etc.

What struck me at that early age was the importance of listening to understand as it laid a solid foundation for authentic communication involving not just words spoken out loud but also emotions, thoughts, and any underlying messages conveyed via listening closely. Tuning into not just words spoken but also emotions allows the listener to catch the underlying messages.

Genuine Listening

Effective communication starts with an intent to comprehend fully. We do this by restating and paraphrasing what others share, connecting their words, feelings, thoughts, and emotions—creating a heart-centered experience between us both.

As life progressed, my listening skills matured, improving my overall communication. Through my leadership journey, I developed an appreciation of having two ears and one mouth in communication— emphasizing listening as a means of understanding.

Steven Covey beautifully articulated this concept: "Listening with an intent to understand, rather than reply, begins true communication and relationship-building."

Communication

Communicating honestly in our communications holds immense value, creating trust, openness, and, ultimately, relationships beyond ourselves. Being authentic in our interactions connects us to something greater than ourselves.

My early days as a United Way of Muscatine board member stand out in my memory: our director highlighted the value of open, honest communication, even when we disagreed. This shift transformed us as individuals while strengthening our organization.

Practical Steps Towards Authentic Communication

For authentic communication, here are three practical steps you should take:

Ask Questions and Listen: Cultivate empathic listening skills and recognize that empathic listening enables you to gain a deeper insight into another person's thoughts and emotions, receiving their deep communication as another human soul.

Create Self-Awareness: Show your attentiveness through eye contact and body language, such as tilting your head slightly to show your intent to listen. Keep your body open, with arms relaxed at your sides or in your lap—no crossed arms, as this signals defensiveness!

Be Transparent and Honest: Trust begins within, so when it manifests in your interactions, it becomes visible to everyone around you. There is no hidden agenda; genuine and transparent communication are hallmarks of success.

"God gave you two ears and one mouth for a reason" reminds us to value authentic communication and embrace its benefits. It calls us to remain fully present when engaging in dialogue with others, taking responsibility for our conversations, and being truly genuine with those we interact with.

Viktor Frankl stated, "Between stimulus and response, there lies a space that gives us the power to choose our response—in turn bringing growth and freedom." Authentic communication that builds connections through listening and understanding allows us to seize that space and make meaningful relationships.

If more people embraced authentic listening, the world would undoubtedly improve. Each soul-to-soul connection made would help build stronger societies.

Remember, authenticity in communication lies in building trust, encouraging openness, and building relationships that transcend individual limitations. At its heart lies mastering the art of listening to connect—an invaluable skill that can transform your professional and personal lives.

So, when someone says, "God gave us two ears and one mouth for a reason," take that as an opportunity to embrace authentic communication and harness its potential.

Authenticity is the foundation of lasting influence, providing mutual understanding between two parties.

DAWNESE OPENSHAW

About Dawnese Openshaw: Dawnese Openshaw is a radically authentic John Maxwell certified leadership coach, trainer, and speaker. At the age of 14, her father had her read Dale Carnegie's "How to Win Friends and Influence People" and she has been a student of leadership ever since.

With over 25 years of experience in small business and non-profit organizations creating and executing plans for growth, Dawnese offers marketing and strategy coaching for small businesses and training for non-profit boards.

Dawnese Openshaw Coaching expanded in 2020 to include families— supporting emotional regulation, communication, and relationship building. She combines her passion for leadership and commitment with strengthening families as a family empowerment coach, primarily serving families with teens. Dawnese empowers families to heal individually and as a unit, creating harmony in their home. She supports frustrated parents to love their kids again and not just like them.

She has been married to her husband, Scott, for 26 years and they are the parents of three amazing children, Randy, Thaniel, and Olivia, and one doodle named Tigger.

Author's Website: *www.DawneseOpenshaw.com*

Book Series Website: *www.TheBookOfInfluence.com*

DEE MANUEL CLOUD

R.E.S.P.E.C.T.

It's more important to be respected than to be liked. Many people want to be liked based on popularity, but when people genuinely know you, they can respect you. That's more important than being like. The Likability Factor is built on a foundation of genuineness and respect. It's essential to be respectful and be someone that people can look up to and be someone that people can admire so that you can attract respect.

It's a different angle to likability and a personal standard you can set for yourself.

Respect vs. Likability

It's achievable to gain respect by giving it to others as well. When gaining respect, your word is impeccable. Being the type of person who lives true to their word invites respect from others. Also, being someone who has compassion and empathy for others will ultimately help you win friends and influence people.

Before discussing the professional, earning or gaining respect over likability can be challenging or simple. Being respected by others can come from presence and composure. It doesn't always have to come from communication, but your appearance does do a lot of talking if you know what I mean. This is not a brag, but I was on a sales call with my sales team recently, and the team leader referred to me as shining. Right after that, when it was just she and I, as other people joined the meeting, another one of the sisters said to me, "Oh, Dee, you're so shining!" And so, I was like, "I don't know if it's the ring light or if it's God in me, but I'll take it."

I like to believe that I show up as someone authentic. I show up as genuine, and I hope people can feel the energy reverberating. Again, I focused on the one thing I can control: me, my mindset, and my appearance.

Respect and earning is a personal mission, something other than something you do for the game. It's just who you are and how you emulate and personify publicly when you're in the presence of other people. It's a beautiful concept. That's precisely it—just being who you are and allowing yourself to attract likability just by being who you are is kind of someone compassionate, loving, empathetic, genuine, and authentic.

These are many essential qualities and attributes you must strive for if you want. Suppose you don't have those qualities and have a negative trait that is often publicly portrayed. In that case, they might still attract a likability from a niche group of people who are magnetized to that negative or the wrong intentions.

On the positive side, far more remarkable outcomes and relationship opportunities can come from having attributes of genuineness. Relationships built on a negative foundation don't last long. Still, relationships built on those positive qualities come from respect first, followed by a more profound sense of likability and influence.

People with a negative or more pessimistic outlook on life may justify their words and actions by just being how they are. The old-dog-can't-learn-new-tricks mindset really can't be a better approach to gaining respect. Enough of us are shining to make a difference in those who have not discovered their shininess.

I felt the most respected in my life in my marriage. I have to be the most receptive. We have genuine respect for each other. So, it shows up in everything we do. It shows how we communicate, care for, and love each other because there's a genuine respect for who we have a person needs.

This is the same type of love and compassion you can have for others in your life that will earn you that feeling of respect.

I have to say the times in my life where I feel the most disrespect have been just being a black woman in America. Sometimes, you can run across people who haven't discovered their shining light, and they could be ignorant. So, these people judge others who are different from them because they haven't had the experience of having somebody like me up close in their life.

Michelle Obama said, "It's harder to hate up close." And, so, when you haven't had an experience with people who are different from you and treat you disrespectfully, it can tear you down, just like I can turn around and say something ignorant unknowingly about someone who maybe has a handicap that I'm not familiar with. It's a straightforward line to cross when you don't know how to behave around people who are different than you, but it's a hard line you cross when you treat people disrespectfully without knowing them. Just like I shared above, to earn respect, one must be willing to give consideration.

Being a black woman in America, being called the N-word has been one of the times that I felt the most disrespect. I was in my early twenties when it was the first time I'd ever been called that. I went to a party with some coworkers who were white to a Country Western Swing event, and some white gentlemen were not happy that I showed up. One man stared me down, walked past me, called me the N-word, and left the party. But now that I have grown older, I can look back at that experience and not make it a bigger deal because they genuinely didn't even know me—it had nothing to do with me. They knew nothing about me other than I'm black.

Being who you are attracts likability. We have yet to learn what other people are going through. Shame on them for their acting out behaviorally! Being who you are could also be disliked. If we know anything about power in the media and influence, sometimes being disliked by others can be a superpower, wicking away unwanted attraction or even bringing more attention to the respectable values you portray.

It takes a lot of growth, acceptance, and forgiveness. I'm proud of the person I've become and how many of my experiences have allowed me to become the radiant human being I am today.

Respect is a beautiful concept and measurement of likability. Many people focus on being liked by creating their likability. Respect has a hierarchy in personal relationships and towers over the surface level of likability. I recommend you give respect to others, and you'll attract more respect in your closest relationships.

DEE MANUEL CLOUD

About Dee Manuel Cloud: Dee Manuel Cloud is a two-time breast cancer survivor, Breast Cancer Recovery Strategist, bestselling author, international speaker, and owner and CEO of Intentional Living Academy.

As a Breast Cancer Recovery Strategist, Dee helps survivors overcome the fear, trauma and suffering of breast cancer to creating a life of peace, joy, and fulfillment so they can thrive and rebuild their lives even better than before.

Understanding the unique life experiences and goals of breast cancer survivors enables Dee to create an action plan that supports survivors in moving beyond breast cancer to create their best life. Driven by the success of her clients, Dee prides herself on creating a personal and meaningful coaching experience that empowers survivors to achieve their goals and make the rest of their lives the best of their lives.

Dee is the author of *Beauty In The Breakdown, Finding Peace In The Midst of Life's Disruptions.*

Author's Website: *www.DeeManuelCloud.com*

Book Series Website: *www.TheBookofInfluence.com*

DIANA SMITH

THAT LIKABLE RESTING B!CHE FACE

"Are you okay? Are you worried about something?" he asked. "No, why?" I asked back. "Well, you look mad and/or unhappy," he said back to me. "Actually, I'm fine. I was just thinking. Thanks for asking," I responded. An absolute stranger asked me if I was okay—why did he ask me that? The nerve!

Now, I know you are never supposed to ask a question with a question, but I did. How could an absolute stranger ask me that? I was just sitting there thinking about my day, thinking about what I was going to do with it, and minding my own business. Did I really look that way? I had to think about this one. This observance certainly made me feel unsettled and shook my confidence.

I asked my daughter if I always looked mad to her, and she informed me that I had a resting b!che face. "*A what? What is that?*" I asked. She let me know that it was just how some people looked when they were just relaxed and thinking. Oh, well, that made sense to me. "Why is it called that?" I asked with great curiosity. "Well, you might just look like you are mad, and it is off-putting to some people or even scary. Just smile more," she responded.

This was absolute news to me because I always felt like I was a friendly person and approachable. I have friends and no one ever said anything about this matter to me at all. Guess not with this news. What do I do about this?

Several of my friends told me that it was normal for me and thought nothing of it. It was just how I was, and they accepted me for who was and how I looked. The question of me having a resting b!che face came to their query and they just laughed at me. "Don't worry about it," I was told. It was right then and there I knew I had a problem.

Inside this one and only flesh structure I have is a warm heart filled with kindness, a brain swarming with ideas, and a face that only wants to wear a smile. When I get irritated, I become another person because there is a solution needed and my words are not always nice. I will throw a few "blankety-blankety-blanks" out there to appease my irritation. That sort of action isn't necessary, but it is just a response to a compromising concern. This is called putting your foot in your mouth, and an apology will generally need to follow after I calm down or the problem is resolved.

So, the RBF-er in me needed to work on this new revelation. What could I do about it? This thought-provoking problem made me think of my mom and her mother. I looked at a few pictures of them and they wore big smiles like they were rays of sunshine. I knew better than that, though, because they both were the queens of scowl. This dilemma was genetic. OMG, I am one of them. NO way!

The mirror would show me more about this inherited defect and reveal the truth to me. "Mirror, mirror on the wall, who has the worst b!che face of all?" I asked as I stared back at myself. Well, it was me. I looked around to see if anyone else was trying to play a trick on me and sure enough, I was alone. Right in front of me was the next generation of the scowl queen. This did not result in a broken mirror because then there would be seven years of bad luck on top of looking like a b!che.

Psychology was never one of my core subjects in school, but I knew if there was ever any issue to be resolved, I would dig deep for the answer and find a solution. Why did I have a constant scowl on my face and what was a reasonable solution to this matter? Hell if I know.

I decided a trip to a public place was in order. I would carefully examine the faces around me and make some clear mental notes. The coffee shop is a great place to find people that are alone. A young woman sitting at her computer with a coffee appears to be quite at peace and her face is not scowlish. The man reading the paper appears to be scowlish, as if the part of the paper he is reading is filled with bad news. A mother with two fidgety children comes in and she has a scowl on her face—I would have one too. Two women are deep in conversation with faces of concern, expressions that could be considered scowlish, but then they smile at each other with delight and agreement.

What is a scowly face? An RBF is relaxed with no true expression of light or life. It is just a face attached to a body that has no reason to shine light to others. There is an obvious sign of life because the eyes are opened. The overall appearance of the face is loose and carefree. Is the person in another state of being, like deep concentration or just really sad or mellow? Who knows, but a careful observer just walks by without any worry about the RBF-er person.

This only revealed to me that anyone deep in thought or conversation could be the wearer of a scowly face. So maybe there is some reasonable explanation behind my unapproachable appearance. It was just how I looked if I was alone or in deep thought. There is nothing wrong with that, I suppose.

I have contemplated this in my mind and found this determination to be true. If I am sad or alone or even deep in thought, I may wear a scowly face, but that, to me, is not a firm sign of being an RBF-er in reality. I am just that way.

When I am surrounded by people, I now try to encourage my mind to fix my appearance. I will raise my eyebrows, put some life in my eyes, and put a small grin on my face because this lifts your cheeks a bit and makes you seem more approachable, so I do not seem RBF-er like. This takes some concentration on my part because it almost seems to be unnatural in some small way.

Fake it 'til you make it, and it will become natural. That seems goofy in my opinion, but some habits are hard to break when you are born that way. A generational change is not a bad thing when it comes to breaking a cycle of something that is apparently not pleasant.

A face like mine is not hard to love but there are times when it is just what it is, a resting b!che face for the world to accept and love just as it is. My dog loves my RBF and so does my husband. The kids don't mind so, I guess, I will just work on how I look when I am around others. It is what it is, a scowly face for the world to take in and for someone to ask me if I am okay.

DIANA SMITH

About Diana Smith: Diana suffered many abuses in her childhood, which left her unsure about her own adulthood and trusting others in her life. By 1979, she had two biological daughters. Poverty-stricken and with nowhere to go, she learned to survive in a world of doubt and desperation. In 2011, Diana's youngest child was killed by a drunk driver on her birthday. Diana suffered grief and severe depression for seven long years.

Diana researched mental health to understand the effects on her own mental well-being. She is writing a memoir of her loss and a book on parenting called *If My Brain Had Wheels*. She is a motivational speaker on mental health regarding depression and childhood abuse.

Diana met and married a wonderful man after her move to Colorado. Together, they have five children, four grandchildren, and two great-grandsons. Life has gotten much better for her.

Author's Website: *www.TheFWord.biz*

Book Series Website: *www.TheBookOfInfluence.com*

EILEEN GALBRAITH

THE MAKING OF A SOCIAL BUTTERFLY

Have you ever met someone and were instantly drawn to them—you just knew you wanted to be around them? Did they make you feel comfortable? Did you feel that they were genuinely interested in you? Were they full of laughter, smiles, and warmth?

Remember the last time you walked into a room and instantly were drawn to that one person who just stood out in the crowd? Their mannerisms, their posture, that smile, and their effervescent attitude were contagious!

It was obvious that you were not the only one mesmerized by this individual, as many were seeking their attention. But why? You don't even know this person, yet you know you must be in their presence.

This, my friend, is the Likability Factor. Some have it, some don't—yet all can achieve it over time.

You can see by how they conduct themselves that they are genuinely interested in those they are conversing with and they just have a flare for creating ease and comfort. There is nothing fake about this person! They truly care.

Oftentimes, people have described me as that person. You see, I am full of life, I love meeting new people, and I have been known to speak with everyone in the elevator! Yes, that's me.

This is rather strange as I grew up a very scared and shy girl. I was afraid of my own shadow and, in a crowd, you could always find me clinging to my mother's skirt. Sometimes, I would just go and hide. I remember being in a very crowded department store when we were kids; all 6 of us were shopping with my mother and I was so stressed out that I hid under one of the clothing racks. Of course, I know now that was not the right thing to do as everyone was worried about me and it took some time to find me.

Do you find yourself doing that, hiding from others because you are so frightened by the crowds? If so, I am here to tell you that all of that can change. I believe it was after high school that I started to come out of my shyness. I was very friendly in school but only stayed around my closest friends. It wasn't until I had my first real job that the shyness withdrew from me.

You see, I never thought I could do anything. I didn't think people liked me; I was bullied and always the butt of someone's jokes. I was an awkward youth, never participating in sports or activities. I didn't realize until much later in life that one of the reasons I was so shy was because, at the age of 8 or 9, my mother was told by my eye doctor that if I was ever hit in the head, I would go totally blind.

Well, can you imagine how a 9-year-old might react to hearing that? This was during a time when I had several operations to correct my blindness in my right eye, as well as trying to straighten this crossed eye.

Unfortunately, neither were a success, so I grew up being blind in one eye and cross-eyed. Bullying was very familiar to me. Apparently, being different was not acceptable to other students.

But all that changed when I got my first job. It was then that I realized that I had many skills and talents and was guided and recognized by my manager at that time. Denise K. was the best manager I have ever encountered in my 42 years of working in retail.

My shyness cocoon started to disappear and a Social Butterfly emerged. I realized that people liked me for who I was, they loved my personality, recognized my abilities on what I could do, and never focused on a limitation.

My Likability Factor soared and allowed me to interact with people I never thought I would meet in my lifetime. As I began to build my coaching business, time after time, people would express to me their desire to work with me because of how they saw me treat others with kindness, compassion, and sincerity. Until I discovered my Likability Factor, I was too afraid to approach anyone! There is hope for all of us to be able to do what we love to do while supporting others in what they want, need, and aspire to have in their lives.

So, what exactly IS the Likability Factor? For me, it is someone that shows an interest in others, someone who supports people, and someone who gives of themselves first. They show empathy, joy, excitement in what they do and how they treat others. They are full of life, and always eager to learn new and interesting things.

How does one develop The Likability Factor? It is simpler than one would think. In the book, *How to Win Friends and Influence People* by Dale Carnegie, he states the following:

> *"You can make more friends in two months by becoming interested in other people than you can in two years by trying to get other people interested in you."*

Simple statement, right? For some, they concentrate most of their energy on the latter.

It is important to note here that you cannot make someone like you; you can, however, show them that you care about them, show an interest in them, and they in turn will naturally like you. Yes, it is that easy.

LIKABILITY FACTOR

Let's define The Likability Factor. I have broken it down into an acronym—for me, it allows me to incorporate the knowledge and principles easily into my life.

Listen: Really listen to someone when they are speaking with you; don't allow distractions to intertwin with the conversation. People want to know they are being heard.

Interest: Show them that you are listening to every word; acknowledge them with small gestures, or a nod of the head. A short reply like, "I agree, I understand" can go a long way. Repeat back certain point so they know you heard them.

Kindness: When it is appropriate, offer help and support, give compliments, and show empathy. Be sure to acknowledge other people's feelings.

Authenticity: Please, above all else, be yourself. Embrace your uniqueness and people will see how comfortable you are to be around. Do not be afraid to be vulnerable, as this fosters a deeper connection with others.

Body language: Many books have been written on this topic! To be sure, your posture, facial expressions and stance will make a difference. Smile, avoid crossing your arms, notice how the other person is standing. The objective here is to look comfortable and approachable.

Initiate conversations: Because I was so shy, this is very important trait to have. Be the first to start the conversation, build rapport and help the other person become comfortable and more at ease. Engage in meaningful conversations about shared topics: Discuss shared interests in-depth, exchanging insights and experiences.

Laugh and smile: This is a favorite of mine—I so enjoy when others are having a great time, as with laughter we all feel more relaxed. Smiles are always welcomed. Most importantly, be genuine.

Integrity: Keep your word: Honor your commitments and follow through on promises. Be honest: Speak truthfully and avoid deceit or exaggeration. Maintain confidentiality: Respect others' privacy and keep sensitive information confidential.

Thoughtful gestures: I believe it to be one of our human traits that we all want to feel appreciated, respected, and acknowledged. Show appreciation when appropriate. Little acts of kindness and showing a genuine interest can go a long way.

Yield the spotlight: We started with *Listening*, and *Yielding* wraps the Likability Factor all together. You don't have to be the center of attention: you should always share that spotlight with others. Be supportive, show enthusiasm, and encourage others to share. Actively listen and you will instinctively know when to participate in the conversation.

By implementing the above steps, you can further develop your Likability Factor and create more meaningful relationships, connections, and partnerships with the people around you.

I will end with this quote, again from Dale Carnegie:

"If we want to make friends, let's put ourselves out to do things for other people—things that require time, energy, unselfishness, and thoughtfulness."

This quote sums up the Likability Factor for me. What would you add to it? I have always believed that if more people would just talk with each other, this would be a much better world!

One Person has the Power to Change Anything—don't ever forget that!

EILEEN GALBRAITH

About Eileen E Galbraith: As a Financial Architect for Business, entrepreneurs hire Eileen to build their influence and scale their profits because most lack essential methods and channels to create success, lack funding opportunities, and may face continuous struggles resulting in business disarray. So, Eileen helps them define, align, and design a visible, credible, and sustaining business. Financial disarray is a precursor to failure—do not let that happen to your business!

Eileen is a Compassionate Kick-ass Coach. She can kick your butt in financial shape and make things happen, but she's also very compassionate. She knows what people need, what they want, and how to deliver it.

Eileen is a Certified FICO Pro, an International Best-Selling Author and Speaker, a sought-after Business Success Coach, and the Founder of Renewed Abundance and Credit Knowhow. She has run multi-million-dollar businesses throughout her career and increased cash flow and profitability throughout her markets.

Recognized as a professional Business Coach, Eileen positions her clients toward optimal possibilities, such as optimizing their personal credit to position themselves to build credit in the name of their business. This all-important step opens the doors to Financial Creditability, Fundability, and Business Growth. Eileen has a high-energy, no-nonsense approach and loves supporting people with their goals. Just look for the Dancing Queen, and you will find Eileen!

Author's Website: *www.CreditKnowhow.biz* & *www.RenewedAbundance.com*

Book Series Website: *www.TheBookOfInfluence.com*

ELIZABETH ANNE WALKER

THE ESSENCE OF LIKING YOURSELF

She sat, hand on furrowed Botox-filled brow, wondering where it had all gone wrong. She had, it seemed, to have them all eating out of the palm of her hand, until one day they just weren't. One person even messaged her saying, "I just don't like you."

Some people have already decided where this story goes, some people relate to it despite me having only written 4 lines, and some people are just about to enter the story.

She had done all the things. She was the it girl, the popular one in school, the one people came to for advice, the one who proved herself over and over. Always striving, always achieving, always winning. She had been there, done that. And every time something she had little knowledge on entered her field, she went and learnt more about it. People hung off her every word. They praised her, sent her gifts, and reminded her every day of just how lovable she was. She had the high score in likability factor.

And it seemed to last for a long time, until, one day, she woke up and no one was listening, no one was watching, and no one was praising. She was a has been.

He spent most of his life inside. Working, discovering more and more of what could further the human race. No friends, no parties—just work. He worked and worked and worked. No one liked him. In fact, no one even really knew him. Until one day they did. He changed their life, he revolutionized the way they did things, and he saved them time. They heralded his inventions and revered him for his tenacity. They demanded more and more and more from him every year. Until, one day, they didn't. He was a has been.

They were the prom king and queen. They went on and had successful careers, got married, had babies, and lived the dream. They were popular, effective, charitable and everyone loved them. Until, one day, they didn't. They were "has beens."

Likability is a trait that has been revered in business for a long time. People who are likable are more likely to be promoted. People who are likable are more likely to be invited to events. People who are likable are more likely to experience greater satisfaction at work. People who are likable are more likely to create great relationships at work. People who are likable are more likely to attract other people who are likable into a team. Managers like people who are likable.

Likability, however, is subjective. It may only work in a certain way for a certain group of people for a certain amount of time.

And I wonder at what point likability becomes a sell-out. Where people, to retain likability, sell out on their values, sell out on their principles, sell out on their hopes, and sell out on their dreams.

The retention of likability can also hold you back. For example, when likability has got you to the point of being a manager and you need to make a decision that is difficult for those you manage. An unpopular decision can damage likability in an instance. And whilst the longevity of likability may allow this damage to repair quickly, it may not. This is where the likable person is shunned by those who previously looked up to him and reveled in his ideas. And the aftermath is horrific.

The previously likable person enters the stages of grief. Only unlike when experiencing the death of someone close to you, it is experiencing the death of you, whilst still having to live every day in what appears to be an unforgiving world.

Everything that used to work to your advantage now seems to work to your disadvantage. Everything you thought to be true about yourself seems to be challenged repeatedly. Everything you believed about others, you now question. Initially, there is denial, and the person will keep going as normal, expecting that people still like them despite the whispers in the hallway.

Next there is anger, and the previously likable person starts to blame their colleagues, their bosses, and the system. The third stage is bargaining, and this is where a recruitment drive will produce unsuccessful results.

And this is the point at which depression sets in. Depression is a challenge that naturally makes one less likable despite a rhetoric of societal acceptance of the condition. For some, this is the end of a life that had so much promise. They become a has been.

For those watching from the sidelines, it can shatter hope forever. And those that have been through it and survived watch from the finish line with a hope filled heart to see this person evolve beyond who they thought they were.

So, what is the evolution from likability? Who do you need to be? What do you need to do? What do others expect of you?

These are all the wrong questions. Here are some better ones:

Who do you choose to be? How do you choose to act? With whom do you do what you do? What is the version of you that you like and enjoy being?

At this point, likability becomes intrinsic, despite societal expectations. Long gone is the need and desire to see here and feel your likability from others. If you like you, others will like you. If you accept you, others will accept you. And if they don't, then move on—you're not a tree; you can literally change your position whenever you feel like it.

Find your people somewhere else—because you liking you, and you being you, and others allowing you to be you is what will create true likability. And often this quest for self-likability leads to incredible destinations.

The tenacity to be all you can be despite what others think will, over time, create greater likability than you've ever dreamed possible. The nature of being principled and holding true to your values above all else will create likability over time. It may not be immediate, it may not be spoken of, and it will create conversations that appear to hold dislike towards you.

These conversations will occur as those that come upon you recognize their failings through their inability to hold their own principles as tightly as you hold yours. You, in effect, highlight their shadow parts. The parts of them that disguise recognition as likability.

And whilst recognition in older times was valuable as it was based on merit over likability, these days it appears to be based on popularity and likability. When awards are a pay to enter scenario and awardees have a close relationship with the award organizers, there's a likability issue as there is likely a better candidate unknown to the organizer personally and therefore unable to be liked.

So, the evolution of likability is truly liking yourself. Many people base their worth on whether others like them. Social media, the internet, and travel have made it easier than ever for all individuals and businesses to be known globally. The job market is a global stage, and supply chains and distribution are global, too.

At the end of the day, you need to be so pleased with your own efforts that you don't need an award. You go to sleep with you, and it is you that will sleep well when you are on target, on mission, and loving what you do, and, even more importantly, who you are.

Whilst likability is useful for initially developing relationships, it is overrated over time. In time, the important things are that you honor your word, show up authentically, deliver on time, create with authenticity for who you are and what the product or service is, and celebrate yourself whilst showing the world what you can do for them.

When you feel like you're a has been, it's just a sign to turn up the volume! Who do you choose to be? How do you choose to act? With whom do you do what you do? What is the version of you that you like and enjoy being?

And to finish in the words of my grandfather, the incredible Angus George Suthers: "Blow your own trumpet, girly—no one else will!"

ELIZABETH ANNE WALKER

About Elizabeth Walker: Elizabeth is Australia's leading Female Integrated NLP Trainer, an international speaker with Real Success, and the host of Success Resources' (Australia's largest and most successful events promoter, including speakers such as Tony Robbins and Sir Richard Branson) inaugural Australian Women's Program, "The Seed."

Elizabeth has guided many people to achieve complete personal breakthroughs and phenomenal personal and business growth. With over 25 years of experience transforming the lives of hundreds of thousands of people, Elizabeth's goal is to assist leaders in creating the reality they choose to live, impacting millions on a global scale.

A thought leader who has worked alongside people like Gary Vaynerchuck, Kerwin Rae, Jeffery Slayter, and Kate Gray, Elizabeth has an outstanding method of delivering heart with business.

As a former lecturer in medicine at the University of Sydney and lecturer in nursing at Western Sydney University, Elizabeth was instrumental in the research and development of the stillbirth and neonatal death pathways, ensuring each family in Australia went home knowing what happened to their child, and felt understood, heard, and seen.

A former Australian Champion in Trampolining and Australian Dance sport, Elizabeth has always been passionate about the mindset and skills required to create the results you are seeking.

Author's Website: *www.ElizabethAnneWalker.com*

Book Series Website: *www.TheBookOfInfluence.com*

ERIN LEY

BE THE SHINING LIGHT

In Dale Carnegie's classic book, *How to Win Friends and Influence People*, he brilliantly states, "The only way on earth to influence other people is to talk about what they want and show them how to get it."

The quickest way to turn someone off is by talking about yourself while showing no interest in the other person. Chapters in Carnegie's book, such as *If You're Wrong Admit It* and *A Drop of Honey* illustrate wisdom from the dawn of time. Likability takes humility. It takes being able to swallow our pride and speak from a place of compassion and empathy.

When I was a little girl, my greatest mistake was that I cared way too much what other people thought of me. The anxiety this caused me was unbearable; I just wanted to be liked. I had zero influence on anyone and I was liked strictly on the basis of conforming to others.

It all started in the 1970's with my introduction to Kindergarten and First Grade. I had bullies for teachers, and they frightened me. I was ridiculed constantly, and physically abused for talking and smiling in class with my friends. I was told I was bringing too much attention to myself. Prior to that experience, I was extremely comfortable within my own skin and had a natural confidence in who I was.

After those two years of back-to-back teachers who obviously had personal issues that they took out on children, I couldn't speak in class for the following six years. If the teacher called on me to answer a question, my heart would race, I'd feel the blood rush to my face, and I'd forget the answer even though I knew it only seconds before she called on me. And right after she called on someone else, the answer immediately came right back to me.

I was the first one to volunteer for the chores to be done in class, whether it was wiping and washing down the blackboards or clapping the erasers outside to get them ready to erase new chalk. I did everything I could to ensure the teacher would like me and treat me fairly. Trying to earn likability in this way is extremely disempowering, coming from a place of fear and not confidence, and offers no influence whatsoever.

This went on from Second Grade to Seventh Grade when I then experienced a bully who was now my peer. She sat right behind me in class. The bully would pull one hair out of my head at a time and thought it was funny. She threatened to beat me up in the park across from the school. This little seventh grader did this for six months. Every time I told my mother about it my mother would say, "Ladies don't fight. I expect you to be better than that."

I dealt with it for six months because I didn't want to disappoint my mother. However, one day I couldn't deal with it any longer. I told the bully I was not going out of my way for this. We will fight each other on the corner on my way home from school.

The crowd formed. Many kids from the all-girls school showed up as well as the all-boys school across the street. The corner was packed. I had so much adrenaline and pent-up frustration that when the fight started, I just saw red. At the end, the bully cried, saying she had to go home. A friend who lived two doors down walked home with me and kept saying, "That was amazing, Erin! That was amazing!"

I looked at my friend and kept saying, "My mother is going to kill me."

I walked through my front door and apologized to my mom. I said, "I'm so sorry, Mom! I fought the bully! I'm so sorry! And I think I broke her nose because it was bleeding, and her mother might call you. I'm so sorry."

My mother responded, "Good for you, Erin! Let her mother call. I have a few words for her."

I thought to myself, *I put up with that for six months when I could have wrapped it up in six minutes?*

The next thing I knew, my Aunt Nancy came out onto her stoop. We lived in attached houses in Brooklyn, NY. My family is very close. Aunt Nancy started offering me high-fives, telling me how proud she was of me. I was surprised by the accolades. I thought I was in deep trouble; however, it turned out to be quite the opposite.

The next day at school, everyone wanted to be friends with me. It was incredible. Fellow students would say, "Erin, can I borrow a pencil?" or "Erin, can we walk home together?" or even, "Erin, can we hang out later after homework is done?" It was absolutely amazing. I learned during that experience that when you are clearly empowering yourself, it leads to becoming an influencer which leads to likability. Likability does not happen from a place of disempowerment or victimhood. The victim mentality only breeds contempt.

That experience was one of the most defining moments in my life. I knew then to deal with adversity immediately, and to always stay in the mindset of empowerment as opposed to the victim mentality.

However, as great as that lesson was, and as empowered as I felt, I was still super sensitive. I personalized everything and it was painful. I'm a Pisces; I'm an empath, a clairsentient. I feel things very deeply. I gave way too much credence to what the outer world thought of me, even more so than what I thought of myself. No one was able to bully me; however, my feelings were still easily hurt. I still counted on others to tell me how pretty I was, how smart I was, how successful I was going to be.

Fortunately for me, I found out at age 25, with a cancer diagnosis of non-Hodgkins lymphoblastic lymphoma, that I was living life of purpose. The diagnosis brought my life to a screeching halt and gave me the time and space to go deep within and become fully aligned with who I truly am.

The opinions of others became irrelevant. I no longer personalized what others think of me. I learned how not to care how others judged me, although constructive criticism is always welcome from trusted sources.

My goal was to not only live but to finally live life on my terms. I got into the driver's seat of my own life. I empowered myself once again. I held my doctors accountable. I became my own biggest advocate. I highly suggest you do the same in life, no matter what your situation is.

As you advocate for yourself, you are encouraging others to do the same without even realizing it. Other cancer patients in the treatment room would see how on top of my protocol I was and the dialogue between my care givers and me was crystal-clear. The other patients shared with me how I inspired them to do the same. Their outlook on life transformed. This kind of likability has massive influence.

I kept living every time the doctors said I'd die during the two-and-a-half-year protocol. I went on to have three children they swore would never happen. The doctors at Memorial Sloan-Kettering Cancer Center began having their patients call me at home in the 1990's and this is how I began Life Coaching. I absolutely love it!

I've been a Life Coach and Business Strategist for three decades, transforming lives and businesses. The most difficult times in my life have always turned out to be the biggest blessings. They've inspired me to stretch, learn, and grow.

Likability starts with you. It begins by you connecting with and loving yourself. This leads to confidence and I'm not talking about the kink of confidence that must be announced. It's just felt by others. It's great energy.

Look to serve others without looking for something in return. Be a shining light in this world. There's plenty of darkness. Don't feed that. There's zero likability or influence in that space if you're looking to live your best life. Make decisions from a place of love as opposed to fear. That's empowering. Empowered people attract empowered people. Like attracts like. Make it so you're creating the best version of you and your best life where the sky is just the beginning.

I have an assessment that will give you a baseline of where you are at regarding the ten top areas of living personally and professionally at *www.LifeOnTrack.club/Assessment.* Take your time when doing this and see where you're at today as you begin to create your next steps walking into the next best chapter of your life, and help others do the same.

Celebrate life and you'll have a life worth celebrating! Always remember to live onward and upward.

ERIN LEY

About Erin Ley: As Founder and CEO of Onward Productions, Inc., Erin Ley has spent the last 30 years as an Author, Professional Speaker, Personal and Professional Empowerment and Success Coach predominantly around mindset, vision and decision. Founder of many influential summits, including "Life On Track," Erin is also the host of the upcoming online streaming T.V. show, "Life On Track with Erin Ley," which is all about helping you get into the driver's seat of your own life.

They call Erin "The Miracle Maker!" As a cancer survivor at age 25, single mom of 3 at age 47, successful Entrepreneur at age 50, Erin has shown thousands upon thousands across the globe how to become victorious by being focused, fearless, and excited about life and your future! Erin says, "Celebrate life and you'll have a life worth celebrating!"

To see more about Erin and the release of her 4th book, "WorkLuv: A Love Story," along with her "Life On Track" Course & Coaching Programs, please visit her website.

Author's Website: *www.ErinLey.com*

Book Series Website & Author's Bio: *www.TheBookOfInfluence.com*

FATIMA HURD

THE GOLDEN RULE: HOW YOU TREAT OTHERS

Dale Carnegie's book, *How to Win Friends and Influence People,* was truly an inspiration to me. Some of his principles aligned with me before I even read his book. His book validated what I already knew and taught me some cool things that I didn't know and now implement in my day-to-day interactions.

These are the following principles:

1. Become genuinely interested in other people.

2. Smile.

3. Remember that a man's name is the sweetest and most important sound in any language.

4. Be a good listener. Encourage others to talk about themselves.

5. Talk in terms of another man's interests.

6. Make the other person feel important—and do it sincerely.

I enjoyed reading this book, and what Dale mentioned in his book resonated with me. I have used these principles many times without intuitively knowing at first that these are the principles Dale Carnegie used to win friends and influence people. The following are examples of how I've used these principles in my life without realizing it. Once I read the book, I realized why I had been so successful, whether to win a friend or influence those around me. It's been a gift and a curse, but after reading Dales Carnegie's book, it's become more like a gift.

Become Genuinely Interested in Other People

Throughout life, I have always been genuinely interested in people. When you show genuine interest in people, you can learn a lot about who they are and how they will align with you, giving you a positive advantage in the relationship or interaction. BEING GENUINELY INTERESTED IN PEOPLE has served me very well in my business.

As a personal branding photographer, getting my clients to talk about themselves helps me understand what they need from me. It helps me understand who they are and intuitively understand their needs regarding my photography service. It paints a picture in my mind of how to photograph them in a way that captures the essence of who they are that aligns with their business/brand in a unique way that makes them relatable to their target audience.

So, even though the shots are similar to others, their essence attracts their target audience. Showing sincerity in them and being able to relate to the vision for their session based on what they told me allows them to trust me and feel safe in my space. Because when you listen and understand what the client needs, it creates trust and loyalty. Like most clients, many don't know what they want until they express it or felt heard, and because of my expertise, I am able to help them understand what type of session they need for their business images.

Smile

Smiling is a commodity that, although valuable to the recipient, won't cost you anything or a fortune if you give it away all day. On the contrary, as Dale Carnegie mentions in his book 'How to win friends and influence people," Smiles can and will bring you dollars every day. Although smiling is physical, it alters your emotion. As Mr. Carnegie explains in his book, Professor William James of Harvard put it: "Action seems to follow feeling, but action and feeling go together. In other words, to be happy, you have to act happy, which can be done by smiling even when you don't feel like it. Just do it!

When working, I tend to get in my head, and then my smile becomes an upside-down frown. It's not intentional, but we should be aware when we do this and shift when we take notice because, honestly, even doing work can feel fun when you allow yourself to smile like I am writing this, and it allows my thought to flow.

Remember that a Man's Name is the Sweetest and Most Important Sound in any Language

Remembering someone's name and details about them is the best form of flattery you can provide anyone. When you are not interested in someone, you genuinely don't care to know them, I have seen many entrepreneurs make this mistake on social networks or when you don't follow up. I attended a workshop with Tim Shurr, and he said something that hit home and aligned with me. He told us how simple it was to make a video message and send it out.

Then I got to thinking about how my friend and mentor Erik 'Mr. Awesome' Swanson makes me smile when he sends a video message. He is the only person that does that. It makes my day that he thinks of me and brings a smile to my face, and I know he does this for all his friends and members because he does this on his SM channels. His video messages are always fun and sincere.

So when I follow up with my connections the next day with a video message or a few months later, it keeps me on their mind. These are not selling video messages. They are heartfelt, hope you are doing well, or celebrating them for doing something great. Use their names and remember an important detail.

Be a Good Listener; Encourage others to Talk about Themselves

"When you talk, you are only repeating what you already know. But
when you listen, you may learn something new."
~ The Dalai Lama

This quote says it all, if you want to learn, especially from those around you, you have to be willing to listen. Again, in my social networking events, I love meeting people, and after introducing myself, I love to hold silence and allow them the opportunity to speak by asking them first what they do. I learn a lot about someone when I hear them speak, and helps me identify ways that I can be of service, either through collaboration or by putting in touch with someone that I know can benefit from their services.

Most of my referrals come from opportunities like these. When people feel acknowledged and respected and know that they matter, they are more likely to refer people to you without you even asking. People always tell you what they need or want by conversation cues that can only be picked up if you listen. You will definitely blow their mind, and they will be eager to refer people to you without you having to ask. Being intentional with your listening and encouraging others through your actions based on what you learned is the best form of flattery.

Talk in Terms of Another Man's Interests

Knowing the interest of people you meet is important for a few reasons. One helps identify if they are your people. What I mean with this is that if you have a similar interest with the people you meet, you are more than likely to build a rapport with them because you share the same interest, therefore making it easy to refer people to them, as they will do the same for you even if they have never used your services.

Second, it gives you motivation to build and nourish those relationships. Entrepreneurship can be lonely, but it doesn't have to be.

Make the Other Person Feel Important—and do it Sincerely

How you treat your clients will determine how well your business will do. In 2015, I built my business solely through word of mouth. This was due to the level of service I provided my clients. When it comes to my clients I go above and beyond for them and usually always over-deliver, which is why they are confident in referring others.

I did this because I knew that they had options. When people have options, you have to set yourself apart so that they keep returning. For me, that was through delivering exceptional service and experience.

I remember when I first started photography, it was a skill that I had to work at, man the newborn pictures were horrible, but you know what? Ten years later, these are still my clients. Most of my clients at the time were maternity, newborns, or family. Treating my new mom-to-be with empathy and respect created a safe space for them. Letting them know that they mattered.

When you have a newborn and you are a new mom, everything is overwhelming, and I, having experienced this as a mom and could relate, gave me the gift of being empathetic to my clients, and they appreciated it so much. If the mom was stressed, that energy only made the child more anxious.

So, my goal was always to put Mom at ease, and the sessions always turned out great. Even when clients can't afford me, they still refer their friends to me. When a client says no to me, "How you treat people is how people will treat you." I have clients who, at the time, can't afford me, but they are my primary source of referrals. Because even if they haven't booked with me or never do, they can still be an excellent source for referrals, especially if you make them feel important by doing simple things like sending a video message about them.

FATIMA HURD

About Fatima Hurd: Fatima is the Owner and Photographer of Fatima Hurd Photography. Fatima enjoys working with entrepreneurs because it allows her to create images that truly capture the essence of who people are by being intentional with their content, so it aligns with their target audience.

She is a partner with *City Lifestyle* magazine and captures the photos of their business partners through Branding and event photography.

With over ten years of photography experience under her belt, Fatima's photography career has evolved into supporting her clients by coaching them to be confident and authentic in front of her camera.

Fatima has an extensive background in energy and self-development work. She is a 10X Bestselling Author in *The 13 Steps to Riches* book series. She has leveled up her photography business by adding coaching to her services. She coaches her clients to feel safe and inspired to create change in their lives and see life through a new lens filled with endless possibilities!

Author's Website: *www.FatimaHurd.com*

Book Series Website: *www.TheBookOfInfluence.com*

FRED MOSKOWITZ

INVEST IN YOUR RELATIONSHIPS BY EXPRESSING INTEREST IN OTHER PEOPLE

Have you ever wondered what is the best way to influence others? My favorite way, hands down, is to begin by simply becoming interested in other people.

Dale Carnegie shares the concept that becoming genuinely interested in others is the best way to win their attention and their time. Another way to consider this is that we can focus our efforts on becoming interested in others, as opposed to trying to get others interested in us.

In this chapter, I would like to talk about some of my favorite strategies for how to lead with expressing interest in others:

- Be a great listener.
- Make it a regular practice to show empathy and genuine kindness towards others.
- Ask good open-ended questions. Invite people to open up and talk about themselves.

- Harness the power in names.

Let's Learn to Listen Just Like Dogs Do

In the book, *How to Win Friends & Influence People*, the author Dale Carnegie tells a brief story about his childhood dog. His dog taught him the valuable lesson that by becoming interested in others we can create great results. In my own experience, I have learned that dogs are some of the best listeners, and we can learn so much by following their example.

Have you ever noticed that just about every dog owner talks to their dog, even though the dog does not understand any of the words? However, we clearly see that dogs are very keen to sense the tonality, vocal inflections, and energy of the voice that is doing the talking. Dogs will sit and listen attentively to everything that we have to say, and they have very little to say in response. Instead, the dog's response is to look intently at the person, and most likely to also wag their tail in agreement.

We can learn so much from observing this unique way that dogs listen, and this is something you can begin to implement today in your next conversation.

Listening Actively

Unfortunately, in conversations, the majority of people are listening to respond, instead of listening actively to carefully receive the message. What often happens is that while one person is speaking, the other person is focusing on composing their response in their mind, and they often miss a great deal of what was being said. It is a form of multitasking during the middle of a conversation. Undoubtedly, it will not take long before the speaker realizes that the other person is not listening to them.

When someone is speaking to you, give them your full and undivided attention. The notion of "listening with your eyes" is a tactic that comes to mind. Use your eyes to observe body language and to make eye contact. The other person will feel this, they will respond to you, and both of you will be fully engaged in the conversation.

And most important of all—never, ever, interrupt the other person. Fully suppress any urge to talk over them, which would have the effect of them feeling like they are not being heard, and this is the complete opposite of what we want. I like to wait until the other person finishes speaking, take a couple of brief seconds to receive what was said, to gather my thoughts in silence, and then respond with clarifying questions or with my own thoughts.

Empathy And Kindness

You may already be familiar with the idea that people prefer to do business with those that they know, like, and trust. Keeping this idea in mind helps to underscore the importance of showing genuine empathy and kindness throughout all of our interactions and encounters.

What does it mean to show empathy? At a basic level, it means that you let people know that you care. In his writing, Dale Carnegie shared a story with us about how he did a project to capture all the birthdays of his personal contacts, and then took great effort to organize them in his calendar with reminders to send a letter or telegram. In today's modern times, instead of a telegram, we might be sending a text message or, better yet, a video message from our smartphone.

However, sending that letter is a unique action that still stands the test of time. Do not underestimate the power of a handwritten note that is sent through the mail. For most of us, the vast majority of what we receive in the mail are bills and marketing letters. When an envelope containing a real stamp and a handwritten address arrives at the house along with all the other mail, you can guess which piece of mail will stand out from the crowd and be selected out of the pile and immediately opened.

Focus on the way you show up during communications and in meetings. While speaking on the telephone and in person, greet people with animation and enthusiasm. The other person will feel your energy and respond in a favorable way. Smile when speaking on the phone. It will come through in your energy and in the conversation.

Do you like to give gifts? The giving of small but memorable gifts that have meaning to the other person is sure to make an impact. Sports memorabilia, a book signed by the author, or even showing up to a meeting with the person's favorite drink or food item in hand are some examples of small gestures that can go a very long way.

Open-Ended Questions

Think about the questions that you are asking in conversation. Show a genuine sincere interest in others. Make the questions open-ended questions. Ask them what they like most about what they do; what do they dislike about what they do? How do they like to spend their time when they are not working? Ask them about activities they like to do for fun.

The simple act of showing interest in others can have very powerful results when it is a win-win for both parties—for the person expressing the interest and for the person having interest shown in them.

As an exercise, set an intention to be cheerful and positive in all your interactions for an entire day. For everyone you meet out on the street, smile. Make a nice gesture. Offer a compliment. Acknowledge the neighbor you see as you are leaving your home in the morning, and the person you see at the gas station. The cashier at the store. The receptionist at the office you visit. The barista at the cafe where you get your coffee. The waiter that brings you your lunch. The sales clerk at the store that helps you. The colleague that interacts with you at work. The customer service agent that answers the phone when you call into the call center.

When meeting someone—make it a memorable experience for the other person.

Be Someone who is 'GREAT' with Names

The most pleasant word that a person can hear is the sound of their very own name—one of the most important things that you can do to build rapport is to remember the other person's name. If you put in the extra effort, it will most certainly get noticed and create a deeper connection with the other person. Remembering names takes some work, and many people simply do not bother, or do not care to learn and remember the names of the people they meet.

But when you do it, you will certainly stand out above everyone else. Make it a point to listen carefully to the name, and repeat it out loud (in conversation) multiple times, so that it becomes cemented in your memory banks. One strategy that I really like is to ask how they spell their name, especially if the name is unfamiliar or of ethnic origin, and repeat it back. Ask for confirmation from the other person that you are pronouncing it correctly. The extra care and effort will not go unnoticed. Everyone deserves to be called by their correct name, and to have it pronounced correctly!

My favorite winning strategies for being good at remembering people's names:

- Do not ever say that you are bad at remembering names. This is negative reinforcement and does not set you up for success.

- When you meet someone, repeat the name back to the other person, and do it several times if it is more difficult. Strive to use the name by addressing the person by name multiple times during the conversation, to help reinforce the name in your own mind.

- Make some mental notes, some associations of the name with facial features or characteristics that will help your memory.

- At the conclusion of the encounter, say their name again as you depart.

- If you ever forget someone's name, do not be afraid to admit it to the person and ask them to remind you. Instead of being annoyed, they will appreciate your effort and sincerity, and then happily tell you their name again. Based on my own experience, it may seem to be the more difficult thing to do, but this has never failed me—ever!

Conclusion

Are you ready to start putting some of these methods into practice today? I invite you to begin right now, while being genuine and purposeful, starting with the next person that you meet today. The people that I have met that are experts at developing relationships all have developed these similar characteristics. Remember that success leaves clues.

Make it a point to listen actively, show empathy and kindness, ask great questions, and be great with names. Then, watch how the world around you begins to respond. I am certain that your relationships will quickly become deeper and stronger.

FRED MOSKOWITZ

About Fred Moskowitz: Fred Moskowitz is a best-selling author, investment fund manager, and speaker who is on a personal mission to teach people about the power of investing in alternative asset classes, such as real estate and mortgage notes, showing them the way to diversify their capital into investments that are uncorrelated from Wall Street and the stock markets.

Through his body of work, he is teaching investors the strategies to build passive income and cash flow streams designed to flow into their bank accounts. He's a frequent event speaker and contributor to investment podcasts.

Fred is the author of *The Little Green Book of Note Investing: A Practical Guide for Getting Started with Investing in Mortgage Notes* and contributing author in *1Habit To Thrive in a Post-Covid World.*

Author's Website: *www.FredMoskowitz.com*

Book Series Website: *www.TheBookOfInfluence.com*

GENESIS GOMEZ

OMG! I DO IT FOR THE LIKES

Likability Factor: Why do some possess it, while others seemingly do not? Is likability the same as popularity? Does being likable mean that everyone likes you? Is it about showing up as your most authentic self or providing people with what they want?

Personally, I have struggled to understand the meaning of likability for most of my life, as I have experienced a conflict with this factor on many levels. How does one feel "liked" when the family she was born into make it abundantly clear that she is unwelcome and unliked?

Yet, wherever she goes, she seems to draw the attention of others. When she takes personality tests, the results always reveal that she has a very likable personality. Yet, conflicts have arisen in her life, even outside of her family, due to her personality—or so it may seem.

Being liked is important in the business world when it comes to opening doors that may otherwise be closed, but how do we achieve that? In this author's opinion, the answer to this is vastly different for everyone, but one thing remains the same: to be truly and authentically liked, you must be true and authentic to yourself above all else. One can only fake what they think others want for so long before the truth will reveal itself, and all will come crashing down around them.

Likability can be great, but to what end if you are simply trying to be liked for popularity, fame, and fortune? When you are liked for who you are and what you stand for, you discover that the people you are meant to be around find you, and the ones who you should not be around float to the surface like dead fish in the lake.

If you are people-pleasing for the reasons mentioned above, you are holding those dead fish in your water, contaminating the supply, and, eventually, your likability factor will diminish because you will eventually be found to act fake with the way you have shown up in the world.

Growing up the way I did, with the heart I have, I so desperately wanted to feel loved and liked, as I had so much love to give. I found myself people-pleasing and ignoring my own feelings, boundaries, morals, and beliefs, so that I might "fit in" and be "liked" by those around me.

However, I also have another side of me that grows tired of injustice, disrespect, and immorality. Being that I wasn't being true and authentic to myself, I would have outbursts of anger and "tell people about themselves" when I felt an injustice had arisen in a situation, no matter how small sometimes, and that would lead to me being the one in the wrong because the behavior the other party exhibited didn't deserve the blow-up.

I have since learned to respond rather than react and have calmed my nerves, but I have also surrounded myself with different, better, less sketchy people than I was hanging out with before.

I have had writer's block with this chapter for a couple of months trying to write this. I kept coming back to write it, and nothing would pop into my head—it would simply be blank. This caused me to procrastinate and allowed my imposter syndrome to become incredibly loud, almost deafening. That all changed when I decided to go to a three-week leadership and development course.

I have been here for a week and a half and have already experienced significant growth in the way I look at my businesses, my mentees, my associates, strangers, my friends, my family, and myself.

I have seen ways that I have been self-sabotaging and not allowing myself to break that next layer in life that I need to break in order to be my whole self. I am learning tools and techniques that can help me coach others in a way that will impact hundreds of thousands of lives, in more ways than one.

The leadership training has taken me far from home. My family's schedules and my schedule don't always allow us to connect, but tonight I was able to talk with my daughter and tell her about the challenges, epiphanies, and small wins I am experiencing on this journey. I explained to her how I have been trained for so long to talk and hold myself in business, but it just will not work for this position.

I also explained how I am seeing a breakthrough in growth by combining the sides of myself that I protect in front of certain people. I can let my hair down, so to speak, and just present the value—if they want it, they want it, but if they cannot see the value, you won't be able to give something that can save the lives of the people, places, and things we care about the most, even for a nominal cost.

As I explained this to my daughter, she said to me, "Mom, you are coming into your own. Think about it: You grew up with people who had a terrible belief system, treated you badly, and made you feel less than. So, you found your way into the corporate, business, and modeling world and realized you had to behave a certain way to get where you needed to go. You have been taking care of people and never really had a chance to be just you without anything else in your head. You are still finding yourself, and that is okay."

Listening to such wise words from my daughter, I remembered a conversation I had with my son a few days prior, where he said he wished I hung out with friends and let my guard down more, that it is good I went out to the club to celebrate one of my colleague's birthdays because I'm "uptight." I had just laughed and gave him a bit of a hard time, but ultimately, I am discovering he's right.

This version of myself that is emerging from this experience at the leadership training allowed me to hear and understand what my kids were saying to me. I also see more where I can come even more into my feminine energy, breathing, and trusting the process.

The people in this program are incredibly special—from high leadership to newbies. I have made some amazing friends, supporters, and challengers. "Iron sharpens iron" has always been something I have heard, and I certainly have sought some iron to help sharpen me, and little by little, I get more refined and sharper myself. This was an entirely new iron set that I have been needing for quite a while, but divine timing is important.

The past year has been a series of challenging events, and I thought to myself, "I am tired of fighting," but I continue, nonetheless. I see where God/the universe/whatever you believe (I chose God) has set everything up for something incredible that is soon going to happen. I simply needed my likability factor sharpened, my finesse tweaked, and to realize 100% that I can do everything right, and there will always be someone who doesn't like you—just move on and find the people that do.

Ultimately, it is my opinion that the likability factor has many different facets depending on who you are and whom you hang around, but one thing remains true: Stay true to who you are, and the right people will find you. You will have more of a likability factor for yourself as well.

GENESIS GOMEZ

About Genesis Gomez: Genesis Gomez is an accomplished supermodel, entrepreneur, bestselling author, and inspiring public speaker, who is dedicated to empowering individuals to pursue their wildest dreams. With her expertise in coaching, Genesis specializes in cultivating a Model Mindset that helps people break into the modeling industry or attain the self-belief and confidence to accomplish their ambitions.

Genesis is the founder and CEO of Model Mindset Mastery Services, a coaching program that focuses on the whole person—from their outward appearance to their mental health, financial success, and business growth. With her wealth of experience in the modeling industry and as a successful businesswoman and entrepreneur, Genesis provides her clients with the tools, guidance, and support they need to succeed in all areas of their lives. But Genesis' coaching goes beyond just helping people look and feel their best—she is also passionate about helping her clients find their purpose and meaning in life. Through her coaching, she has helped hundreds of people discover their true potential, manage their finances more effectively, finance their dream homes, and grow their businesses.

With Genesis as your coach, you can be confident that you are working with someone who truly understands the challenges and opportunities that life can present. Her experience, expertise, and passion for helping others will inspire and motivate you to take action, overcome obstacles, and achieve your wildest dreams. So, if you are ready to transform your life and create a better future for yourself, look no further than Genesis Gomez—the coach who can help you master your mindset and achieve success in all areas of your life.

Author's Website: *www.GenesisAshleyGomez.com*

Book Series Website: *www.TheBookOfInfluence.com*

IAN STERMER

TO LIKE OR BE LIKED... GENUINELY

. . . .

"All things being equal, people want to do business with their friends. All things being not quite so equal, people still want to do business with their friends."
~ Jeffery Gitomer

We all have a restaurant we like to go to, even though they may not have the best food or the best prices. For me, it was a little Japanese place near my office called E-Sushi. The E stood for Elvis. The chef had a 4-inch high pompadour, and the walls were a mix of Hokusai Prints, cherry blossom paintings, and Elvis album covers and movie prints. How could you not love the place? The food was only average, and a bit overpriced, but that didn't change the fact that I liked going there.

That raises the question, can we be liked by others even if we can't make a spicy tuna roll while singing "Viva Las Vegas"?

As important as likability is, it can be hard to pin down. The plain truth is that we won't like everyone, and not everyone will like us. That doesn't mean we dislike others, or they dislike us. It means we may not easily build a connection with everyone, especially right away.

Sometimes the connection is quick and simple. In high school, I mentioned the name of a rock band I liked to a friend (for the curious-minded among you, it was Jethro Tull). Another student happened to walk by at that moment and overheard me. He stopped and said he loved them, too. We've been friends ever since. That one commonality sparked more conversations, and other commonalities were discovered, deepening our friendship.

Other connections may take longer and are less obvious. Will Rogers famously said, "I never met a man I didn't like." While I strive for that, I can say that I've never gotten to know a person I didn't like. A past coworker had a few mannerisms that I found difficult to work with, and maybe even grated on me a bit. In time, I began to see past this exterior to who he was on the inside, and he gradually moved from coworker to work friend and eventually to just friend. Aside from work, there was little commonality, but there was a human-to-human connection.

Given time and an open mind, I find something to like about everyone I get to know. By focusing on the things we like about another, and downplaying the things we don't, it's not hard to like anyone, at least a little bit.

Once we learn that we can like others, the next question is how do we get others to like us? The two-word secret to this is simply, "We can't." We can't make people like us. There are ways we can become more likable, though.

You can't pretend to be someone you are not, just to get someone to like you. We've all seen the SitCom TV show where the character pretends to be a doctor or millionaire to impress some guy/girl, and it never ends well. Real life is the same. It's a staple of TV comedies because we all do that to some extent, and we've all had our own house of cards collapse from it. People can tell if you're faking it, and it will turn them off. Even something as simple as faking an interest in a client's favorite football team can eventually come out, and, instead of a closer relationship, you end up looking dishonest.

Before you say we are doomed by our own honesty, let me give the example of water. It is the nature of water to flow downhill. That is unchangeable. However, water can be redirected to gently irrigate a field, provide a swift powerful current to turn a waterwheel, or become a raging flood to destroy a village. All of these are the nature of water.

A former manager of mine would always drill in my head the mantra, "Listen, don't talk. Ask, don't tell." Don't dominate the conversation with your own ideas and opinions. Listen, and let the other direct the conversation once it's started. Listen to them, and let their enthusiasm infect you as well. Maybe infect is a strong word for it, but find that genuine interest or curiosity, and let them tell you more.

Be a good listener. Actively listen to what people have to say and show that you are paying attention. Listen with the goal of understanding the person and learning more about them. Make the conversation about them. If we instead listen for opportunities to insert comments to show off how smart we are or look for places to insert sales pitches, we will push people away.

At a business networking meeting, I met a woman and agreed to have a coffee meet with her. I'll confess I wasn't too excited, as she was in an industry I did not see as complementing my own. In short, I didn't think I would benefit. My selfishness almost convinced me to cancel this meeting.

At the meeting, we just started talking. Even though our businesses were quite different, we realized that we both faced similar challenges in our careers. As I let down my defenses some and opened up to her, we began to know, like, and trust each other. We began meeting every month or so, to discuss how business was going, share advice, and seek input. We became a sounding board for each other's ideas. We congratulated our success and consoled our failures.

In short, we became friends. While eventually opportunities arose, and we each became customers of the other, the friendship we developed has been far more valuable and continues to this day. Because we took time to genuinely get to know each other and build a relationship, we ended up with both a friendship and a customer. Had we tried to pitch our products to each other at the beginning, we would have had neither.

At a similar business networking group early on in my career, I was invited to another coffee meet with a young man. He began by asking me what I did. As I explained, he paid close attention and asked several very good questions. With his apparent interest, I started to get excited about a sale from him. All the signs were there.

After about ten minutes, he abruptly changed his demeanor and said he would now like to tell me about himself and his services. The next twenty minutes was a hard-pressure sales pitch from him. I quickly realized he had faked his interest in me in an attempt to build trust. His only goal was to sell to me. Rather than building the trust he expected, his attempt at manipulation immediately made me distrust him, and, by proxy, his services.

Finding genuine commonality builds trust. Building on fake commonalities breeds distrust. One door-to-door salesperson I knew had the last name Kimball. Every door he knocked on he would try to look inside and see if they had a piano made by the Kimball Company. If they did, he would say something like "I see you have a Kimball piano. My name is Kimball, too."

There were a few flaws in his approach, though. Most people that had Kimball pianos did not buy them because of the brand. He was not related to the Kimball's that made the pianos. He did not have much background, talent, or interest in pianos, so couldn't carry much of a conversation if they did show interest. It was simply a manipulative sales technique designed to build trust, but it was based on a false premise.

Let me contrast that with the corporate trainer at a company I used to work for. He would often greet me with a compliment on my necktie. He even pointed out a couple of his favorites that I wore. It always made me feel good to be noticed. In a training meeting, he let on that he always tries to compliment men on their ties. He does this for two reasons. It makes the man feel good, and he genuinely likes ties and pays attention to them. It may be a sales tactic, but as it's something he genuinely likes, it helps build commonality rather than creating distrust.

Likewise, I have seen many women meet and start a conversation with something like "I like your shoes." Almost instantly a bond begins to form. I don't mean this to sound sexist, or that women only care about shoes. As a generalization, many women put effort into choosing an outfit. Complimenting a person on that effort shows an interest in them and an appreciation of their efforts. This is essentially what my former trainer did with men's neckties.

The previous book in this series was about "Authentic Communication." In that book, I stated that authentic communication meant that both parties were genuinely open to an exchange of ideas. That is the foundation of likability, as well. We need to genuinely want to know about a person, and get to know them personally if we want them to like us. Don't hide behind tricks and techniques. If you take the time to genuinely care about them, more often than not, they will begin to like you in return.

IAN STERMER

About Ian Stermer: Ian is a serial entrepreneur, international speaker, corporate trainer, and business coach. He cut his teeth in the hospitality industry, where he gained a love of helping people smile a little more.

Ian has spoken before thousands from New York to San Francisco to Hong Kong. His decades of real-world experience and his unique perspective on life have made him a popular speaker with businesses, civic groups, and professional organizations.

He has created training programs on customer service for some of the top hotels in the world, including the Mandarin Oriental and Marriott Hotels. Solopreneurs, salespeople, and small businesses have sought his expertise in training themselves and their staff on customer service, sales, and creating collaborative partnerships. He is currently teaching courses on financial literacy and how to use humor to reduce stress and improve sales.

Ian has facilitated small business and entrepreneurship workshops ranging from improving skills and mastering new techniques to mindset shifts and leadership training. His unique coaching method has helped numerous business owners improve sales and customer satisfaction.

Ian has successfully started and ran businesses in the Customer Service, Human Resources, Business Coaching, and Finance Industries. He has turned around failing businesses and created new growth markets for existing businesses.

He currently runs Stermer Financial, a financial services company. In addition, he is on the Executive Team for Champion Circle. This networking association provides high-performance-based networking activities to create connection capital and increase professional prosperity.

Aside from business, Ian is most passionate about his family. Nothing is more important than building a happy and healthy family. No other success in life will compensate for failure in the home.

Author's website: *www.IanStermer.com*

Book Series Website: *www.TheBookOfInfluence.com*

JESSA CARTER

MAGNETIC LIKABILITY

In a world where most people strive to be authentic or likable, go beyond. I challenge you and invite you to *Be Magnetic*.

Think of being magnetic as next-level authenticity or likability. To *Be Magnetic* means to possess the power or ability to attract. If you like the idea of being magnetic, how do you go about it? Where should you start?

My warm yet bold recommendation is to look in the mirror, an honest look in the mirror. Look into the eyes of the person staring back at you. Do you like the man or woman looking back at you? More importantly, do you LOVE the man or woman looking back at you?

Magnetic Likability is not in a book, in this chapter, online, or anywhere else in the world. Magnetic Likability is an inside job. Don't worry, I won't leave you hanging; I'll absolutely shed some light on how to begin your journey of becoming magnetic, but before I do, I'd first like to share this:

While researching for inspiration to write this, I searched to see what the web had to say about authentic likability. I read several different articles. What I found was a superficial display of horse manure.

It's not my nature to be negative. "A superficial display of horse manure" is the most honest and polite way my brain can describe what I was reading.

Quick Bonus Lesson: One of the principles of being A Peaceful Millionaire is, "Worrying is praying for something you do not want." That said, I strongly encourage you to work on decreasing and eventually eliminating worry from your life.

This is extremely powerful. No matter what you find to worry about, you are praying for something you do not want. I vividly recall a time in my life when I was worried about getting into a car accident. You can imagine what happened, right? I got into an accident.

Throughout years of study and dedication to becoming a better version of myself and having a better life, I discovered that I was a far more powerful co-creator of anything I desired than I previously understood was possible. Here's the thing: You are a powerful co-creator of anything you desire, too, but that means you are equally powerful at co-creating things or circumstances that you don't desire.

Remember that I said to *Be Magnetic* means to possess the power or ability to attract. Your ability to attract is synonymous with the finesse at which you co-create things that you desire versus things you don't desire. Like attracts like. The catch is, you don't attract what you want, you attract *WHO YOU ARE*.

Which takes us back to the mirror. Do you like the man or woman looking back at you? More importantly, do you LOVE the man or woman looking back at you? Are you excited to be around the man or woman staring back at you?

If you answered no or cringed at the mere thought of being this vulnerable and present with yourself, it doesn't make you bad, unlovable, or unworthy, it simply shows you an opportunity to go within. At times you might not love or like the person staring back at you, at times you might feel unlovable or unworthy, but I assure you that's not the truth.

You might have heard one or more of those negative comments at some point in your life; if you did, it likely became part of your internal dialogue that can play like a broken record in your head anytime it feels like it. Still, I assure you it's not the truth. It's not the truth of who you are, and it's not the truth of what you're capable of.

Anything the inner critic or 'negative Nancy' voice in your head says is not the truth. It's all externally sourced and it's false.

I firmly believe that how I show up for myself is how I show up for the world, personally, professionally, romantically, and financially. I believe the same to be true for you. Here's how I navigate. When people or circumstances show up in my life that are unpleasant, I take an *internal inventory*.

I ask myself, "Have I thought, said, or done something to attract this?"

If the answer is yes, I take radical ownership and responsibility and correct who I'm being or what I'm thinking. I also ask myself, "What is this person or circumstance showing me? What am I meant to learn? How am I meant to grow?"

If the answer is no, I still ask myself, "What is this person or circumstance showing me? What am I meant to learn? How am I meant to grow?"

If I'm not proud of how I showed up for someone else or how I showed up in a situation, the only person who can correct that is me. If I don't agree with a situation or how someone showed up for me, I am responsible for how I respond and how I allow it to make me feel. There are times when someone else elicits feelings of sadness or anger that are unavoidable, but the question I ask myself is, "How long am I willing to allow this person or circumstance to disrupt my joy and peace?"

Speaking of joy and peace and not allowing others to disrupt it, I'd like to visit happiness for a moment. Happiness, similar to being magnetic, is also an inside job.

Which brings me back to the mirror one last time. If you deeply love, honor, and respect the person staring you back in the mirror, or at least like him or her, you have one of the inner secrets to being magnetic. If you are happy with yourself and with your life, you will be magnetic.

When you deeply love, honor, and respect yourself and your life, you will exceed happiness and find true joy, bliss, and peace. When you reach this place within yourself your life becomes a reflection of that and you automatically become super magnetic for anything you desire or choose to have in your life, including that special someone. However, when it comes to that special someone there is one small caveat, you can't override anyone else's free will. If it's meant to be, you'll each choose to have each other in your life and the magnetic force between the two of you will be undeniable and unstoppable.

Again, you don't attract what you want, you attract *WHO YOU ARE*.

I don't have space in a single chapter to dive deep into the metaphysics or energetic imprint behind how all of this works; however, I do want to touch on what I mean by energetic imprint briefly and use it to debunk one example of the superficial display of horse manure I found before writing this.

Albert Einstein said, "Everything is energy. Match the frequency of what you want and you can't help but have that reality." Energetic imprint refers to the frequency at which something vibrates. Everything is energy including your thoughts, beliefs, feelings, emotions, or words (spoken or unspoken).

Here's one example of the superficial display of horse manure I found before writing this, "Smile. Smile. Smile. Studies have shown that people who smile are perceived as more sincere and competent, as well as a whole lot more likable."

This superficial nonsense is frustrating to me. You can't just smile and expect someone to like you. Why? Because not all smiles are created equal. I'm not saying that to be a jerk, I'm saying that because what you're thinking and how you're feeling is the energy behind your smile and other people can feel the difference.

If you pay attention to someone's energy in addition to their smile you can learn a lot, whether it's your best friend or a complete stranger. Let's say person A and person B are meeting for coffee. Person A just found out they landed a huge promotion at work and is feeling on top of the world. Person B just found out their cat passed away. Person A and Person B show up for coffee, smile at each other, and exchange common pleasantries while standing in line to order a coffee. They pick up their coffee and make their way to the nearest empty table. By now Person A has noticed something that feels off about Person B and compassionately says, "Hey, you don't seem like yourself today, what's going on?"

There's no judgment either way, however, if a smile is always covering up pain, stress, guilt, shame, lack, self-doubt, or insecurities it shows. You can't fake it. The reason you can't fake it is the energetic imprint of pain, stress, guilt, shame, lack, self-doubt or insecurities carries a low energetic frequency compared to feelings such as joy, love (including self-love), bliss, faith, gratitude, etc. which carry a much higher energetic frequency. When the frequency of your inner world (your thoughts, feelings, and beliefs) vibrates at a higher frequency you naturally become magnetic.

Quick Bonus Lesson #2: Throw away the old saying, "Fake it until you make it." I've just explained why that isn't effective. I invite you to adopt a fresh perspective and instead, "Faith it. Faith it until you make it."

One last time, you don't attract what you want, you attract *WHO YOU ARE*.

Remember, Magnetic Likability is not in a book, in this chapter, online, or anywhere else in the world. Magnetic Likability is an inside job.

If you'd like support becoming magnetic and co-creating your next-level wealth, peace, fulfillment, or financial freedom, I'm your girl.

In the interim, Live Boldly, Love Deeply, Laugh Often, and Be Rich Always in All Ways.

JESSA CARTER

About Jessa Carter: Jessa Carter, The Peaceful Billionaire, is the world's most highly sought Life and Wealth Strategist for High Achieving Leaders and Entrepreneurs who are missing fulfillment, joy, and passion in life despite their massive outward success. As the founder and CEO of The Peaceful Billionaire Institute of Wealth Creation™, she excels in redefining and reinventing yourself, your life, your business, your relationships, and your bank accounts to soaring heights that defy logic so that your time on earth is by Intentional Design, never by default.

A Certified Physician Assistant with a Master of Medical Science degree and a 10-year career in Neurosurgery, she went on to become a Quantum Energy Practitioner, Master Coach, Holistic Health Practitioner, and Certified ThetaHealer®. Her expansive expertise integrates powerful personal, professional, and spiritual development to unlock the unlimited potential within the subconscious mind.

Working with Jessa is an experiential, bespoke playground where the worlds of science, energy, and spirituality collide to entice depths of the mind, heart, and soul's intelligence often left untouched. Jessa is a beacon of light illuminating a disruptive path beyond societal norms, beyond the status quo, and beyond limitation. She is your unwavering constant, your cheerleader, and your advocate for feeling exceptional while co-creating a life and legacy beyond your wildest dreams.

"It is the plunge deep within the ocean of self that expands one's capacity to experience the vast depths of others and the world around us." ~ Jessa Carter

Author's Website: *www.ThePeacefulBillionaire.com*

Book Series Website: *www.TheBookOfInfluence.com*

JILL LUBLIN

YOUR FIVE MOST IMPORTANT LIKABILITY FACTORS

There are few things that tie into your success more than **likability.**

At the base level, your likability determines whether people trust you and choose to work with you over the competition. It is what will make your previous customers or partners decide to refer new business to you given the choice. Over time, your likability will also determine how quickly you're able to grow your media presence.

It is so true...*your network certainly does determine your net worth.*

As the author of the bestselling book, *The Profit of Kindness,* I've been fortunate enough to make a career out of helping businesses get more publicity, while exploring the specifics of how kindness can be measured everywhere in their business.

From years of research and "boots on the ground" service to clients, these key factors tie into your likability, the public's perception of you and your business, as well as how kindness pays dividends in all that you do.

Likability Factor 1: Connection

Connection is defined as your ability to connect with others in service of your vision. This connection is critical with everyone you interact with on a daily basis, including your teammates and customers. Although connection is generally driven through communication, your ability to connect typically starts with an internal focus and answering some key questions:

- How easily are you able to communicate your vision?
- What strengths do you have as a leader that show that you're secure and focused on your vision?
- What weaknesses or distractions might pull you away from your ability to connect with others?
- Are there particular areas within your business or daily work that might cause you to fall into anxiety, avoidance, or chaos?

As a leader, you've likely attempted to answer these questions before or had them presented to you in some way. Despite how many leaders regularly work on themselves, bad management and feeling unappreciated is still the number one complaint that most team members and customers mention when they're moving on to new opportunities.

This means that maintaining a focus on your connection to your most critical team and resources is vital to your success over time. Make the time to regularly evaluate how you're feeling about your relationship with others. Ask yourself if you're providing opportunities and prioritizing these relationships on a regular basis.

An easy way to manage this is to consistently take an inventory of your connection with those most important to your business success. Rate how connected you're feeling to these people to see where you might have opportunities to extend a little kindness, go the extra mile in your communication, or understand more of how further connection can be developed.

A little bit goes a long way and showing focused effort will make a big impact.

Likability Factor 2: Gratitude

Over the past 5 years, the understanding of the impact of gratitude and the further integration of Emotional Intelligence (EI) into businesses has demonstrated both the psychological and business benefits of actively practicing gratitude on a daily basis.

Just as with your ability to connect, your gratitude process should start from within. The simplest way to integrate gratitude into your routine is to simply make a list of 3 to 5 items that you're grateful for in your life—make a list each day at the beginning and end of your day. Ideally, this practice should be completed in a quiet environment where you have the opportunity to spend time thinking and reflecting.

By focusing on this process for a minimum of 21 days, you'll find that your attitude will improve while your mindset adjusts to focus on the positive aspects of any situation rather than the negative.

As you become more focused on gratitude in your internal world, you'll want to transition those thoughts into actions in your daily routine. Extend kindness and gratitude to teammates and customers as often as you can. Be generous with your recognition, praise, and compliments. Focus on the positive aspects of your relationships and how they create opportunities for you on a regular basis. When these opportunities come to fruition, don't forget to thank those who helped you along the way.

Gratitude has a measurable impact on your success and your likability. Don't underestimate how much of a difference it will make for you!

Likability Factor 3: Patience

Leaders and entrepreneurs may struggle with perfectionism more than any other group. This perfectionism tends to seep into organizations and create a culture where goals feel unattainable, and problems feel insurmountable.

As your focus turns to connection and gratitude, developing your patience becomes a practical application of how you want to be perceived by others.

Patience is best developed by taking an extra moment before any interaction with others. Take a moment to think, review, and reflect on the intention of your communication. How do you want to be received? What's the goal? How will this increase mutual understanding?

Distractions in the workplace have never been higher, which means that important communication sometimes gets sent out hastily or without adequate time to process the impact. When you're communicating with others, it's often best to do so in an environment where you're devoting time that's specifically scheduled to responding or requesting. This allows you distraction-free moments to remember that there's a person on the other end of that text or email.

Although conflict may seem inevitable in a business or workplace, even the worst situations can be turned around with enough perspective.

Just like with gratitude, it's important to remind yourself that effective relationships are built on optimism, humility, and forgiveness. The more patient you become, the more patience you will see reflected at you.

Likability Factor 4: Generosity

Everyone likes someone who makes them feel seen and appreciated.

Generosity isn't always limited to "gift giving" or literal gestures. Your ability to be generous with your time, words, and focus is a big factor in how you will be perceived and received. When you demonstrate a willingness to give more than expected (especially if that was previously the bare minimum), you'll find that relationships improve dramatically.

Everyone is busy throughout their day-to-day routine. Generosity of time doesn't necessarily mean constantly breaking your focus or stopping what you're doing to focus on others. But what it does mean is that during scheduled time, meetings, calls, or connection points that you are fully focused and devoted during that time. Put your cell phone away. Don't be easily pulled away by other priorities or distractions. Value the time you're spending with others and they'll value their time with you.

Generosity also extends into your relationships. As you develop your network, you'll regularly find opportunities to connect people. Be generous with your referrals. Make it clear that you're resourceful and willing to help create relationships when you have the opportunity. Have an awareness of how your presence impacts your network as much as they support you.

Once you've mastered the art of being generous with time and attention, don't hold back on compliments or opportunities to express your appreciation. This develops loyalty, which is one of the key components of likability.

Likability Factor 5: Positivity

In the era of social media and 24-hour news cycles, you might worry that people are becoming increasingly disconnected or jaded by the state of the world.

The reality, however, is much different.

People are still drawn to positivity and people who make them feel good. Orienting your thoughts, actions, and conversations around positivity will make you truly magnetic in any environment.

As much as possible, don't allow outside influences to drag you down. When you can, avoid complaining or dwelling in negativity traps. Spend your time with others as the valuable and important opportunity that it is.

Bringing positivity into any environment only takes one person or leader who is focused on maintaining that feeling.

As you adopt the practices and focus that I've shared throughout this chapter, staying positive becomes a far easier task. Maintaining your own peaceful stream of thoughts that are focused on your vision, relationships, and how you benefit others keeps your attitude in the right place.

When you feel yourself slipping into negativity or conflicts, don't be afraid to seek out counsel from mentors, coaches, friends, or anyone who can help reset your thinking. If you take out that energy in the wrong place, you risk long-term damage where it hurts the most.

Remember that, as humans, we're programmed to focus on threats and fears. A long-term obsession with these influences creates toxicity. Who wants to deal with toxic behavior on a daily basis (other than other toxic people)?

Although much of what I've discussed in this chapter may seem like common sense, it's easy to fall into patterns that sabotage every one of these likability factors. Taking regular time to check-in with yourself, review these areas, and make sure you're paying attention will make a measurable and significant difference in your life and business.

Don't underestimate just how powerful the power of kindness and likability is in your life.

You deserve to show up as your best self in all of your interactions with others. Now, show the world just how much you have to give!

JILL LUBLIN

Jill Lublin is an international speaker on the topics of Publicity, Networking, Kindness, and Referrals. She is the author of 4 Best Selling books, including *Get Noticed...Get Referrals* (McGraw Hill) and co-author of *Guerrilla Publicity and Networking Magic*. Her latest book, *Profit of Kindness,* went #1 in four categories. Jill is a master strategist in positioning your business for more profitability and market visibility. She is the CEO of a strategic consulting firm.

She has over 25 years of experience working with over 100,000 people, plus national and international media. Jill teaches a virtual Publicity Crash Course and consults and speaks all over the world. She has spoken on many stages with luminaries such as Tony Robbins. Jill also leads an intentional kindness community. Visit publicitycrashcourse.com/freegift and *jilllublin.com.*

Social Media links:
LinkedIn: *linkedin.com/in/jilllublin*
Twitter: *twitter.com/jilllublin*
Instagram: *instagram.com/jilllublin*
Facebook: *Facebook.com/jilllublin*
Facebook business page: *facebook.com/publicitycrashcourse*
Clubhouse: *clubhouse.com/@jilllublin*
Website: *JillLublin.com*
Website: *PublicityCrashCourse.com*
Jill's Publicity Action Guide: *PublicityCrashCourse.com/freegift*

Author's Website: *www.JillLublin.com*

Book Series Website: *www.TheBookOfInfluence.com*

JOANNA JAMES

THE DOUBLE-EDGE SWORD

A lady appeared at the classroom door and, after gently knocking, announced that I was wanted in the principal's office. My heart flew into my throat: I was 7 years old, and I was in trouble. The walk to the other end of the school grounds was never ending. The concrete seemed to go forever and ever and you could cut the air with a knife. I was terrified.

Reaching the door, the lady signaled for me to sit on a seat inside. The room smelled of old school lunches and there were bars on the window.

The Principal slowly stood up. "Sit down," he said. "Do you know why you are here?"

"No," I fumbled, trying not to cry.

"You're not in trouble," he said. I looked at him, confused. "Your mother came to see me, because you don't have any friends."

The start of a new school had been difficult, and I spent most of my lunchtimes alone. Every day, I went home and cried.

"Well, not to worry. Come with me and we will sort this out."

I didn't dare ask what was about to happen—rather, I just obediently followed him to the classroom. My teacher was sweet and kindhearted, and she smiled at me as if to say, "It will be okay; don't worry." I was petrified.

At the front of the room, I could see all eyes upon me. The dialogue in my mind had the volume dial turned right up. I couldn't bring myself to look at anyone.

"Does everybody know who Jodie is?" The kids began to nod their heads.

"You'd all agree that Jodie is a nice girl?" There was a long pause.

"I want you all to make an effort to like her," he said, repeatedly nodding his head. As if in a trance, slowly the kids began to nod, too.

"Great." And, just like that, he gestured for me to sit down.

What happened next was bemusing. The bell rang and I stood up shakily to walk out, but this time I had a swarm of people asking me to sit with them. I was exactly the same person, nothing had changed, and yet everything had.

In that moment, I felt an intense dichotomy—joy and disgust. I wasn't sure if it was my intense desire to be liked or my contempt for the fickle nature of humans that had impacted me the most. One thing was clear: Likability is a double-edged sword.

Fast forward a decade and I found myself sitting confidently in the Dean's office at the University of NSW. This time, I was on the front foot as I had been the one to schedule the meeting. The room was a definite upgrade, smelt fresh, and had a nice view from the window.

"Thank you for taking time to meet with me. You see, I have just graduated high school in the United States," I explained. "My family has returned to Australia and I wish to study here; however, I have no Australian HSC score which is a prerequisite for university entrance here. I have my full academic record, including my SAT grades, and other achievements for you to consider."

"I see," the Dean said. "Why do you want to study Architecture?" he asked, flipping the pages of my transcript.

"During school, I did work experience at a local firm and just loved it—I designed the new school sign and it's already been built. As you can see, I graduated with Magna Cum Laude Honors and have been accepted to several Ivy league schools. I have reviewed the other universities here in Sydney and I am very impressed by your program offering. I'd like to see if it's possible for me to attend here."

He stopped flipping through the lengthy document I had given him. What happened next was gratifying.

He looked me square in the eyes and said, "If I offer you a place here, will you guarantee me that you will list our university as your top choice?"

"Yes, of course," I replied.

"Congratulations, then; we will see you next year."

In that moment, I felt intense joy. I had just used the skill of likability to secure the future direction of my career.

Fast forward another decade.

It was 8 weeks before my wedding and things at work were crazy busy. We had just bought a building for our new office, which had been an old pawn shop in a corner position in an up-and-coming part of town. The timing was really tight, and we needed to do a quick renovation before the big day, so the team could move in and we could relax and enjoy our honeymoon.

It was an ambitious timeline, yet possible, so I had been negotiating with the real estate agent to allow us to gain access to the premises to start work. The only hitch was that the building contract was not due to be settled for another 3 weeks.

I looked the real estate agent straight in the eye and said, "Don't worry; we will settle this contract and any work we do here will be adding value to the property. You have my word."

He turned to me, handed me the keys, and said, "Just don't tell the owners."

That was just the beginning of a series of miraculous events arising from the conscious practice of likability.

"You need to have it done by when?" the contractor asked.

"7 weeks" I said.

"That's not a lot of time and we are already very busy," he replied.

"I know you must think I am crazy, but I am getting married in a few months and if you could simply agree to meet me on the site to discuss what options might be available, I would really appreciate it."

There was a long pause. I could hear the subtext conversation inside his mind—what type of crazy person would even make such a phone call?

"Okay, I'll meet you tomorrow morning at 8 am." The dial tone disconnected.

The next few weeks were a flurry of activity to reach settlement with lots of building activity. Some things went according to plan and a lot of things didn't. Lifting up the carpet led to the discovery of old train tracks and resulted in jackhammers and new tiles prior to settlement.

Regardless of what presented, we were determined to hit the deadline, and as each contractor joined the build, somehow the momentum grew as a team of optimistic people in the pursuit of a happy ending.

It was as if the project evolved on its own and they felt a key part of supporting my wild idea to attempt the impossible. Many commented that they agreed against their better judgment simply because I seemed like a genuinely nice lady.

A few weeks later, we settled the contract and a few more weeks after that, we moved in right on time. In that moment, I felt intense gratitude for the understanding that likability operates well beyond the logical. It's a miraculous ingredient in the process of working with people.

A sword can be used for good or evil—the choice is always yours. Swordsmanship is a skill and there are techniques that you must learn as you weave your way through life. However, the mindset of the swordsman holds the defining power if one is to be a master. Likability is an art form that brings rich rewards.

JOANNA JAMES

About Joanna James: Joanna James is known as a revolutionary difference maker in the Design, Construction and Banking sectors and is featured in publications such as Entrepreneur, USA Today, The Advisor, MPA, Australian Broker, Flaunt, CIO and Insights Success.

As Australia's youngest registered female architect & builder she is known as creator of the world's first 'Bio' home, featured on TV series 'I Own Australia's Best Home.'

Joanna created the Shambhala@byron retreat which welcomed celebrity singer Sting as her first guest. Her book Mind Body Spaces raises awareness around our health and the spaces that we live in.

A pioneering entrepreneur for the Mortgage Ezy Group of companies, her contribution shines through the 32 Industry awards including 3 times BRW fastest company.

A passionate advocate for women in business, Joanna has also been recognized as Principal of Year (WIFA), Top 100 Female Entrepreneurs and Top 100 Female Mentors.

Contributing to the FBAA Artemis Forum, she works to raise opportunities for Education, Advocacy and Awareness for women within the Australian Finance Industry.

Author's Website: *www.JoannaJames.com*

Book Series Website: *www.TheBookOfInfluence.com*

JUSTIN MORRIS

WHAT HAPPENS WHEN VILLAINS & HEROES MAKE UP?

It was one of those "train wreck" moments that we can't look away from. That American Idol moment when a contestant comes on the screen and you just seem to know that it will be one of "those" auditions—the auditions planted to keep the show *interesting*. The singer confidently stands in front of the judges, faces the camera, and unleashes a herd of screaming cats and seagulls into the ear drums of the listeners. The camera pans to the laughing judges and the oblivious singer continues confidently as long as the judges allow them to.

Well, if American Idol was filmed in 1994 and if it were a high school talent show and if that high school was in Idaho—that singer would have been me.

I had never sung in front of any crowd before. So, naturally, I selected my debut to be in front of the most forgiving crowd possible: the entire student body at the High School Talent Show. But really, I had everything going for me. I was singing a duet with a super cute and amazing singer, and we were singing the hit song, "A Whole New World" from—you guessed it—Disney's Aladdin. What could possibly go wrong? Oh yeah. Puberty. That, and I couldn't hear the piano.

Guess what happened, I dare you.

I have to hand it to my skinny 92-pound Freshman self. I finished that song. I may have been out of tune for 92 percent of the song, but I was totally in character! I may have not heard the piano, but I sure heard the laughter—for the next three years of high school.

You would think that experience would cure me of ever wanting to sing or perform or speak in front of anyone. Ever. Again. However, strangely, it fueled me.

I have often reflected on that moment, wondering how I ever could have finished that song even though in my heart of hearts I knew it was not going so hot. I was embarrassed. So embarrassed. It was one of many dark moments of my high school career. Oftentimes, it shadowed the triumphs that I also experienced. Yet, now I look back and I smile at that young man. I am proud of him. I like him. He's cool. He's someone I want to know and be friends with.

Here's the deal. And, trust me, this is a really, really good deal. You're going to want in on this action.

To be liked, *truly* liked, to acquire that "it factor" as Simon Cowell would say, requires just one ingredient: YOU must *really* like YOU. I'm not just talking about the pretty "Instagram selfie" qualities of you, I'm talking about liking *everything* about you. The good and the not so good. The fabulous and the interesting. The strengths and the weaknesses. The spiritual and physical gifts and the lack thereof. All of it.

Self-Love = Loving your own villain and hero.

Yes. I know. This may go against every fiber of social self-preservation but obtaining the Likability factor (charm) requires us to be—you guessed it—SEEN. Unmasked and uncensored. To allow yourself to truly be seen requires courage and confidence.

Confidence is a by-product of self-love.

I'm no "Pollyanna," and I understand that it's a delicate balance to love yourself whole-heartedly—especially when there are real life situations and life-long emotional, spiritual, and physical challenges that will be a part of your life without any hope of healing or relief. But I can tell you this: Loving both your light and shadows is absolutely possible and is totally FIRE!

Now, please don't tell me that you are one of those "throw it out to the Universe and forget it" kind of folk. Don't get me wrong. Sending our dreams goals and desires to God / Universe / Source is a key component to manifestation and creation!

BUT.

It's not the ONLY step. But that is a topic for another day.
Let's just say that to manifest this Likability Factor or Charm requires something from each of us.

1.   Be willing to look at both your light and your shadows.
2.   Stand eye to eye with your light.
3.   Gracefully face your darkness.
4.   Magnify your light.
5.   Discover the gifts offered by your shadows.
6.   Stand confidently in the life of your design.

Being willing to look at both your light and your shadows is like taking extra time to iron your clothes really nice, put on your favorite shoes, comb your hair like a movie star, put on an extra spritz of cologne and strut out the door like you are John Travolta—all while sporting a huge ripe zit on the tip of your nose.

It requires courage to stand confidently and own your strengths but also the courage to be vulnerable and acknowledge those things that you could improve. To quote Marianne Williamson, "Our deepest fear is not that we are inadequate. Our deepest fear is that we are powerful beyond measure. It is our light, not our darkness that most frightens us." I find it interesting that it is easier for us to look at our flaws rather than face our light; however, we must be willing to face all of it in order to truly begin to love who we are.

It is easy to overlook the darkness and weaknesses of those we love. We just love them. Especially babies. They poop. They burp. They throw up on everything. They stink (sometimes...strange that even when they stink, we still sniff and smile) and they keep us up all night. But, we love them. We coo at them. We dress them up like little trophies. We become different people when we are talking to them. Seriously—a phenomenon. My question is this: If we can overlook others' shadow moments, why not look more graciously at our own shadows?

One of the cool unintended consequences of being willing to stand eye to eye with your strengths and your light is that you naturally begin to use your gifts! Using your gifts intensifies them and magnifies them and allows them to flourish and grow. You know...like muscles. The more you work them out and break them down—the bigger they get. At least that is what I am told. I have never seen my abs.

However, the secret sauce to truly knock your own socks off and truly love *all* of you is to discover the gifts that your shadows have offered you—to look at your perceived weaknesses and ask, "What do you offer me?" "How have you blessed my life?" "What gifts have you given me?" Then wait for the answer. Have your pen and paper ready, because the answers are going to be deep. They are going to be life-altering. They will shift how you see yourself and your life's journey.

A few years ago, our family travelled to the site of my parents' death. We had never been there before. I was agitated and snippy and not pleasant to be around. My emotions were all over the place. However, when we arrived at the specific spot, we knelt down and just had a moment of silence and prayer. In that moment, I asked myself, "What did growing up without my parents gift me?" The answer was life changing. "It gave you your family."

I would gladly go through the confusion, the loneliness, the pain, the endless wanting, if it meant I could stare into the beautiful dark eyes of my wife and six children. I would do it again. And again. And again. And again. And then...I would do it all over...again.

As I knelt that day in the field of my parents' last breath, my life drew in a new breath. I recognized the seeds of love, family, faith, knowledge, and experience that I had planted in my season of darkness had blossomed into the most beautiful crops that I am still harvesting today. Suddenly, the villain and the hero hugged and made up and became best friends. My light truly had little meaning without its contrasting darkness and shadows. Because without the darkness and shadows, I would never really be able to fully appreciate the light.

Somehow, I just don't believe that you have ever suffered the level of *self-induced* consequences of social suicide from a high school talent show "whoopsie" moment like I did in 1994. But, if so, please let's be friends and swap stories. And as my new friend, I would want you to know this.

Dance on the stage of your creation. It's fine if you mess up in front of everyone; make your "mess up" spectacular! Everyone's already looking...so give'em a show!

What I see is your goodness and your humanity.

What I feel is your desire to be seen, heard, and understood.

What I admire is your desire to be better and progress even when things are poopy.

And, I love you just as you are.

Do you?

JUSTIN MORRIS

About Justin Morris: Justin Morris is the creator of The Color Alignment Protocol, and brand new, groundbreaking energy alignment modality which utilizes the energetic power of color. He has used color to create physical spaces of healing for the last 20 year in his career as a professional interior designer in spaces like corporate offices, homes, resorts, and temples for the Church of Jesus Christ of Latter-day Saints.

Justin has taken his life-long study of color, psychology, and an incredible intuitive gift for seeing the colors inherently attached to a person's soul and use them as a guide to get to the core issues people are facing. As a Life Coach, and International award-winning keynote presenter, he now teaches people to be the designer of their own life and use color to bring out the highest version of themselves.

Justin has been married to his wife, Nancy, for 23 years and together they have 6 amazing and talented children. They currently reside in Ogden, Utah.

Author's Website: *www.JMSpectrum.com*

Book Series Website: *www.TheBookOfInfluence.com*

LAUREN COBB

UNVEILING THE KEYS TO BEING LIKED & DEALING WITH JEALOUSY

In a world that values connections and relationships, likability plays a pivotal role in personal and professional success. Being liked by others not only brings about a sense of acceptance and belonging, but also opens doors to opportunities and collaborations. When someone is liked, they most often also have some haters.

It took me some years, deep soul-digging, and a change of heart to really explore the factors that contribute to likability and be able to discuss strategies for handling jealousy when faced with individuals who harbor such feelings.

The easy thing to do is to shrug your shoulders and tell yourself it isn't your problem—WHICH is true, but understanding where the jealousy is coming from makes it easier to truly move forward and not harbor any negative feelings deep down.

Some Factors That Make People Like You:

- Being authentic and genuine
- Embracing one's true self

- Demonstrating sincerity and honesty
- Building trust through reliability
- Active listening and effective communication
- Empathy and understanding
- Having a positive attitude
- Being optimistic
- Responding to people with compassion
- Treating others with respect and kindness
- Being supportive of others' endeavors
- Creating a positive and enjoyable atmosphere
- Being intuitive to others needs
- Being vulnerable

When someone displays these characteristics, others can interpret it as overconfidence, usually to those who lack self-confidence.

I can recall a couple times in my life where I had been the center of unwanted attention, all because someone who I did not know very well but knew someone close to me decided that watching my life from a far was their business. Ultimately, they started to spread rumors about me, making very big assumptions based on what they thought they saw, or who they saw me with, rather.

This went on for months behind the scenes. When it came to my attention, those closest to me who were given this information KNEW it was not true and ultimately went to bat for me without hesitation. They were not vicious or mean, but they appropriately put a stop to those things being said. These accusations and rumors could have done a lot of damage to my personal life; thankfully, it did not. There was no apology given and I reached out to this individual first to clear the air.

But what was interesting to me was those who felt the need to defend the other individual, suggesting I needed to apologize for what went down, that it was my fault that I got so much attention. There was a good solid two-hour conversation and what it boiled down to was that this person "didn't know why so many people liked me and my husband," why people gave us praise and thanks publicly. Ya'll, I was speechless! I have never done anything to seek out the attention of others and to get praise.

My whole life, I have been taught to serve without expectations. My Dad was the biggest example of this in my life. He passed away when I was 18 from cancer and I had the privilege to help take care of him the final 9 months of his journey. I live every day to do my best and be the best version of myself because of his example. I do acknowledge that, because I strive to do so, I have benefited greatly from those in my life. If you serve others with no strings attached, then it comes back to you tenfold. I truly believe it.

How does one understand the root causes of jealousy? When faced with jealousy, it is important to respond with empathy, focus on personal growth, and seek constructive solutions to diffuse negative dynamics. Those who stir the pot or spread rumors often have insecurities that they have not dealt with in their lives. They feel the need to compare themselves and will LOOK for the fault in other people.

Some people do it for attention, others it is just the environment they grew up in. They have a fear of inadequacy and do not understand their own self-worth.

Now that you can recognize the emotions behind such actions, you can offer up support and ultimately make some changes in your organization or in your personal dealings that might help cultivate personal growth and awareness for those around you:

1. Encourage open and honest communication

2. Offer support and understanding

3. Cultivate self-awareness and self-improvement

4. Avoid feeding into negative dynamics

5. Practice humility and modesty and refrain from bragging or flaunting success
6. Be mindful of others' feelings
7. Encourage collaboration instead of competition
8. Share knowledge and resources
9. Avoid talking about others
10. Promote a supportive and inclusive environment.

When you surround yourself with a network of individuals who also hold these values, then it becomes easier for you to work on yourself as well. Seek mentorship and guidance.

The likability factor is a crucial aspect of personal and professional relationships. By embracing authenticity, empathy, respect, and positive attitudes, you can enhance your likability and foster stronger connections with others. Surrounding oneself with positive influences further strengthens one's ability to navigate through jealousy and maintain healthy relationships.

Ultimately, developing and nurturing the likability factor empowers individuals to not only build rapport but also create an environment that supports personal and professional growth.

LAUREN COBB

About Lauren Cobb: Lauren Cobb is a wife to her amazing and supportive husband Tyler. A mother to 3 beautiful daughters who've taught her more in the last 12 years than she has learned in the first 23 years of her life.

At a young age Lauren knew she had a lot of ambition and drive. As she became an adult, she knew that entrepreneurship was her passion and thankfully married someone who supported that! Together with Ty they own a graphic and media design company that they've built from the ground up. Growing and seeing the successes from their own efforts has been one of the most rewarding experiences!

Self-development and leadership have been a big part of Lauren's life since she was 14. She traveled and taught leadership to youth across the country throughout her high school years. She knows first-hand how self-development is crucial to success in life. Knowing who you are and finding your purpose and passion is important.

As Lauren and her husband Ty are building their businesses and seeking a network and friends who are aligned with their values, they've found in Champion Circle and learned how to properly mastermind. Lauren is a member of the corporate executive team at Champion Circle Networking Association, founded and led by Jon Kovach Jr. Masterminds have changed her life and their business for the better.

Author's Website: *www.TyCobb.MyPortfolio.com*

Book Series Website: *www.TheBookOfInfluence.com*

MALEAH BLISS

LOVE YOURSELF

As a child, I was not well-liked. In fact, I was bullied so badly that my mom pulled me from school and homeschooled me for 2 years. When she allowed me to return to school, she held me back, so that I was no longer the youngest person in my class. I repeated fifth grade for non-academic reasons, but it really did not help.

In seventh grade, there was a group of girls that I had befriended. I spent most of the six months that I went to school there hanging out with them. Two days before the last day of school that year, they all stood up in unison as we had been eating lunch, ran over to the trash can, threw away their lunches, and then ran away from me. I still remember the way one of the girls turned around and looked at me momentarily before deciding to continue with the course of action they had planned.

That was an emotionally devastating day. I had been bullied most of my childhood but had never been blindsided by people that I thought were my friends, especially in that way. That day I went home sobbing and did not return to school that year.

Now, as an adult, I am considered a "super-connector," and am greeted by a chorus of joyous welcomes and open arms in almost every room I walk into.

What changed? I did. But likely not in the way that you are thinking. Did I learn communication skills? Yes, absolutely; and I will share those. However, the change that mattered the most was how I viewed myself.

You see, as a child, I externalized my self-worth. I wanted so badly for other children to like and accept me, but they didn't, and somewhere along the way, in my little kid's brain, I decided that meant that I was unlovable and that I was the problem.

It took me years to unlearn that. But that unlearning was my turning point.

I realized I was different from most people at a very young age. I was the weird kid in the eyes of my peers. I understand now that it was my neurodivergency, but at the time it was painful and confusing. All I wanted was to be friends with the other kids and to be allowed to play with them. But most of the time, this was not to be. I had to work much harder than most people to learn how to communicate with others in a way that made them want to include me.

As a teen, I set out on a journey to learn how to "win friends and influence people." I even read a book by the same name (maybe you've heard of it?). So, let's start with the communications skills I have found to be the most valuable, and then we will move on to the one thing that I believe to be the most important skill when developing your likability factor.

The thing I've found that sets people apart in networking, business, or any kind of interpersonal relationship is whether they truly care about other people. If you go into an interaction trying to get something from the other person, people will feel it and they don't like it. If, on the other hand, you are there because you truly care about them, you will create stark raving fans. But you actually have to care—it is not something you can fake.

As a very neurodivergent child, I absolutely cared about people; however, I didn't know how to show it in a way that others understood it. I would often talk about things that *I* cared about, instead of things that they cared about.

I had to learn how to show other people that I was interested in them. This meant that I had to learn how to ask questions. I also had to learn to not interrupt as often as I used to. I'll be honest, this is still something that I work to improve daily. When I get overly excited about a topic, I still interrupt people, but I have learned to apologize and to return our conversation back to what they were saying. It's important to remember that "a person's name is to that person, the sweetest and most important sound in any language" (Dale Carnegie). The longer you can keep attention on other people, the better.

A lesson I learned in my 20s was to stop waiting to be invited to go "play" and instead be the one inviting others. When you have fun and include others in that fun, it creates opportunities for friendships to grow. People also start to see you as someone they can trust. Be inclusive, be excited to meet new people, and in all social situations, be as welcoming to the newcomers as you are to the people that you have known for years.

All of these tools helped me to create more friendships, but without this next change, my life would not be what it is today.

I had to learn to love and value myself as much as I loved and valued others. Throughout my youth, as I said, I hated myself. I thought that I was broken, unwanted, and not good enough. I remember the first time a friend told me to look in the mirror and tell myself, "I love you." I couldn't do it.

I sat in front of that mirror, sobbing for what felt like hours. I was 19 years old and felt that nothing I ever did could make me someone worthy of the acceptance and love I so sought. I was in my mid-30s before I discovered that the path to happiness, connection, and a community of people that love me was through learning to love myself. It was a long path. But of all the things I've done in my life, it is the thing that has made the most difference in my relationships. (I have a list of resources that helped me learn to love myself listed on my website, *maleahbliss.com*.)

When you aren't looking to others for your value, you are able to show up for them. You stop worrying about whether you look silly or you did something stupid. You are able to share and be vulnerable, which will encourage others to share and be vulnerable. This is the path to true friendships.

In my opinion, your likability factor comes down to your ability to communicate how much you care about the people in your life. If you're stuck worrying about whether or not people care about and like you, you will never be able to be vulnerable enough to show people how much you like and care about them.

As I learned to love myself, I found it important to cultivate a positive attitude and mindset, both for myself, because managing the voice inside my head was paramount to protecting my self-value, and because people are naturally drawn to those who radiate positivity and optimism.

This doesn't mean that I have to be happy-go-lucky all the time, but rather that I approach situations with a solution-oriented mindset and focus on the good rather than dwelling on the negative.

Anytime I found the voice in my head being hyper-critical, I challenged that voice. If you find yourself beating yourself up inside your head, please challenge it. You deserve to have only peace and love in your head space. You are just as worthy as I am.

If you love yourself, the world will love you right back.

MALEAH BLISS

About Maleah Bliss: Maleah Bliss loves to share her passions and journey with others. As the owner of Salt City Payments, Maleah has a wealth of experience in business and finance, but what truly ignites her passion is personal development, mycology, and connecting with people.

Maleah loves learning and she is currently in school to become a Doctor of Medical Qigong. She is an author and speaker teaching about business, personal development, and how to achieve your full potential. She also loves to paint.

Maleah believes in the power of connection, and she is always looking for ways to positively impact the lives of those around her. Whether through her writing, speaking engagements, or business dealings, Maleah is driven by a desire to help others reach their full potential.

Author's Website: *www.MaleahBliss.com*

Book Series Website: *www.TheBookOfInfluence.com*

MARIS SEGAL & KEN ASHBY
LIKABILITY: A SONG FOR SUCCESS

Am I likable? This is a question that many of us ponder. Dale Carnegie noted that "likability" is a central aspect of success. We agree! Likability begins with a connection and that connection is the first step to building a relationship that prospers personally and professionally. In today's world, with all the social "likes" we face on so many platforms, the importance of authenticity and being present with people both online and in person is more important than ever.

Some key likability traits and insights offered by Carnegie include being genuine, approachable, making others feel valued, avoiding criticism and complaints, being flexible and adapting to the need and preference of others.

Likability is a path to influence. On any given day, how we feel about ourselves inside is how we will show up to others outside. To build trust and have others see us as likable, we must first see and "like" ourselves. We're a proud husband and wife duo, married fifteen years, living, loving, and working together 24/7 as business consultants, executive event producers, coaches, and trainers. We choose each other every day as partners in life and in business. So, it would stand to reason that we find each other "very" likable... on most days!

Inevitably, people ask us, "How does it work to have a love relationship and be able to work together without making each other crazy…and still have a personal life?" We had never analyzed our relationship, thinking that if we pulled it apart, we may break it! What we've always known is that there is a rhythm and a flow that works between us. In our work, we have identified four key universal rhythms that, when working in sync, create harmony and alignment at home and at work.

These rhythms—Respect, Responsibility, Reframing, and Resilience—sit at the core of who we are as a couple and as professionals. We've learned as well that when these rhythms are out of sync and expectations are not in agreement there may be arguments, illness, business deals gone bad. Working with our public and private sector clients over the years, we realized that these four harmonic rhythms are consistent with most, if not all, thriving and prosperous relationships.

If we consider the rhythm of our "personal and professional relationships," like any rhythm, it works best when it's in flowing and melodic. We are all aware that "likability" is so much more than the words we say! It is the underlying music that people we are connected to really hear. It is our full being that resonates the melody and vibrates "in" or "out" of sync with another person and forms what we call a "song for success." The "likability" factor is a foundational beat that sets the tempo for the song and the music we are putting into the world.

You may not think of yourself as a songwriter, but we've got some news for you. Your words are the lyrics and your voice the melody. We are all writing songs everyday with everything we say. Words matter and we can't take them back! So, what is the music you are putting into the world? We always have a choice, and our choices determine our future. We think of this as the Song for Success!

Every hit song has three core elements: verses, chorus, and bridge, and they are the framework for this "song for success."

The Verses

In our relationships, eliminating criticism and complaints is the first verse of our "song for success" and leads to more meaningful levels of connection.

Criticizing ourselves, someone at work, at home, or in friendships causes discord in the relationship. Complaints only breed more of the same. The verses of the "song for success" that are written around eliminating judgment and blame promote responsibility and support the harmony of interaction and possibilities.

When we approach an obstacle situation or challenging relationship from a place of curiosity and solution finding, the possibilities can be inspired and empowering. The fastest way to have someone disconnect is to focus on their flaws and dwell on their debacles.

In many cases, the blemishes we call out in others are the projection of our own weaknesses. We are, after all, perfectly imperfect humans, and we are good at it! In a Navajo court of law, the judge will remind you that when you point a finger, there are three fingers pointing back at you. Others are often mirrors for our own behaviors.

The Chorus

People are more inclined to like you if they feel good about themselves when they are around you!

Finding and celebrating the good in others is the foundation of any strong relationship and is not only uplifting for the other person, but also a source of joy for you as well. The chorus of any song is the focal point and what we want people to keep singing and coming back to. Being the trusted person in a relationship that repeatedly contributes to another person feeling good about themselves is the soul of all great love songs and the heart of good business deals.

When we show up and listen, we build trust and amplify a relationship! All significant relationships are built on respect. It is improbable to experience and hear the joy in a relationship if we cannot respect the other person. It is even more impossible to respect the other(s) in a relationship if we do not respect ourselves. The unifying chorus raises all voices. An expedient way to foster respect in others is to make a list of the attributes you respect in yourself. This one exercise can open your ears to hear the ways you sing respect to someone else.

The Bridge

The ability to be flexible and adapt to the needs of others is consistent with the bridge for our song.

The bridge always exposes a new emphasis or a new perspective to complement our likability tune. We can resist the inevitability of change and disregard the fact that change is the only constant in life, or we can surrender to the new transitional movement in the bridge to lead us back to the chorus. Flexibility is about reframing and resilience: Moving through change, flowing into the bridge to the next verse.

When we are truly present with people and hear them, meeting them where they are a new perspective emerges and we're often better for encouraging a collaboration. This reframing also continues to build trust. As change occurs, we stand up to it with resilience. This builds the harmonic likability. Adaptability and flexibility are the "bridge" and the transition of that rhythmic progression of "becoming!"

Our Song for Success

We are grateful in our relationship, both personally and professionally, to practice finding the "good," "avoiding criticism," and "adapting." The melody isn't always perfect because sometimes old stories get in the way and drown out possibilities. In our marriage, we pay close attention to and stay mindful of singing in unison, as one voice, in everything we "be" and "do."

One thing that supports this in our living is a daily chorus of "gratitude." Reflecting on our most valuable assets—family, health, possibilities, and love—is the rhythmic "count in" that starts every day on solid footing.

The music gets amplified, and we sing in unison. Collaborating, communicating, celebrating and being grateful for accomplishments, large and small, for whatever shows up is our "song for success."

We are all connected as humans first and that's where the bottom line begins.

A true likability song goes beyond the elements of a verse, chorus, and bridge. It connects us all. The deeper music of "likability" means living in generosity and embracing the "song for success" as a crucial aspect of thriving in both personal and professional relationships. Our daily playlist of songs support building stronger connections with others, increasing our influence, and ultimately achieving our goals. Whether you're looking to make new friends, improving your love relationships, or succeeding in your career, focusing on "likability" is the "song for success" in all relationships.

We invite you to ask yourself, "What is my song playlist?" *Am I just replaying the oldies, stories of past failures or limiting beliefs coming into my head? Am I just listening and singing along to programmed melodies on a repeating playlist of self-doubt?* Or, are you curious about new beats and tempos and reframing and rearranging those over-played and worn-out melodies?

We all have the ability and internal beats and rhythms to create the background music of our lives. We have choice in how we live into the four universal rhythms of Respect, Responsibility, Reframing, and Resilience. Show up every day, at home and at work, committed to creating your own "song for success" with a "chorus" that looks for the good in others, "verses" that avoid being judgmental and critical, and a "bridge" that adapts quickly, opening the door to successful relationships.

We have one life to live, one body, and one planet. Isn't it time that relationships move front and center on the global stage we call life? Likability is a "song for success" that is worth singing every day.

MARIS SEGAL & KEN ASHBY

About Ken Ashby & Maris Segal: Ken Ashby and Maris Segal, "America's Master Connectors," coach, consult, and collaborate with executives, entrepreneurs, celebrities and rising leaders to identify and bring their professional, personal, and philanthropic vision to life. Spanning four decades and forty countries, they combine their relationship marketing expertise with head and heart leadership to build meaningful connections and impactful strategies that drive their client's internal and external success.

Ken and Maris live by the philosophy that "We are all connected as human's first and that's where the bottom line begins."

Together and individually, working across the public and private sectors, they have served a wide spectrum of local and global leaders, consumer and financial brands, causes, and policy makers. This dynamic duo also leverages Ken's international award-winning singer songwriting gifts to develop collaborative teams with a songwriting workshop series. From board rooms and classrooms to Harvard, the White House, and Super Bowl Halftimes, Ken and Maris are also known for uniting diverse populations with innovative cross-cultural marketing and personal development programs.

As certified Executive and Relationship coaches, their latest book, *The RFactor; Universal Rhythms for Leading Prosperous Relationships* and their **DRIVE method:** Desire, Relationships, Intention, Vision, and Empowerment sit at the core of their work. Ashby and Segal set a path for every client to build high performing businesses and elevate personal and professional leadership for maximum impact and a 360-degree thriving life! As authors they have been featured in thirteen Amazon best-selling leadership centered books. They speak regularly and were recently featured on the TEDx Farmingdale stage.

Author's Website: *www.SegalLeadershipGlobal.com*

Book Series Website: *www.TheBookOfInfluence.com*

MICHELLE CRITES
CARE THROUGH AUTHENTICITY

. . . .

"The only way I can get you to do anything is by giving you what you want."
~ Dale Carnegie

"Nobody cares how much you know until they understand how much you care."
~ President Theodore Roosevelt

"The only way I can get you to do anything is by giving you what you want."
~ Dale Carnegie

"Three-fourths of the people you will meet are hungering for sympathy. Give it to them and they will love you."
~ Dale Carnegie

MICHELLE CRITES

About Michelle Crites: The founder of Live Your True Calling, Michelle's desire is that every person realize the full potential of their God-given destiny. She is an Author, Speaker, Empowerment Coach, founder of several summits, award-winning actress, and her greatest role to date is being a mom!

Michelle has spent the past 12 years serving in Deliverance Ministry, breaking down strongholds and helping people heal and get free from the pain of the past that has kept them from being all that they were intended to be. She is an advocate for health and wellness and teaches classes on natural ways to supplement a healthy lifestyle.

She is currently working on her next book and creating a podcast to inspire everyone to live their best life. To see more from Michelle, please find her on Facebook at Live Your True Calling.

Author's Website: *www.linkedin.com/in/Michelle-Crites-86389563*

Book Series Website: *www.TheBookOfInfluence.com*

MICHELLE MRAS

CHARACTER IS KEY

The likability factor of an individual is based on their connection skills. Many people come into a situation and begin to dominate the conversation in order to be accepted. That person may get the most attention, but it's the one who listens and relates that leaves the biggest impression. It seems contradictory, but that is how relationships work.

"To be more interesting, be interested."
~ Dale Carnegie

Children experience strangers with wide-eyed curiosity. It is rare to see a toddler look at a new person with fear. This is quite the opposite of how an adult approaches a stranger. Adults have a skewed reality in which they expect something negative to occur, so they approach strangers with trepidation or not at all. The likability phenomena is best explained through the eyes of an innocent child.

Toddlers quietly observe. They naturally scan for a face that responds. If they like or are not threatened by what they see, the next step is to make eye contact. They offer a coy smile towards the stranger, wait for the reciprocal smile, then wave or say, "Hello." This interaction occurs as naturally as breathing. The best way to witness this is to see two or more groups of young children on a playground. Within milliseconds, children go through this entire process. Once they exchange names, it is as if they have been lifelong friends. Children instantly like another person until they are proven wrong.

Life experiences cloud our willingness to like other people with open abandon. Our teen years are when likability take on a new role: Popularity. Most people equate likability with popularity. I believe this perception is not true. Likability tends to be more long term and is who and how you are received as a person through your personality and demeanor. Popularity is limited and tends to be a determined by what you possess that others want.

Reflect on your high school years. The popular crowd didn't always have the highest grades, serve in student government, or hold positions to create change. They were the sports heroes, cheerleaders, homecoming royalty, and the like. They were the ones with a following. The ones who everyone in the school knew because of what they did for the school's reputation, not for their ability to relate to the masses that followed them.

The popular kids were not necessarily the most liked people. They simply held a popularity factor because of what they had, not for who they are. A test of this can be done at your high school reunion. See how popular they are now that their looks or athletic ability have passed. Remember, likability is based on reliability that lasts.

As we age, our sights are set on more lasting relationships. We learn to be more discerning with whom we bestow favor. We still fall into the popularity trap, but far less than we did in our teen years. Likability becomes more of a player as it creates an employee or co-worker who is reliable. Popular employees do not tend to produce. I was once asked what I thought about someone in regard to a job. My question back was, "Personally or professionally?" They were taken aback by my answer until I explained that I liked them as a person but would never hire them because they failed to get things done.

This reminds me of a job I held in the early 1990s. I worked under a very popular woman who had been promoted to branch manager based on her past skill set that helped create amazing advancements for the credit union. To me, her lack of leadership skills were glaringly obvious. She never recognized the incredible work performed by the small group of employees at her branch. She rarely listened to those who worked for her.

Don't get me wrong, she was quite pleasant to customers and other workers. Her personality was likable. She was incredible at technology. Her skills in the technology aspect of the credit union made her incredibly popular. Her likability factor was high for those who had not worked directly under her. It was her popularity that got her the leadership position.

My crisis came to me in the form of quarterly performance reports. There were complaints about "the new girl" messing up transactions and "not being competent." This branch manager would call me in for my quarterly review and tell me that this feedback was "troublesome." I was initially confused because I had great repartee with all the customers and my coworkers. Then I figured it out. I informed her that those comments were not about me, rather they were about her. She was so rarely in the branch, that the members though she was the "new girl," not me.

Nevertheless, she wrote me up. This infuriated me. She knew it was her, and still marked it onto my employee record as she giggled about the confusion. I ended up leaving the credit union because of her. In my exit interview, I set the record explained that I could not work under the conditions she was imposing and neither should anyone else at the branch. After checking my story, they begged me to come back but I refused and recommended one of the other employees. The popular but incompetent branch manager was pulled back to work IT at the main branch while my recommendation was promoted. It was amazing how quickly the branch turned around.

I learned several things from this experience: 1) A management position does not mean you were a leader, 2) Popularity does not mean competent, and 3) Likability is based on what is perceived to be true.

It is far more important to gauge a person on their personality and character rather than what can be gained from your interaction with them. Likability becomes more of a character development, rather than the popularity response of how many people can I impress for a short amount of time.

LIKABILITY FACTOR

"Fame is a vapor, popularity an accident, and riches take wings. Only one thing endures, and that is character."

~ Horace Greenley

MICHELLE MRAS

About Dr. Michelle Mras: Dr. Michelle Mras is an award-winning, internationally recognized inspirational speaker, published #1 Best Selling Author, intuitive leader, wife, and mother who has been stirring audiences and individuals to action through her compelling message of self-leadership, resilience and living a life of intention. Michelle's infectious presentations and coaching inspire her clients to rise above negative self-talk to reclaim their inner grit.

Michelle encourages you to be your best version every day and live unapologetically. Her fiery spirit and passion drive her to candidly share the key moments that transformed her into the irresistible force she is today. Learn more about Michelle and her writing at her website.

Author's Website: *www.MichelleMras.com*

Book Series Website: *www.TheBookOfInfluence.com*

MORGAN TAYLOR RUDNICK

CHANGE FOR YOURSELF, NOT FOR OTHERS

"Until you make the unconscious, conscious, it will rule your life and you will call it Fate."
~ Carl Jung

Likability—a word with so much power behind it. Being liked seems to be conditioned in us since we were young children. Remember being on the playground and wanting the other kids to come and play with you? In middle school and high school, it seems to be a popularity contest as to what individual or group will be liked and admired by their classmates.

This continues into adulthood, that desire to be liked by our clients, employers, employees, peers, etc. Reflect on a question for a minute: "How does it feel when someone does not like us? What internal feelings come up?"

Let me share a story about my client, Luna, and how she learned to not only like herself but love herself and how this changed her ability to move through the world with a new perspective.

Luna and I explored some beliefs she held about herself as she was going through a huge transition in her life. Having a domestic violence restraining order against her soon to be ex-husband kept her in a constant state of fear, locked away in her house and terrified to go outside or engage with anyone. She was left with just the voices in her head and these voices got louder and louder as the days went on.

The world around her became unsafe and started to crumble. She went into hermit mode and shut herself off from the world. Who had Luna become during her marriage? She did not like the person that was staring back at her in the mirror; she realized that person was someone she did not recognize any longer.

She struggled with self-hatred, and thoughts of how she could be so stupid to not see the signs of someone who was gaslighting her. She would continue to ask herself how she could have missed the signs. She struggled with the guilt of her dog being abused by her ex and hated herself for not getting out sooner.

Who was Luna? Everyone had liked her but was she people pleasing? Was she standing behind someone that wasn't her? Did she not feel aligned with her career path anymore? The life she thought she wanted was no longer making her happy.

She realized she had to explore her morals, values, integrity, and belief systems to ensure they were in alignment with the woman she was blossoming into. Luna spent months diving into her unconscious or what I like to call "the void:" Just being present and sitting with the overwhelming feelings without judgment or criticism.

After some time, diving into her shadow self, Luna started to realize her own unique gifts and the more time she spent feeling these negative emotions, she could never express these gifts to the world. When she started breaking out of her shell again, she realized that there is a whole world out there waiting to be explored. No one was going to take that away from her.

If she wasn't going to be liked, she realized that was okay because she loved herself and that was the most important gift she could've given herself during this time.

Luna no longer relied on others for external validation; she started relying on herself for internal validation. She had these beautiful qualities within her—they've been with her all along. Sadly, it sometimes takes a traumatic or life changing event to go within and find these likable qualities, not for others, but for ourselves. Once we do this, we can become whole again.

Luna realized if she couldn't love herself, who else was going to love her? The most important thing is to love yourself first because you will never receive the authentic love you desire. You can only love someone else into the depths you can love yourself.

It's hard to realize that not everyone will like you or your brand, your ideas, or your opinions, but that's okay. The people that are meant to find you will. Don't change for anyone—change for yourself. Don't just like yourself, but love yourself and others will be attracted to that frequency.

We are all unique beings here with a purpose to serve that may not look like everyone else's mission here on earth.

Take a good look in the mirror today and tell yourself, "I love you!"

MORGAN TAYLOR RUDNICK

About Morgan Taylor Rudnick: Morgan graduated with her Master's in Psychology, with an emphasis in Marriage and Family Therapy. She felt a special calling to focus on helping those with past traumas overcome them while lessening the trauma's impact in the development of mental illness and addictions.

Prior to earning her Master's in Psychology, Morgan studied Kinesiology and Nutrition and earned a certification as a Health and Wellness Coach. She believes that the mind, body, and soul are interconnected, and we cannot treat one without addressing the others.

Morgan is the Co-founder and Chief Executive Officer of a substance abuse and mental health facility that strives to create a customized approach to recovery. Her goal is to bridge the gap between western and eastern practices to create a holistic-based approach to treatment.

Additionally, Morgan and her business partner serve as Energetic Branding Consultants, helping business owners align with their unique energetic type and build a brand that honors that.

Morgan and her business partner also service clients looking for a more spiritual approach that includes services such as: human design, astrology, numerology, tarot and oracle cards, and other spiritual practices to help map out a unique blueprint for each individual.

Author's Website: *www.CustomizedConsultingServices.com*

Book Series Website: *www.TheBookOfInfluence.com*

NADIA FRANCOIS

HOW TO WIN FRIENDS: MY JOURNEY

Through my life experiences and insights, I have come to comprehend the complexities of human connections and likability. From miscommunication with my mother to discovering authentic expression through expressive arts therapy and beyond, my journey echoes Dale Carnegie's principles of influence relating to making people like you, drawing upon my experiences and insights to further explore these principles.

Do This, and You'll Be Welcome Anywhere: Authenticity

My fallout with my mother wasn't about what she said but how it was delivered. Carnegie advised that I show genuine interest in others; once my mother and I revisited our misunderstandings sincerely and eager to understand each other's viewpoints, our relationship began healing.

Being genuine means more than simply speaking the truth: it means communicating it in such a way as to show thoughtful consideration for another's feelings and perspective.

How to Leave an Impression: Respect & Integrity

While considering past experiences that led to strife between friends, I understood the invaluable role respect and integrity play in making an impressive first impression. Carnegie advocates giving sincere compliments to build positive relationships—had our truths been communicated more empathetically and with greater appreciation, there wouldn't have been so much friction among us all.

Building Lasting Good Impressions Requires Showing Respect and Sincerity

An Easy Step to Becoming a Good Conversationalist: Listen

Over time, I have come to appreciate listening as an integral component of effective communication—echoing Carnegie's principle: "Be a Good Listener; Encourage Others to Talk About Themselves." Having given this concept more thought over time, my mother revealed new aspects to our story as I paid her more attention when listening intently.

Listening effectively involves more than simply hearing words; it requires understanding the emotions and motivations behind their exchange.

How to Interest People: Empathy & Understanding

Empathy has always been my go-to for dissolving various misunderstandings. Carnegie advised speaking directly about someone else's interests when conversing. While my experiences have taught me that mutual understanding often comes through shared perceptions, my connections deepened exponentially when I focused on grasping another's viewpoint in conversations.

People respond well when we genuinely try to understand and align ourselves with their emotions and perspectives.

How to Instantly Make People Like You: Bridge Communication Gaps

Carnegie emphasized the sincerity in making someone else feel valued and important, which is essential in building my mother-daughter bond and creating connection and growth. Understanding both perspectives was vital for breaking through communication gaps that separated us further and helping me develop my mother-daughter relationship more rapidly. "Bridging communication gaps fosters connection, influence, and growth" has always been my core philosophy and value.

Bridge building in communication fosters immediate connections and likability. Therefore, every interaction should start with the goal of understanding and connecting.

My experiences serve as an illustration of Dale Carnegie's principles. They show how authenticity, respect, active listening, empathy, and effective communication are keys to becoming likable—which in turn leads to more substantial personal relationships and influence and leadership across various areas. Real communication has played a massive role in my success!

NADIA FRANCOIS

About Nadia Francois: Nadia Francois is a serial entrepreneur with a heart for people. A hairstylist by trade, Nadia holds current licenses in Cosmetology and Barbering, a B.S. in Business Administration, and a certificate in Women's Entrepreneurship. The Louisiana native began her entrepreneurial journey at the age of 19 and has used her experiences and knowledge to help other business owners start and grow their ventures. In 2018, Nadia served as the inaugural Ms. Black Louisiana Empowerment representing her state by serving at several community projects and by hosting outreach activities.

The Beautypreneur and non-profit founder became a first-time author in August of 2018. In 2019, she was nominated for Business Woman of the Year by the Greater Southwest Louisiana Black Chamber of Commerce. July 2020, the What's Your Super Power Empire began with an anthology and expanded into the digital TV world. In 2021, Nadia continued to enhance her digital footprint with the addition of *Power Conversations Magazine & Podcast* which are additional extensions of her WYSP Digital Media which caters to minority entrepreneurs and their advancement.

In 2022, Nadia was awarded the "Game Changer" award by the Beauty Industry Community Awards Organization, has spoken on various global platforms and is launching her newest #1 Best-Selling Book, *A Mother's Prayer* anthology. This goal-getter contributes her success to grace and mercy. Her number one assignment is being the mother and sole provider for her four sons, the driving force behind her persistent hustle and diligent pursuit of greatness.

Author's Website: *www.NadiaFrancois.com*

Book Series Website: *www.TheBookOfInfluence.com*

NANCY DEBRA BARROWS

LIKABILITY UNLEASHED: CONNECT, INFLUENCE, SHINE!

There are those people to whom we are immediately drawn. People who make everyone in the room feel like they're the only person there, just as easily as they keep a crowd riveted. They emanate warmth and are welcoming. They somehow feel "familiar." Why do we feel that way? How do they do it?

In Dale Carnegie's *How to Win Friends & Influence People*, he talks about likability and ways to make people like you:

- Smile.
- Show genuine interest in others.
- Make people feel important.

Seems obvious. Intuitive, even. But it isn't, for some people. Some people do not learn the hidden rules of conversation by simply observing. Others possess the skills but lack the confidence, experience anxiety, or have had negative experiences in their past that keep them from being able to employ/demonstrate these skills when engaging with others.

As humans, we want to be accepted and welcomed by others. Many clients come to me, as an Empowerment Coach, asking, "How do I compel others to like me? Can I influence how people receive me?" The response is, "Absolutely. It's not about you! It is about how others feel when they're around you!"

We all have a voice. Have you found yours? Are you comfortable using it? I have the privilege as a speech language pathologist and "The Chick with The Toolbelt" Empowerment Coach to be witness to my clients discovering what was inside of them all along.

Using my 20-plus years as a Speech Language Pathologist focused on Social Cognition, I started "The Chick with The Toolbelt" to help people find success in every interaction they enter. Notice, I did not say, "In every conversation?" It goes beyond the words. It goes beyond the direct interactions we experience. The communication you have with others is a critical piece of "Likability," and you have the power to influence how you are seen in the eyes of others.

We all have thoughts about other people. Think about it: In all your communities (work, family, friends, school, etc.) you are aware of who knows all the best gossip. You know who you want to collaborate with because they are a team player. You know who will NEVER be on time. You know who to call if something needs repairing. You know the person who's 'bossy' and inflexible.

It happens all the time. It happens in an instant. Let me reassure you that this is normal and that you have the power to influence the thoughts people have about YOU!

Here are 3 "Chick Tips" that give you the ability to do just that. Ready?!

Chick Tip #1: You Have to Like People

Um, durrr. But it's true and it matters! You must be genuinely interested in others, if you want them to be interested in YOU!

When you pretend to be interested in others, but aren't interested in what they have to say, they'll know. Let's say you meet someone for Happy Hour and they order a certain drink, and you casually ask, "Is that your go to Happy Hour drink?" It gives you an opportunity to learn about them, yes, but not just for the moment.

In that moment, it makes you personable and likable, but if you file the information away, and the next time you meet for Happy Hour, you order their 'go to' drink before they arrive, or you can say to them, "Your usual, right?" as you order, you instantly become the person who makes others feel seen, heard, loved and valued!

It demonstrates that you're someone who values and respects others. YOU are the person people want to spend time with because they feel important around you and that makes them want to get to know you! They're now ready to invest time in you and the relationship, because they genuinely like you.

Chick Tip #2: 'Speak' Without Words

I want you to do a little experiment. It will require putting down the book, but it will be here waiting for you when you've finished. I want you to walk past someone, make eye contact, smile as you approach them, and give them a compliment as you pass by ("You have a great smile," "I love that sweater," "That is a great color for you"). How do they respond? How does that response make you feel?

Not done yet! Now, find someone else, give them a sideways glance and keep your face expressionless as you approach, and 'harumph' as you pass by them. How did they respond? How did THAT response make you feel?

As demonstrated, your body language speaks **volumes** about you, so make sure it's sending the **right** message. When you are with people, you want them to know that you value their time and who they are as a person!

Allow me to illustrate.

Standing or sitting up straight shows that you are energized by their presence and the content of the conversation. Crossed arms send the message that you are defensive, guarded, holding back, judging, and closed off. YIKES!

Think about what it looks like when 'people of power' come together: Uncrossed arms are an invitation 'in,' like they are opening the door and saying, "Welcome! I am so glad you are here!"

Move your arms and hands when you speak. Lean in slightly to show you are engaged in the conversation and invested in your conversational partner(s).

I told you it was more than the words! It doesn't cost anything. It doesn't take away from your day. It only makes it better for YOU and EVERYONE your smile, your eyes, and your body language touches. You make people **feel**. Emotion is a powerful place of connection, as well. It connects people without uttering a word. As Maya Angelou wisely said, "People may forget what you say, but they will never forget how you made them feel."

And remember, a smile makes someone else's day BETTER, and makes YOU feel better because of it!

You are now the person to whom others are immediately drawn. You are captivating, likable, and exude warmth.

Chick Tip #3: Appreciation, Connection and Celebration!

A genuine compliment is the least expensive gift you can give! Appreciation is a strong heart-nourishing emotion to experience. It lifts people up. It demonstrates that they are valued for who they are. When we offer another person sincere, unconditional love and unconditional acceptance, we are offering appreciation—the feeling of being valued.

There is ALWAYS something positive to comment on, such as someone's contribution, positivity, a recent accomplishment, or how you really enjoy their company! Go beyond the surface, physical, and observable. Comment on what makes that person special.

More than likely you have at least one shared interest or experience that creates an opportunity for an authentic point of connection.

For example, look for common ground with the other person, a hobby, favorite sports team, or a mutual friend. This can provide a good starting point for conversation and help you establish a rapport with the other person.

Don't be afraid to share about yourself!

Our willingness to be honest with one another creates a strong connection. Walking away from an interaction feeling like we didn't learn anything about our communication partner(s) creates a feeling of disconnect and limits the depth of connection made.

People who ask questions and encourage others to reveal information, while sharing nothing about themselves, are rarely described as 'likable.' More typically they are talked about like this: "I don't know. I couldn't get a read on them. It was weird. It made me uncomfortable." As humans, allowing ourselves to be vulnerable is scary and when people do not reciprocate, we feel 'exposed.'

Caution: I am not advising you to crack open your chest and share every secret you've ever held. That is not real or genuine and will be just as poorly received as sharing nothing or worse! Sharing ANYTHING about ourselves as humans, creates a moment of vulnerability. It can be a picture of your fur baby, a story about your favorite place to travel or recounting something that happened to you that was funny! Radiating Real and connection starts small, by being relatable.

We each have a story. A powerful, impactful, important story, which makes us who we are. Stories that are meant to be celebrated, shared, and appreciated as much as the human who has taken the journey!

BONUS "Chick Tip:"

Above all, it's important to be genuine, authentic, and true to yourself. People can sense when someone's being insincere or trying too hard to impress them. They're ingenuine and the incongruity makes us uncomfortable around them. They are the opposite of likable. Instead, be genuine, honest, and enjoy your interactions with others. In other words, be YOU! This will help you build trust and establish a strong foundation for positive relationships.

Likability isn't about manipulating or deceiving others. It's about building positive connections based on mutual respect, trust, and genuine interest. The techniques included in the "Chick Tips" work to create a positive first impression and establish a strong foundation for positive relationships in any situation. In other words, you are likable! Now it's your turn to give it a try!

NANCY DEBRA BARROWS

About Nancy Debra Barrows: Known as the Queen of Engagement, Co-Founder of peakAboo analytics, and named one of the Top 50 Most Impactful People on LinkedIn and a LinkedIn Top Voice, Nancy Barrows, a #1 Best-Selling Author, a 20+ year Entrepreneur of a thriving private practice, Keynote Speaker and Coach who, using her 20 years of experience and expertise in Social Cognition, developed her program, The Chick with the Toolbelt. She partners with clients on showing up, finding their voice, and fully engaging their community across platforms and media, guiding them to reach their personal and business growth goals and build robust revenue streams, while sharing tools to maintain these changes independently.

Highlighted on ROKU TV, LinkedInLIVE, Apple Podcasts, Spotify, YouTube, Twitter, Anchor, GooglePodcasts, Stitcher, AmazonMusic, Audible, VoiceYourVibe.com and more, Nancy's LIVE every Wednesday and Saturday, co-hosting the Global Award-Winning Live Shows #WhatsGoodWednesday and #ShoutOutSaturday, which have been featured on NASDAQ, *Forbes*, *Thrive Global*, *Yahoo Finance*, ROKUTV, AmazonFire, The CW, multiple #1 best-selling books and syndicated on a SmartTV Network. Nancy has thrived through adversity and employs her experience to help others find their voice.

By telling her story and creating the #RadiatingReal movement, she is making a positive impact, encouraging and inspiring others to do the same. Book your FREE 15-minute consultation with Nancy: *calendly.com/nancybarrows*
Author's Website: *www.linktr.ee/VoiceYourVibe*

Book Series Website: *www.TheBookOfInfluence.com*

DR. ONIKA SHIRLEY

THERE'S POWER IN KNOWING LIKABILITY REALLY MATTERS

The desire to be liked is such a powerful force in the world today: It has such an influence that it can push you to think differently about your behavior; it will make you take a second look at your appearance, and even the relationships you're a part of. But despite all the things you do and even after putting in your very best efforts, no one really has a say in how much other people like them.

During my lifetime, I have personally found that likability is a moving target. It can be thought of as an invisible checklist that we house in our hearts, and we allow it to sometimes take up space in our minds but others around us do the checking on our checklist. As a woman with a career in manufacturing and an entrepreneur, I have discovered that the stake of that checklist is even higher as a woman of color in a career that's thought to be a man's world.

When you're a business owner and you're surrounded by competition, you're asking yourself, "Is the thing I am offering or service I am rendering worth the potential trade-off in likability?" You're asking yourself, "Do I trade off being myself to fit in or do I stand true to myself and standout?" I will tell you that I found that standing true to myself and standing out has been rewarding and life changing. Although we don't have a say in how much others like us, there are some things we can do to make ourselves more accepted and likable.

Likability can be used as a catchall for other biases, and it can be viewed through several lens. When I think about it, I think about labels. I think about categories, and I think about some form of segregation. So, for example, a Black woman who shows up as confident will often be read as arrogant or cocky. When people say to you, "I don't like you," very often what they are really saying is, "You did not meet my expectation of how a person like you is supposed to show up in the world, on a job, in a business."

See, this can open another door as a Black woman with a career in manufacturing. Likability can sometimes catch you off guard, especially when you walk into a place with a mind of just wanting to help and wanting to make a difference in the organization, in the world, and honestly in your own life.

I think people would know how to respond if it was visible or if it was simply said. The problem is, a lot of this is hidden behind clicks, groups, and association that you're not privileged to be a part of. Likability is one of those areas where you must constantly question yourself: "Am I not worth it? Do I not have anything to offer that will bring results? Am I doing something wrong? Why do they not like me?" The capacity it takes to keep asking these questions can be very time consuming and, honestly, mentally draining.

Fundamentally, though, this is not about people simply being liked—it's more about prioritizing building an environment where people feel like they can show up as themselves while offering a life changing product or service. There's a saying that goes, "People buy from those they know, like, and trust." Being liked is a great path to overall success.

For women leaders, likability and success can go hand-in-hand. Likability contributes to a path of influence, leadership, and, overall, a great social life. Likable people have diverse traits and there's no definitive set of attributes that makes one likable, but they carry a magnet of attractiveness.

I know this to be true because I am a likable person, but can I share with you what's really going on? Sometimes, high-achieving women experience negative social responses because we are successful, and we are looked down on specifically because of the behaviors required to create the success. Some feel that it's going against the grain. It violates society's expectations about "how women are supposed to behave."

Society has a list of expectations of how women are supposed to be behave and we are expected to be agreeable, affectionate, amiable, and nurturing.

Thus, if a woman acts confidently or competitively, if she pushes those under her leadership to perform, if she holds her team accountable, if she displays decisive and forceful leadership, she is deviating from the social blueprint that dictates how she "should behave."

By violating society's beliefs about what women are like and what women should be like, successful women experience pushback from others for not measuring up, not being feminine enough, and being too masculine.

The world seems to be deeply uncomfortable with powerful women. In fact, oftentimes people don't really like us. It's not that we can't do what need to do. It's not that we are not making an impact and getting results. It's simple: We are not meeting certain expectations set by certain people. We have a choice, and we must weigh our options.

Likability and success have worked well for me. When I aspired to be in a position of power in manufacturing over fifteen years ago, I knew it was totally my choice whether I acted in a way that will have people continue to like me or not. I knew that it was vital to get this right because getting it wrong could be taxing. When I say taxing, it could have prevented me from being promoted or it could have contributed to me not being paid for the work performed and the results I was getting.

As I went into a place that I knew nothing about, I knew I needed to be in touch with me. As a black woman in manufacturing, I knew I needed to be likable, but I had to stay in touch with myself and not allow myself to be lost in the noise of a list of expectations. I knew that if want to be liked, I had to genuinely like people. I discovered that being likable meant people would help you get more done, and they will stick with you if you stick with them.

I have seen and experienced that highly likable people have more. They have more opportunities, they get more deals, and they have more fun. People want to know likable people. They want to work with them, they want to be around them, and want to do business with them. As production operations manager, I quickly noticed how likable people were easier to work with and they were great assets to team projects.

I put in the efforts to be likable and, in return, I attracted other likable people. We can't make people like us but there are some things we can do. We can put in the efforts and shape how much other people like us. It's time to be intentional and make likability a priority. Here's some of the things we can do:

1. Simply be authentically you.
2. Build on the qualities that are essential to being a successful leader, despite your gender.
3. Know that we're obligated to future generations.
4. Find your voice and serve those around you.
5. Be collaborative.
6. Support others and encourage their success.
7. Make eye contact when speaking.
8. Smile naturally when you are speaking.
9. Use a tone that conveys warmth and enthusiasm.
10. Work on being compatible on social networks and in social networking events.

In closing, likability can be leveraged to persuade and to influence. Have you ever used it? Have you seen it used by others? Likability is powerful and it makes people want to interact with us, work with us, do business with us, and buy from us.

When people like us we can more easily influence them, and our words will carry more weight with them, and they are simply more likely to listen to our recommendations. We can cause people to like us more by paying more attention to them and their needs.

DR. ONIKA SHIRLEY

About Dr. Onika L. Shirley: Dr. Onika L. Shirley is the Founder and CEO of Action Speaks Volume, Inc. She is a Procrastination Strategist and Behavior Change Expert known for building unshakable confidence, stopping procrastination, and getting your dreams out of your head into your life.

She is a Master Storyteller, International Speaker, Serves in Global Ministry, is an international bestselling author, International Award Recipient, Serial Entrepreneur, and Global Philanthropist impacting lives in the USA, Africa, India, and Pakistan. Dr. O is a Motivational Speaker and Christian Counselor.

Dr. Onika is the Founder, and Director of Action Speaks Volume Orphanage Home and Sewing School in Telangana State, India, and the Founder and Director of Action Speaks Volume sewing school in Khanewal and Shankot, Pakistan. She founded, operated, and visited an Orphanage home in Tuni, India, for four years. She supported widows in Tuni, India. She is the Founder of Empowering Eight Inner Circle, ASV C.A.R.E.S, ASV Next Level Living Program, and P6 Solutions and Consulting.

She has served for 13 years as a therapeutic foster parent. Of all the things Dr. O does, she is most proud of her profound faith in Christ and her opportunity to serve the body of Christ globally.

Author's Website: *www.ActionSpeaksVolum.com*

Book Series Website: *www.TheBookOfInfluence.com*

RACHEL DIAMOND

THE DEEP CONVERSATIONAL ROUTE

The Deep Conversational Route is that the only way to make friends is by being one. Likability is an intangible quality that most of us intuitively grasp yet can find difficult to define or explain. At its core, likability involves building connections and invoking feelings of warmth, trust, and comfort—but how can we cultivate it? The key lies in deep conversation.

Dale Carnegie, one of the foremost experts on human relationships, provided us with an invaluable principle in his groundbreaking book, *How to Win Friends and Influence People*: "Be Genuinely Interested in People." It seems simple enough, yet most people need help to fully appreciate its power.

Reflecting upon my relationship with my teenage daughter, from our shared moments to silent nods and snuggles, it is clear that our bond, or "likability quotient," is founded in genuine mutual interest. We have fostered an environment where both sides listen with open ears and attentive hearts.

Building Likability Habits

Authenticity Is Key: At the core of likability lies authenticity. As we saw earlier in my anecdotes, being true to ourselves opens doors for deeper relationships. Being vulnerable also sends a powerful signal about trust—that you trust me with my truth—permitting others to open up. In return, this may also give them the courage to open up.

Active Listening: One key to being likable is being an excellent listener. I remember hearing my daughter's slight sniffles and knowing something wasn't right immediately—without magical hearing! Instead, this was about tuning into her, actively listening even when no words were being said back at me.

Create Safe Spaces: Establishing an atmosphere where people feel safe to open up about their deepest thoughts and fears is a mark of your likability; just being there as I was for my daughter can sometimes serve as support.

Understand and Respect Different Perspectives: It is key to realize that being likable doesn't require always agreeing with everyone around us; it involves understanding and respecting diverging perspectives. My household engages in tough conversations without turning away; our aim is not just reaching an agreement but understanding and respecting each other's points of view.

Deep Conversations as the Key to Likability

Deep conversations combine authenticity, active listening, safe environments, and the desire for understanding into one cohesive whole. They go beyond superficial conversational topics into more deeply personal topics involving vulnerability, dreams, fears, and aspirations—providing the gateways into heartfelt connections.

My relationship with my daughter didn't happen overnight—it took years of authentic, in-depth conversations for our bond to develop genuinely. Through regular dialogue, we learned about each other's unsaid words and hidden emotions behind them, creating a space where our thoughts and emotions could flow without judgment—this deep understanding fostered trust and likability within both parties.

Make Deep Conversations Part of Your Routine Start with Authenticity: Don't be intimidated to share your vulnerabilities; this makes you relatable and opens doors for other people to open up about themselves.

Engage: Like when I asked my daughter if she was okay, always create opportunities for dialogue between two individuals. A small prompt can often open up floodgates of emotion.

Engage in Active Listening: For successful conversations, active listening is paramount. Listen with all parts of yourself: heart, intuition, and eyes - paying particular attention to nonverbal cues or emotions hidden beneath words.

Make Sure They Feel Secure: Assure the other person they can confide in you without fearing judgment. Be their anchor without judgment being passed on them.

Likability doesn't just depend on charisma or being the center of attention; it's about genuine connections, understanding, and deep conversations that form the cornerstones of lasting bonds. Fostering authentic communication and acknowledging unspoken realities allows us to touch lives in significant ways—something Dale Carnegie expressed perfectly when he said, "You can make more friends in two months by showing genuine interest in others than by trying to get others interested in you."

My journey has taught me that the key to likability lies in genuine interest in others and deep conversations. Remember, being likable is more than a trait; it's an approach and way to live life—authentically.

RACHEL DIAMOND

About Rachel E. Diamond: For more than 30 years, Rachel has been touching lives and sharing her gifts in the Architecture and Construction industry. Her award-winning Interior Designs can be experienced in public/private facilities and residences across North America and Europe. She has written and contributed to industry-specific articles published in Architecture and Construction magazines. Utilizing this collective experience, she continues to leave her creative fingerprint on the world as the Visionary and Owner of Radiant Artistry and Design, providing planning, design, photography, and artistic services. Additionally, Ms. Diamond is in the process of creating Radiant Life: Wellness and Coaching.

When asked about her life vision, Rachel will passionately express her deep desire to discover, capture, and express the heart, soul, and dreams of each person whose life and energy intersects her own; share the beauty of our human experience, and empower humans on their journey of self-discovery and creation of their best life. She is an advocate and contributor to various non-profit organizations who also share her vision for leaving the world a better place than they've found it.

Rachel is a mother of a teenage daughter and two senior rescue canines, an entrepreneur, nature lover, adventurer, romantic, and creator of beauty and magic in the world around her. You can contact Rachel: *RadiantArtistryandDesign@gmail.com*

Business Website: *www.RadiantArtistry.Design*

Book Series Website: *www.TheBookofInfluence.com*

ROBYN KAYE SCOTT

BUILDING AUTHENTIC TRUSTING RELATIONSHIPS

Our interactions with others often hinge on that crucial first impression, a first encounter. As I started on my mentorship coaching journey, I gained insight into the immense significance of first impressions through Dale Carnegie's timeless principles. Through Jon as my accountability partner, this lesson forever altered my perspective on making friends and building authentic connections.

Simple Text with Profound Connections

At first, meeting my accountability partner, Jon Kovach Jr., was both nerve-wracking and exciting. Amplified Minds (the coaching company) guided its accountability coach program to ensure we remained on course toward our goals. Yet, I felt overwhelmed at having some stranger dig deep into my most intimate goals.

Jon boasted a list of skills in his bio, such as Accountability Coach, Business Strategist, Motivational Speaker, and Entrepreneur. But I had one lingering question: What could this young entrepreneur teach me about my own journey through business?

Jon was my Accountability Partner from Amplified Minds. From our initial text message exchange, he exuded kindness, friendliness, and genuine interest in getting to know me and my goals better. Our initial interactions were brief—innocuous "Hey theres" and "How's your week so fars"—but as I revealed more about myself to Jon, his inquiries quickly evolved into more thoughtful questions that dug deep.

Display Genuine Interest

Make an excellent first impression by showing genuine interest in another person. Begin with simple greetings like friendly handshakes, then progress into more profound inquiries as the connection deepens.

Positive Thinking Can Reap Benefits in Times of Strife

Jon was so kind as to send me an encouraging text during one particularly trying week that read: "Hi, Robyn. I hope you are having an amazing week! What cool things have inspired you to pursue your goals this week?" His overwhelming positivity caught my attention immediately, and when I didn't reply promptly, he continued his encouraging words by writing back saying: "Robyn, I believe in your success and your goals are important—what can I do to assist?"

Jon was an enormous source of positivity during a difficult week for me. Finally responding, our connection grew deeper—his unfaltering support, encouragement, and friendly demeanor transformed a virtual partnership into a genuine friendship.

Accept and Celebrate Positive Energy

Be the source of positivity in all your interactions. Provide encouragement, compliments, and support when others need it most—positivity will foster strong bonds even during difficult times.

Grace Achieved Revealed

Years passed, and I realized the extent to which Jon had helped me achieve my goals and complete the certification program. Expressing my appreciation led to a surprise: Jon revealed that most of my classmates had yet to thank their accountability partners for their assistance; this left me questioning how so many could miss an opportunity to connect on a deeper level with someone they were accountable to.

Jon and I bonded deeply when we met face-to-face at a networking event. His friendship felt just as genuine in person as through text messaging, and after sharing an emotional hug, I knew we'd remain lifelong companions.

Appreciating Others

Extend your gratitude when someone has made an impactful difference in your life. Affirmations can strengthen connections and lead to lifelong friendships.

Building Real Friendships: Harnessing the Power of First Impressions

First impressions form the cornerstone of true friendships. How we present ourselves can enormously affect whether or not we establish long-lasting bonds. Consider this: When meeting someone new, their appearance, demeanor, and body language leave an indelible mark; similarly, your presentation influences whether someone wants to get to know you better.

Present Your Best Self

Showcase your strengths and show who you truly are by emphasizing them and being authentic. Showcase your best qualities, such as humor, intelligence, kindness, or creativity—authenticity will draw people in!

Establish Trust Through First Impressions

Positive first impressions create trust within seconds of meeting someone new. Confidence, friendliness, and approachability can lead others to trust you and feel comfortable opening up to you; conversely, negativity or standoffishness could sabotage forming meaningful connections.

Build Trust

Prove confidence, friendliness, and approachability; these traits can build trust that forms lasting friendships.

Setting the Stage for Long-Term Engagement

Positive first impressions set the stage for future interactions and demonstrate your desire to form connections and be invested in them. Communicating, exchanging stories, and reciprocating engagement are essential to developing genuine friendships.

Promote Long-term Connections

Establish conversations, share stories, and reciprocate engagement— these actions help ensure continuous dialogue essential to building meaningful friendships.

Make an Impressive First Impression | Tips for Establishing Positive Initial Impressions

So, how can you ensure positive first impressions? Here are a few points to keep in mind:

Be Authentic: Be yourself; authenticity is the cornerstone of building genuine connections.

Be Friendly: Smile and make eye contact as you greet others warmly while showing genuine interest in getting to know them better.

Listen Actively: Pay close attention to what others are saying and respond thoughtfully; be genuinely interested in their stories and experiences.

Stay Positive: Maintain an upbeat outlook by sharing positive experiences and stories.

Dress To Impress: Your appearance can leave an indelible mark, so dress appropriately for each event and occasion.

Positive first impressions are essential in creating genuine friendships. By being yourself, remaining friendly, listening actively, and remaining positive while dressing appropriately, you can form lasting connections that enrich your life and extend beyond this encounter. So put forth your best effort—amazing relationships are out there waiting to be discovered!

ROBYN KAYE SCOTT

About Robyn Kaye Scott: Robyn Scott is a coach, speaker, bestselling author, entrepreneur, female empowerment leader, and a networking queen. Robyn helps manage a prospecting program for Divinely Driven Results. She is a Habit Finder Coach and has worked closely with the president, Paul Blanchard, at the Og Mandino Group. She is also a certified Master Your Emotions Coach through Inscape World. Robyn is commonly known in professional communities as the Queen of Connection and Princess of Play. She has been working hard for the past nine years to hone her skills as a mentor and coach.

Robyn strives to teach people to annihilate judgments, embrace their own stories, and empower themselves to rediscover who they truly are. She is an international speaker and also teaches how to present yourself on stage. Her first book, *Bringing People Together: Rediscovering the Lost Art of Face-to-Face Connecting, Collaborating, and Creating* was released in August 2019 and was a bestseller in seven categories. She is also a national multi-number one bestselling co-author in the historic hit series *The 13 Steps To Riches* based on Napoleon Hill's work in *Think and Grow Rich*.

Author's Website: *www.RobynKayeScott.com*
Book Series Website: *www.TheBookOfInfluence.com*

RYAN FRITZSCHE

WINNING FRIENDS & INFLUENCING YOURSELF

Gaining the admiration and trust of others is paramount in our daily interactions, yet how often do we lie to others and ourselves? It's ironic; while we seek genuine relationships, often at our own cost, we end up being our worst enemy. Taken as inspiration from Dale Carnegie's book, *How to Win Friends and Influence People,* let's embark on an introspection journey toward self-understanding and reflection.

Do This, And You'll Be Welcome Anywhere: Authentic Self-Reflection

Recall my morning alarms? One was set for 4:30 A.M., while my secondary one arrived at 4:40 A.M. They serve as a valuable symbol for how often we tell ourselves falsehoods: whenever we delay taking action or shirk responsibility, our authentic selves fade further into the distance.

To be genuinely accepted anywhere, it is first vital to accept yourself, recognize your vulnerabilities, and address any "skeletons in the closet." Accepting some people might like you, and others can also help; the key is being honest with yourself first and then the world.

Personal Standards as an Effective Means of Making an Impressive Impression

Our standards define who we are as individuals. Mine include being true to my values, prioritizing my needs, and accepting that perfection doesn't mean the absence of flaws but accepting them all as part of life's beauty. Think about it—when we encounter genuine people, it makes a lasting impression, and it is easier for us to form instant connections with them!

An Easy Approach to Becoming an Engaging Conversationalist: Listening and Processing

My principle for becoming a good communicator is listening first, thinking second, and responding third. Active listening doesn't just apply when speaking with others—it applies when talking with yourself, too! By listening to yourself—listening for stories you tell yourself or excuses or fears you have—active listening can transform not just into a good conversationalist but also an effective communicator.

How to Engage People: Share Personal Journeys

People love stories they can connect with. When I shared my daily routines or my mind wandered off track, my intent wasn't for self-promotion but to highlight a universal human experience. Recounting your journey of self-discovery—including its wins, losses, and reflective moments—sparks interest and builds bonds—which is an effective strategy to engage others and influence.

Staying True To Your Code

Living by your code doesn't mean being rigid—it means being consistent and reliable, drawing people in immediately when they see you're being true to yourself, and operating from a place of authenticity. When making difficult choices or decisions, take a step back to reflect upon who you are so that your actions align with this identity.

Journey Forward

Attaining personal and relational growth depends upon being true to oneself and authentic in relationships. Chadd Wright explained, "Your mind may be telling lies about who you are; when we address these lies by acknowledging them and changing narratives, accordingly, not only do we change ourselves but we impact those around us as well."

As human beings, we're engaged in an endless battle not with others but against ourselves. This journey begins by being honest with ourselves about any self-deception and taking steps to ensure our external actions reflect our inner truths.

Being influential and likable means being genuine with oneself first. So, when making an impression, remember to make an impactful statement. Remember: be true to who you are—don't try to put on another facade for people's benefit; your authenticity can help others as well as you. Not only will you win friends by being true to who you are—but you may also learn the art of loving and respecting yourself more deeply in return!

RYAN FRITZSCHE

About Ryan Fritzsche: Ryan Fritzsche is the Founder and CEO of MSS Pay, a full-service merchant service company, helping thousands of businesses accept payments from their customers. Specializing in meeting the needs of the business with the software, hardware and payment types, Ryan uses this expertise to continue to consult and serve businesses nationwide.

Prior to founding MSS Pay, Ryan consulted with and co-owned many Chargeback Management companies and was responsible for helping businesses manage their risk and analyze data to improve business practices and customer satisfaction.

Ryan also spent 8 years working in different facets of the payment industry from sales, customer support, technical support, management and served in executive positions. This experience truly allows Ryan to run and operate a successful company today.

Ryan is an entrepreneur, professional in the payments industry, adventurer, philanthropist, father of four, husband, and an active person in his community.

Author's Website: *www.MSSPay.com*

Book Series Website: *www.TheBookOfInfluence.com*

SALLY WURR

WHAT MAKES US LIKABLE

"We are far more revealing by the questions we ask than the answers we give. Answer briefly to sense where their questions are heading."
~ **Unknown**

I believe that, as humans, we want to be liked and accepted by others. Sadly, that does not happen as often as it should. From the very moment that we are born, we are judged. By this, I mean that when each of us was born our physician gave us what is called an "Apgar" test. It lets everyone know, based on your height and weight, what percentile you are in compared to other babies the same age. If you are taller and heavier you might be considered to be in the 95%; if you are smaller and lighter, you are below 50%.

This follows us throughout our lives. Within the first few seconds of meeting someone, we have judged them based on their looks, their clothing, how they carry themselves, and how they talk. It is simply human nature.

What differentiates us is whether we disregard that person based on how we have judged them. I believe it is simply the first impression. You need to spend time with them to figure out if what your eyes and ears saw and heard make them a positive or negative person for you.

Being a "likable" person, I have found, does not come naturally to everyone. One of the greatest aspects of being likable is asking people about themselves. People like to share who they are, but few really care about a person's details. Most want to know if you will fit in with who they are and the direction their life is going and if you can help them.

"We all take a different path, but we help each other along the way."
~ Sally Wurr

When I meet people, I like to figure out if they are coming into my path for a Reason, Season, or a Lifetime. When I can categorize them in one of these areas, I am better able to be a resource.

In addition, I like to ask them enough questions to find out if they will be there to help me in some capacity or if they need my expertise.

The days of simply hanging out with our friends is long gone. For those of us that have built or are building a business, our time is spent meeting people that can help us grow. We want to find common ground with those that have reached a higher level than ourselves so we can learn. We also want to be aware of those who come to us to learn and grow.

Not one of us has be able to achieve and be where we are without the help of others. Sometimes we feel like we are on an island by ourselves, but we are not. Someone gave their time and expertise so we could have success.

People do not know you care until to tell them you do. Each one of us has our own journey through life. We choose to spend time with people who we know, like, and trust. This is the Likability Factor! Once we step past the person's mask and get to know them, we can figure out whether they are someone we can spend time with.

I remember a story a friend shared with me. Tom (fictitious name) and his wife went to a theme park with her brother and sister-in-law. Tom is a quiet introvert and does okay most times around people. He simply sits back and listens versus joining the conversation. After hours in the theme park, he was feeling ill and felt a headache coming on. He wasn't sure what his issue was as they were having a great time! He excused himself and went back to the hotel. After being by himself in a quiet room for a few hours, he felt he could join everyone for dinner.

What Tom discovered about himself is that, as an introvert, when he spent too much time around people that have a much higher energy level (extroverts) than he did, it created havoc for his system, and he shut down. It made him physically ill. You see, Tom's brother-in-law was an extrovert personality type and it depleted Tom of his energy. Tom needed to learn to monitor his energy levels, as did his brother-in-law.

Studies have shown that introvert personalities enjoy spending time alone. They also like to think before they speak and always appear to be more reserved or standoffish. Extrovert personalities, on the other hand, gain energy from being in social situations. They make quick decisions and are seen as outgoing and personable.

I was born an extrovert. I have learned to read people's body language and how they react in a crowd to decipher how to approach them, if at all. We are all different degrees of introvert and extrovert, depending on the situation we find ourselves in. As an extrovert, I make sure to drop my energy level to better match up with others if I need to. It really just depends on the situation.

I talked earlier about a quote I wrote, which says, "We all take a different path, but we help each other along the way." I said this because none of us are able to walk in each other's footsteps. We can walk in similar ones but not the exact same one.

Each of us has been born with what I like to call "tools in our toolbox." It is a set of traits that you were born with. As you grow, you learn new tools to add to your toolbox. For example, we all have heard of young children who will step up to a piano and simply begin to play. They have had no training. They were simply born with a natural knowledge of sound.

Most of what we need in life we can learn and add to our personal toolbox. But if you were not born with the aptitude or natural ability to do some things, no amount of training and tools will allow you to do those things. For example, not everyone has the aptitude to be a singer or rocket scientist. No amount of practice or learning can change the fact that you can not carry a tune or that you do not understand physics.

When we are looking at the likability of those around us, it is important to understand their personality and energy type. It is very easy to judge someone with a high energy level as flighty or a know it all, just like it is easy to judge a lower energy person as lazy or they have bad attitude because they don't engage. Usually, neither of these judgements are correct.

No matter who the person is in front of you, ask them questions and engage them in a conversation. It is only then that you will get a better idea of whether you will engage with them again.

We all like to hear and see our name. Social media has certainly changed the way we interface with each other. When I see other people posting, I like to look and see if it is only about them or are they also reposting other people's news and great moments in other people's life journey.

If they share the triumphs and events of other people, then I am more likely to follow, like and share theirs. When someone sends me a "friend" request, if I have not already met them, I go to their account and find out about them. If they have days of posts that are all about them, I will typically not allow the friend request. I prefer people who understand how to help and nurture others.

When we lift the wings of other people, we all win! When people see that this is your goal, you also become someone they want to know more about. People are watching other people all the time. You never know, when you take an action, what those ripples can create along the way.

Most of us only want to show our positive attributes. Our wins in life. But many times, it is when we share our losses or our mistakes that we become human. No one has a perfect life. We all have good and bad things happen to us almost daily. Make sure you share some of those more vulnerable moments.

I will close with a favorite quote by Maya Angelou:

"People will forget what you said, people will forget what you did, but people will never forget how you made them feel."

SALLY WURR

About Sally Wurr: Sally Wurr is an international speaker and multi-book author.

Sally is known as the "Storm Whisperer" because her message is about how to prepare for life's storms. Each person has trials and tragedies, but it is how we react to those events that help us grow and survive in our business and personal activities.

By sharing her expertise with stories, she teaches you how to embrace change and how to face life's struggles head-on. Simply put, she likes to teach others how to problem solve.

Sally embraces the knowledge that those who can must be the ones that do. She shares her stories so that others can find their true purpose.

In addition to writing and speaking, Sally is the President and Founder of SW Insurance Corp. She has helped thousands of CEOs develop employee benefits programs to attain and retain employees. It is her problem-solving and attention to detail that have made her successful in this arena for many years.

Author's Website: *www.SallyWurr.com*

Book Series Website: *www.TheBookOfInfluence.com*

SARAH LEE

THE MANIFESTATION OF INFLUENCE

There are so many aspects to likability and influence. It is a challenge to just pick just a few items to focus on.

Getting someone to like you is mostly three things. It's a version of having fun, getting them to like themselves more when they're around you, and you being a constant reminder to them that you like them, until they trust you.

This might sound counterintuitive to some, and you might think that likability has something to do with you being likable, but it really doesn't. Likability today is a kind of perception of being likable, accessible, and giving value without asking for too much in exchange. It has little to do with the reality of whether you are actually liked.

Let me give you an example.

Tip and Sarah Principle #1: People like people who make them feel good. People like people who validate them and who make them feel seen, heard, and understood.

Remember the adage, "Seek first to understand vs to be understood." The basis of communication is making the other person feel seen, understood, and heard. When you cannot make another person feel seen, heard, and understood, they will not feel validated, and they will not trust you and thus they will not allow you to have influence over them. This is basic to human understanding.

I want to remind you I was trained as a Clinical Behavioral Psychologist in a hospital setting at UCLA, in addition to some other places. I was also trained, from the time I was a child, in communication, compassion, and working with and leading various kinds of people. So, what I am about to say comes from years and decades of knowledge, practice, study, and sacrifice. And my goal in sharing it with you is to help you avoid some of the time and pain I went through to learn and apply this knowledge.

People like people who make them feel good about themselves. Period. This is true in Sales and in Sales Management. It is true in leadership and leadership development. This is true in friendships and in interpersonal relationships with your husband, your wife, your spouse, or your significant other. This is true in business, media, and in social media. Since my goal is provide value, I will start with how likability affects your ability to build a Brand and how you market yourself and your services for sale.

Regarding the importance of getting known and liked on social media, people always say, "In order to be successful on social media," like I am (implied), you will hear the phrase, "you have to be known to be like and trusted" to be purchased from (implied).

But that is not really the whole story. What I am about to tell you is *the secret of why most people fail at Social Media Marketing.*

In order for someone to buy from you, **they first have to feel like you have seen and understood THEM as the buyer.** What does that mean?

Well, first, it means that your marketing not only has to be about **them** instead of you, but has to show **them** that you understand **their pain** and that you have a 1) quick, 2) easy, 3) simple, 4) proven, 5) effective system to help them move past *their pain* into success. If they do not see this or understand this from you quickly, they will not **"trust you"** and thus, **"they will NOT buy from you"**—even if they are aware that they

1) have the problem and 2) believe you might be able to solve it. This is basic to how humans work.

Tip and Sarah Principle #2: Marketing and social media conversions, which happen through *conversion conversions*, are two different things.

Tip and Sarah Principle #3: The basis of all effective communication (a baseline of trust) comes from Validation.

When your spouse or significant other does not feel seen, heard, understood, and validated they will give you a hard time, often for what appears to be for no reason (or what seems like no reason to you). Men, can you relate?

So, when someone is giving you a hard time for what seems like *no reason* to you, try to find out if their feelings are hurt, or if they feel like you have insulted them by not validating them on something that they found was very important to them.

A lot of times when a child or an adult is acting up and you don't understand why, it is because you did not validate one of their core values, or maybe even violated one of their core values, and no matter how skilled the other party is, a lack of validation leads to resentment, and resentment leads to a "*lack of influence*" in any kind of relationship.

When your spouse doesn't clean up after themselves, and you do not perceive yourself as *a maid* or their maid, you will start to resent that person after a period of time, no matter how much you see, value, or love them. It is the same in any type of communication regarding influence.

Let's take this further: When your spouse *does* clean up after themselves, like when you come home from a business trip and the house is clean and the kids are calm and they have a plan for how to spend time with you, and your favorite drink is in the fridge, how does that make you feel? For most people, it makes them feel respected, and when one feels respected, you also feel understood and validated. Thus, you feel it is now safe to allow that person to have some influence on you at that moment.

The best social media marketing, whether funny or serious, allows the audience to relate to you. They want to see that you are *just like them*, and have the same kind of struggles they have, or the same goals and have overcome those struggles, and that your program delivers the same results that you get or got (in the past) to them.

When you create an online business, or any business, if you do not understand the basics of influence, you will not have very much success in business, no matter how good of a "technician you are" at solving the problem. This *is* a problem.

And this misunderstanding is one of the reasons why I agreed to participate in this book series about influence.

Because it took me, trained as a Clinical Psychologist, some years to understand how my brick and mortar understanding of people translated to social media influence, and I don't want my audience to have to spend the years it took me to understand it this deeply. I want to help you avoid the pain that I went through and the struggle I went through trying to figure out why people that I knew who were successful in some ways, but not in others, didn't understand the basics of this concept. But I digress...

One of my pet peeves, as a coach and mentor, is when another coach, who is successful, famous, or rich, wants you to pay them for a result, but once you start working with them you realize that they were just famous because people could relate to them, but they were not going to ever get more famous because they actually don't understand their audience and actually had no sense of how to solve the problem that the audience and clients experience.

Many of you have experienced these kinds of coaches and have wondered to yourself, "Why did I pay this person money when they didn't actually know more than I did or could not actually get me the results I was looking for?"

We have all been there.

My assertion is: Even if they were likable, known, and trusted, that coach or mentor who is perceived to be successful already, might actually not even know that they don't know, because of ignorance, arrogance, or ego. Ouch!

When people are learning new information, they go through four basic stages of learning.

We all start at: Unconscious Incompetence, where don't know that we don't know.

We move to: Conscious Incompetence, where we are aware that we don't know but are learning.

Then we move to: Conscious Competence, where we have to think about everything we do but we get it!

And if we keep going, that leads to: An Unconscious Competence, which is another word for **Mastery.**

But if you don't know that you're incompetent at something, especially if you BELIEVE you already have MASTERED IT, you could spend 10,000 hours, or 10,000 years even, thinking that you were competent, practicing the wrong things (ideas and habits), holding on to the wrong ideas, and wondering why, after all of that work, time and effort, you don't get the result that you are seeking.

One of the primary reasons you don't get the result is often a mix of the two things that I just illustrated: A failure attributed to the wrong thing (cause and effect); and a coach, mentor or leader who doesn't know what they don't know, but thinks they do. In both cases, the people can **NEVER LEARN.**

The coach or trainer may not know that they are missing a piece of the puzzle, especially when they are successful or well-known. Because it is not just their ego that won't allow them to learn it, but their identity or self-image won't allow them to. They already see themselves as a Master, which makes learning new things somewhere between challenging and impossible for most people, but what's worse, is it goes against people's *self-image.*

Identity is the thing most difficult to change and get people to see and understand about themselves. They will defend who they "think they are" to the death. This is one of the most illuminating things to understand about self and people, and success and influence.

Tip and Sarah Principle #4: *Lack of self-awareness, even in the self-proclaimed self-aware, is a business killer.*

Marketing and converting those people to clients through conversation are two different skills.

Helping people achieve a result as a technician, where they copy your thought process and pattern in one particular problem area is a different skill.

Being emotionally intelligent and aware enough that you are unaware is a different skill. Having people in your life who will tell you the truth when you are messing up is a different skill.

It is difficult to have influence over other people if you have not mastered the ability to have influence over yourself.

When we talk about being likable and known in marketing, we are only talking about a very small part of the puzzle, and all or almost all of the pieces have to be there to be a very successful coach or mentor—which is why we build and have teams.

People that have done enough personal development often achieve more success.

If you see someone being successful in social media or being successful in the personal development business, they have probably examined themselves more in a day a week or a month than most people have in their lifetimes. That's why we say that **successful people are lifelong learners.** They have to be lifelong learners to do what I just suggested and if they want to be considered likable and influential enough to even get started, they need to know what they like about themselves, and they need to know that they're not alone in that journey. It's a process for us all.

The self-development business is not for everyone. It takes a special kind of person to want to put themselves through that type of self-examination in order to help other people get results.

But on that note, I wholeheartedly believe that every single person has something they can teach others, and every single person has a natural audience that they can speak to without ever needing to be likable or famous or influential outside of that.

Each one of us is naturally influential to our own markets.

My hope in presenting this material is to encourage you to teach what you know to other people, but also to not get disappointed when you do not have the same influence as someone else that you perceive to be similar to you, especially if you have not done the internal development work I just outlined, and have not taken all of the steps that I have outlined above to heart.

My last last point: I like you.

I like you just by the fact that you're reading this, which means you respect me or someone else in this book enough to give us a few minutes to even just consider the content we are providing to you.

Self-development is a lifelong journey, and something that is to be respected, because it *is* work and it works. The only way to help another is to help yourself first.

As Earl Nightingale would say, "In order to be perceived as the person who can do the thing you want to do, you must BECOME the person who can do the thing you want to do." That's manifestation.
The manifestation of influence.

SARAH LEE

About Sarah Lee: A brilliant educational psychologist and leadership expert by education, Sarah Lee is the innovative author of "Rock Soup - An Innovational Idea in Leadership." By profession, Sarah has been teaching financial literacy for the last 15 years using her own firm as a platform. She is a full-service financial advisor and manager of her own Securities Branch of a national firm.

In addition, she networked with 100 Brokers all over the US. Sarah has an MBA in Finance and Social Impact and is 14 months shy of a Ph.D. in Educational Leadership. She is also the founder of multiple other companies and brands; some sold for profit, some she learned from, and some she consulted on other businesses. She is now mostly currently focused on her production company with her husband, MONEY MENTOR, LLC™.

She has been advocating and speaking on large issues like financial literacy, literacy, mindset, clean water, and service to the world (hunger, water issues, poverty, and literacy) for her entire life. She is the child of a public servant. Her father was a writer (he wrote textbooks on risk and insurance practices), a city councilman in a small town who taught Sarah civic duties, service to the public, and how the national political system works. She learned how to serve others, run a nonprofit volunteer group, and make a community impact. That led to an opportunity to be "on TV (not streaming) weekly as a host" as a nine-year-old. The opportunity became more interesting when they asked Sarah what she would like to produce for Kids-4 TV.

She said, "I would like to host a consumer reports show, where I would interview local business owners and see how I could highlight them while giving them ways to give back and make a difference." She was nine. That led to a life of public speaking, running endowments, and working with local universities on educational issues. She developed her world-famous business philosophy during this time: "Business is just like Rock Soup..."

Learn more about Sarah Lee, MBA, and follow her on FB: @coachmeSarahLee, @moneymentormethod
Instagram: @moneymentorcompany, @coachmeacademy.
For Money Tips, you can text the words "MONEYMENTOR" to 55444 for a free gift or visit our webpage: *linktr.ee/MoneyMentorMethod*

Author's Website: *www.MoneyMentorFreeGift.com*

Book Series Website: *www.TheBookOfInfluence.com*

STEPH SHINABERY

CONTAGIOUS ENERGY & THE NEUROSCIENCE OF LIKABILITY

"Guess why I smile a lot? Uh...cause it's worth it."
~ **Marcel the Shell**

In the charming animated movie, *Marcel the Shell with Shoes On,* Marcel's optimism, outlook, and hope are irresistibly contagious. I giggled and smiled while watching the film, enchanted by his childlike innocence, openness, and curiosity about the world.

Contagious energy is the driving force behind likability. When someone radiates positive energy, they create an uplifting atmosphere and a sense of warmth that helps others feel comfortable and drawn to them. Harvard Business Review refers to these individuals as "positive energizers" who possess honesty, humility, compassion, gratitude, and willingness to recognize others for their contributions.

Likability is the secret sauce for building robust relationships, expanding our networks, and positively influencing others. It's a magnetic force that draws people in with warmth, genuine interest, and contagious energy. This energy is not just a feel-good phenomenon; it's rooted in the fascinating world of neuroscience and psychology. We can explore contagious energy and its connection to likability through the lens of science.

Meeting someone enthusiastic and uplifting can lead us to experience a surge of feel-good emotions. The activation of different regions in the brain is what causes the release of specific neurotransmitters and explains the neuroscience behind these emotions. For example, when we experience joy or pleasure, the brain rewards us in the form of dopamine. The release of dopamine encourages us to seek out that positive stimulus again. Therefore, engaging with positive people can improve our mood and often motivates us to seek out interactions with these folks again.

Another neurotransmitter in this process is oxytocin, sometimes called the "love drug." Oxytocin contributes to connectedness and well-being, fostering trust and promoting bonding. By understanding these mechanisms, we can better appreciate the importance of positive social interactions and their impact on us and those we interact with. It's profound and exciting that my thoughts and attitude can positively influence someone else's biology and well-being!

I bet you can think of examples from your life when you've been around positive or negative energizers, people who light up the room or suck the air out. I once worked with a woman who showed me how not to be, but also the importance of protecting my energy from others' negativity.

She was like a dark storm cloud casting a shadow over our workplace. When she retired, we took on an increased workload and took more call.

Call for anesthesia, that is. This means being tied to a "beeper" or pager 24/7. It puts you on hyper alert. It stresses your nervous system. Even though we were working more and taking MORE CALL, it was easier than working with a negative force. As someone sensitive to others' energy, I'm naturally drawn to positivity and try to distance myself from negativity.

Conversely, my friend Leslie is a walking confetti cannon, bursting with fun, friendliness, and enthusiasm. She's the kind of person who can brighten any room with her infectious energy. So, when she shared how a documentary impacted her, I was inspired to watch it, even though I'd struggled to get into it on two different occasions. I committed to the movie because of her influence this time and was grateful I did.

As a nurse anesthetist, my job is demanding and fast-paced, requiring unwavering focus and vigilance. In this high-stress environment, it's easy to lose sight of the importance of human connections and social interactions. However, through my experiences with Cheryl, the wife of one of my favorite colleagues, I have witnessed the transformative power of meaningful connections. Cheryl's warmth and genuine interest create an aura of likability that encourages deep, meaningful conversations.

I loved popping into her office to say hello. Often, after fifteen minutes later or so, I would leave wondering how and why I had just shared so openly and vulnerably with her.

My colleague wasn't surprised when I mentioned this to him. He said that Cheryl has this effect on people wherever she goes—at the gym, the grocery store, or even while traveling across the world. People naturally open up to her and share their life stories.

Cheryl makes people feel at ease with her genuine interest, attentive listening, and ability to find common ground. She exudes a warm, bubbly energy, accompanied by a bright smile and infectious laughter. She is the embodiment of high-vibe positivity.

So, how can we tap into the magical world of contagious energy and likability, harnessing the power of neuroscience and psychology to impact ourselves and others? By recognizing and embracing the traits we admire, we can become more influential in our personal and professional lives, spreading a ripple effect of positivity.

Our vibration has a significant impact on our likability factor. We can use our neuroscience knowledge to alter our brain chemistry and create feel-good neurochemical cocktails to benefit ourselves and others.

How can we sustain a high vibe?

- We can be about as likable as we decide to be. What traits do you admire in others? Their smile? Their genuine interest in you or others? Their tone? Confidence? We can decide what traits to cultivate and how to show up for others.

- Thoughts are powerful energy generators. Our thoughts and beliefs affect our vibration. We can entertain the thoughts we choose and let go of the ones that aren't serving us. We are all unique vibrating balls of energy influencing those around us. Positive-vibers are more approachable.

- Gratitude is a powerful tool that generates a positive state. When we appreciate the good things in life, it expands and leads to a chain reaction of positivity. With gratitude, dopamine and serotonin are released, which contribute to a sense of pleasure and well-being. Gratitude is a muscle: You can strengthen it with use, and make it a habit. Bookend your days with a short gratitude practice, before your feet hit the floor and before your head hits the pillow. The key is to feel the emotions of what you are grateful for.

- Humor makes life more enjoyable. Laughter triggers the release of endorphins, more feel-good chemicals, and promotes overall well-being.

- Protect your energy. I try to distance myself from negative influences but also try not react to these sources. When we react, we give this negative energy our power. It's not just the people we are around, but what we read, watch, listen to, and think about.

- Smile! Thich Nhat Hanh said, "Sometimes your joy is the source of your smile, but sometimes your smile can be the source of your joy." A smile's simplicity can change how we feel; it activates dopamine, serotonin, and endorphins, which are contagious!

Neuroscience explains the world of contagious energy and likability. By understanding the neuroscience and psychology behind these emotional connections, we can actively choose to embrace this philosophy, thereby improving not only our own lives but the lives of those around us.

When we commit to these principles, we create an environment that facilitates personal growth, robust connections, and a deeper understanding of ourselves and others.

Just like Marcel, we can smile a lot because it's worth it, creating a ripple effect of positivity that benefits us and everyone we encounter.

STEPH SHINABERY

About Steph Shinabery: Steph Shinabery is The World's Best Possibility Coach, Nurse Anesthesiologist, Artist, Speaker, and the Founder of GENIUS CODE ACADEMY.

After spending much of her life in a career that lacked the inspiration and fulfillment she knew was available to her, she began a journey to answer the question: "what is it I truly desire?"

Her journey led to creation of the Genius Identity Code™, a process for unlocking your gift, purpose and path, and helping people see, believe and execute their unique genius to achieve miraculous outcomes.

Steph works with creative experts, entrepreneurs and coaches to help them embrace their authenticity and create a life that gets them excited to jump out of bed every day!

You can find her talk, "Wake Up Your Genius Machine" on Amazon Prime Video's Speak Up: Empower Your Ideas, Season 4.

Author's Website: *www.StephShinabery.com*

Book Series Website: *www.TheBookOfInfluence.com*

SUSAN CARPIO

SHINING THROUGH LIKABILITY

Time is often our most valuable commodity in professional life; therefore, making meaningful connections and achieving long-term impactful relationships with those we meet can be challenging. One solution lies within Dale Carnegie's timeless wisdom on "How to Win Friends and Influence People." Here, we will delve into building genuine connections and discovering the transformative potential of leading with heart.

Take This Approach, and You Will Always Feel Welcome No Matter Your Destination

Dale Carnegie's fundamental principle is becoming genuinely interested in other people. This principle is deeply fulfilling as I've always emphasized genuine interest and appreciation as crucial to genuine human connections. While some colleagues may prefer adopting more formal personas to get things done more quickly, authenticity has proven more successful in opening doors to success for me than rigid approaches to business relationships.

Being genuine doesn't require political maneuvering or superficial flattery; it means appreciating people for who they are, acknowledging their efforts, and sincerely showing your thanks. Simply saying "Thank you" or "You're amazing" can go a long way toward creating an upbeat work environment and increasing morale.

Making an Impression Fast

One day, I hosted a Zoom call with a colleague who was having difficulties. Together, we worked through his issues while I expressed my sincere thanks for his remarkable skills and dedication—an act my colleague later noted had an enormous effect on our conversation.

This incident served to emphasize how humility and gratitude can leave a lasting impression. When we lead with heart and express genuine appreciation, our sincerity shines through, making us more approachable and trustworthy.

If You Don't Take Steps Now, Trouble Will Soon Arise

Humility and authenticity are essential traits in building long-lasting relationships. In my professional journey, I've had the honor of working alongside brilliant minds for whom I always made an effort to recognize their talents and contributions.

Recognizing and appreciating each person's gifts can lead to mutual respect and admiration between colleagues, which in turn increases opportunities for personal and professional growth. Failure to do this could rob us of potential connections and growth opportunities.

Easy Way to Be an Excellent Conversationalist

Dale Carnegie's principles extend far beyond the workplace and our personal lives. To be an engaging conversationalist, one must genuinely show interest in others—something I've witnessed firsthand through my daughter-in-law, who always manages to find time for her children and family despite a demanding job and packed schedule. (See previous chapter in *The Book of Influence: Authentic Communication.*)

Her ability to create an inviting home environment stemmed from her kindness and genuine nature. When she initially doubted her skills in side-hustles and online marketing, I saw potential and extended an offer to collaborate. Her journey from challenging herself to success stands as a testament to the transformative powers of genuine support and belief in others.

Interest and influence go hand-in-hand, so when we lead with our hearts and show genuine curiosity for others, they become naturally engaged, and we gain their attention and interest without resorting to manipulation —it's about building meaningful connections!

My daughter-in-law's experience entering the world of side hustles is an example. At first, she doubted her abilities but ultimately excelled due to my firm belief in them and unwavering support—ultimately leading her into this field of endeavors. When we invest in someone's growth and well-being, they become more likely to reciprocate our interest and offer reciprocal assistance.

How To Instantaneously Win People Over

Integrity is the cornerstone of instantaneous people-pleasing. People sense when you lead with integrity and show genuine care for others, which resonates with them deeply.

My professional experience has exposed me to people who, at first glance, appeared distant or stern, yet once they revealed their genuine, caring side, it was like a breath of fresh air breaking through the clouds. Smiling confidently even in challenging circumstances and accepting responsibility for mistakes with grace makes an individual instantly likable and trustworthy.

As The Heart Shines Through me in an industry that often prioritizes business over humanity, leading with your heart can be the difference. People remember kindness; it forms the basis of lasting relationships. By showing genuine care for others and making an effort to acknowledge their contributions, you create a positive chain reaction that has the power to transform lives.

One senior director I encountered took note of my alteration in demeanor during Zoom meetings—proof that when we approach interactions with authenticity and warmth, people notice.

At its core, leadership means leading with love. When you truly care for others and take steps to uplift them, your kindness shines through in each conversation and interaction, making the world a better place. So, remember Dale Carnegie's principles, but more importantly, lead with your heart—authenticity will win friends and influence people more easily than anything else!

SUSAN CARPIO

About Susan Carpio: Susan has worked in the high-tech industry for more than 30 years, starting her career with an electrical engineering degree. Her experience encompasses deep technical roles in electronics labs, front-line project management, and senior-level leadership roles in the commercial, aerospace, and defense sectors. Currently, Susan is a technical business development manager for integrated test systems supporting aerospace and defense applications at Keysight Technologies based in Loveland, Colorado.

While working for technology companies, she also has an entrepreneurial spirit and heart. Her son, Jase, his wife, Shilo, and their three children are the light of her life, and watching that young family start on their own has created her dedication to helping young mothers find a sustainable income so they can stay home with their children.

Susan is a cancer survivor and a thriver for 10+ years. She attributes this to the mercy of Jesus Christ, the loved ones who surround her, and her heartfelt thankfulness for life!

Author's Website: *www.SusanCarpio.com*

Book Series Website: *www.TheBookOfInfluence.com*

TEASHIA FRENCH

CREATING TRUST IS CRUCIAL

Likability is a crucial factor in building trust and establishing successful relationships, especially in sales. I am a firm believer that people buy with emotion and justify with facts. This means that customers are more likely to purchase from someone they like and trust, even if the product or service is not the absolute best in the market. Customers want to feel heard, respected, and valued.

In my own experience, I used this most often in the sales process. When I transitioned from marketing to sales, early in my career, I entered the field with little experience in sales. I knew the products I was selling very well so there was a level of confidence there, but I knew if I was going to succeed, I had to be humble, ask a lot of questions, and ensure that my potential customers felt heard and valued.

This approach proved to be very effective and helped me to build strong relationships with my customers. By being genuinely interested in their needs and concerns, and taking the time to understand their challenges, I was able to provide them with customized solutions that met their specific needs. This not only helped me close more sales, but also resulted in customer loyalty and repeat business.

I was also born very inquisitive and shy. This isn't always a winning combination. I was interested in everything but too shy to ask questions or speak up. As I got older, my courage grew, and I found myself able to ask more questions in the things I was most interested in. I could sit and listen to lectures or other people talk for hours without the slightest desire to inject or give my two cents. I always listened more than I spoke, as I genuinely enjoy listening to what others have to say.

You have to find a field or an industry that interests you so much that you genuinely want to learn about it. The people you interact with will feel your passion. On average, when interacting with someone, if they speak more than 50% of the time, they will rate the interaction as being more positive than if they speak less than 50%. This is an easy way to keep those odds in your favor.

Moreover, I found that my likability factor also helped me to negotiate and close larger deals. When customers felt comfortable and trusted me, they were more willing to make bigger purchases and were open to negotiating better terms and conditions.

So, how can you become more likable? Here are some tips based on my knowledge and experience in professional sales:

1. Be Authentic: As you mentioned, telling the truth, no matter how difficult it is, is a key factor in building trust. People can tell when you're not being genuine, and this can turn them off from doing business with you. Be yourself and be honest in your interactions, even if it means admitting your mistakes or limitations.

2. Listen More Than You Talk: Effective communication is a two-way street. Make sure you take the time to listen to your customers' needs and concerns, and respond accordingly. By actively listening, you demonstrate that you care about their opinions and are invested in finding the right solution for them.

3. Be Empathetic: Empathy is the ability to understand and share the feelings of others. When you demonstrate empathy towards your customers, it shows that you are genuinely concerned about their well-being and are willing to help them achieve their goals. This can go a long way in building trust and establishing a strong rapport.

4. Find Common Ground: Look for commonalities between yourself and your customers, whether it's a shared hobby or interest, a similar background, or a common goal. By finding common ground, you can establish a connection and build a stronger relationship with your customers.

5. Show Gratitude: Showing appreciation towards your customers can make them feel valued and respected. Simple gestures like sending a thank-you note or offering a discount on their next purchase can go a long way in building loyalty and establishing a positive reputation

6. Be Positive: Positive energy is contagious, and it can help to establish a more optimistic and productive environment. Maintain a positive attitude, even in difficult situations, and look for the silver lining in every situation. This can help to create a more relaxed and enjoyable experience for your customers, and they will be more likely to want to do business with you again.

7. Be Respectful: Showing respect towards your customers is essential in building trust and establishing a strong relationship. Be mindful of their time, their opinions, and their boundaries, and make sure to treat them with the same level of respect that you would want for yourself.

Overall, likability is a critical factor in building trust and establishing successful relationships, especially in sales. By being authentic you can become more likable and build stronger relationships with your customers. My likability factor has been shaped by a combination of my inquisitive nature, passion for my field, ability to empathize with others, and effective communication skills. By focusing on these key areas, I have been able to create positive relationships and achieve success in both my personal and professional life.

TEASHIA FRENCH

About Teashia French: Teashia French, MBA is a seasoned professional with over 15 years of experience in the Medical Device and Pharmaceutical industry. She has held various leadership positions, including Marketing Manager and Regional Vice President of Sales. Teashia's dedication to her career is matched by her commitment to education.

She holds a bachelor's degree in communication from the University of Washington and an MBA with a concentration in Finance from Washington State University. Additionally, Teashia has received a digital marketing certificate from Rutgers University.

More recently, Teashia has leveraged her passion for design and her expertise in marketing to start her own interior design business, Visceral Design. As the founder of Visceral Design, Teashia creates intentionally minimalistic spaces for busy women who want beautiful homes. She combines her eye for design with her marketing skills to create functional and aesthetically pleasing spaces for her clients.

When she's not working, Teashia enjoys spending time with her family. She is a proud mother of two beautiful children and is happily married. Teashia and her family reside in Paradise Valley, AZ, where they enjoy the sunny weather and outdoor activities. With her diverse background, education, and entrepreneurial spirit, Teashia is a true force to be reckoned with.

Author's Website: *linkedin.com/in/TeashiaNelson*

Book Series Website: *www.TheBookOfInfluence.com*

TERESA CUNDIFF

EVERYBODY WANTS TO BE LIKED!

Dale Carnegie states, "There is one all-important law of human conduct. The law is this: Always make the other person feel important." I believe it is from this principle about likability that the other five principles flow. However, doing this is sometimes more easily said than done. We all have our own egos and the desire to stoke it, but *Winning Friends and Influencing People* has no space for our own egos. But it seems to me that if we accomplish the great task of winning over lots of friends by applying Mr. Carnegie's principles, that our egos would indeed be bolstered. It truly is as simple as applying the Golden Rule as a mantra for life even though we all know that there will be those who do not reciprocate.

I remember a time in my own life when I stopped using the Golden Rule. I didn't stop being kind or anything like that, but I didn't put myself out there either for fear of being hurt in both friendships and relationships. I felt like I was the one always giving while seldom receiving the benefit of the other person making me feel special. It gets tiresome after awhile. I was the one always putting the planning into doing things. I was always the one making the connection. In other words, our "friendship" was very one-sided until the other person needed my help with something. That never feels good, does it?

Whether it's business, friendships, or romantic relationships, we all want to feel like we are important to someone. In fact, it feels like it takes quite a lot of effort sometimes to be continually giving while being taken from or just taken for granted. There have been periods of my life when I have been quite cynical about it. I'm not even sure what brought me out of that cynicism, but I currently don't feel that way now.

I suppose it's how we really purpose in our hearts that we want to be. It certainly takes no effort to give your smile away to someone without one. Or, to say good morning to someone when you pass them on the street. Sometimes it is difficult though to sit back and be the listener in the conversation when you want so desperately to jump in and contribute because you think that what you have to say is important. I am certainly guilty.

One thing I have always been fanatical about is getting peoples' names right. If I have any question whatsoever about how to pronounce it, I will ask for the person to say it for me. I will also ask for the spelling. I think saying a person's name correctly and pronouncing it like they prefer shows respect. This stems from people not spelling my own name correctly even though the most famous person with my name, Mother Teresa, has no H in her name. Even so, the struggle rages on! LOL!

I believe that everyone wants to be liked for who they are. Sadly though, people will do things around certain individuals or groups that they think they must to gain favor with those people. Sometimes I think it's a purely subconscious act as well. We humans do the strangest things sometimes to make people like us. And what's unfortunate is that lots of people probably do like us, but we are too much in our own heads to realize it. We give our power away so easily sometimes. Or maybe I'm just projecting!

When I was in 6th grade in elementary school, I had a best friend named "Sally." We were as thick as thieves and were partners in crime. We did everything together all day long. We sat together at lunch, we were always together at recess and P.E. and our desks were beside each other in the classroom. We made certain to not get in too much trouble so the teacher wouldn't separate us. Then one day close to bus time, Sally leans over and whispers in my ear, "Janet's my best friend." I was gutted, but I played it off! It was my way to never let my hurt feelings show.

You see, in my house I had been conditioned not to cry about anything. If I cried about something that my mother deemed unworthy of tears, she would say, "Well, that's silly." Thus, leaving my feelings unvalidated and me thinking that I shouldn't be feeling the way I was feeling. I felt certain she would say that Sally telling me that Janet was now her best friend was something my mother would put in the silly category. But for me, it was devastating. I've only ever told a few people this story until now.

When the school day ended, and I finally got home and all the afternoon and evening activities were concluded and I could finally be alone in my bed, I cried and cried and cried and cried! My heart was so broken that I can still feel it as I recount it for you now. What was going to happen at school now? Janet was in another class, so I couldn't understand why Sally had ever told me that. They lived near each other and played after school, but that didn't change how things went AT school.

Still, I felt the only choice I had was to just pretend that I didn't care at all and that I wasn't hurt. I couldn't talk to my mom about it although I probably could have talked to my older sister about it. This just added to the loneliness and isolation I was already experiencing at home because of the terrorizing sexual abuse I was suffering at the hands of my half-brother. That began in the 4th grade and is a story for another time.

This dreadful experience with Sally colored how my friendships would go for some time. I wondered if I would have any friends that I could trust or if I would have any friends period. I felt like there was something wrong with me and wondered if anyone would ever like me just the way I was.

Our home burned down in 1975 as my 7th grade year started and we moved across town. We may as well have moved across country given the fact that everything was totally new. And even though school had only been in session for two weeks, I was still the new girl reporting in at every class. It was one of the most miserable times in my entire life. I went on in junior high to be bullied as well. I did have some friends, but kids can be so cruel. I had lived a sheltered life out in the country, but now my life was completely turned upside down. One amazing thing, however, was that the abuse had ended because my brother went away to the military.

I'm not the only person with terrible stories from childhood, nor do I purport to be. I'm sharing because we are not defined by such things and can take action to rise above the pettiness of Sally and the bullies of junior high and mature into wonderful, caring humans! I will tell you truly though that I was in college in a psych class when I heard the professor say, "You are entitled to feel any way you want to!"

This may sound very basic to you and like a no-brainer, but it was an absolute revelation to me! You mean, I could feel any way I wanted about something, and that was okay? I felt so empowered with that information that I was liberated from a prison I didn't even know I was in at the time!

When does the time actually arrive when a person decides he or she wants to win friends and influence people? Is it a conscious decision? I look back at when I thought I could never win any friends to where I am today. It all begins with kindness in my opinion. From there, I smile at people. I show a genuine interest in people and always make a supreme effort to get their names right! I also think that a firm handshake with eye contact is important when first being introduced to someone. I always try to pay a genuine, sincere compliment.

My areas of improvement are being a good listener and talking more about what interests the person to whom I am speaking. Having a heightened awareness to this though is more than half the battle I think. And I also think it's important that my heart is in the right place when engaging in conversation with others. I do want to be liked by the people in my life as I think everyone does. Life would be so lonely without people who like us. The question is, are we doing things and showing those whom we like that they are important to us?

TERESA CUNDIFF

About Teresa Cundiff: Teresa hosts an interview digital TV show called Teresa Talks on Everyday Woman TV. On the show, she interviews authors who are published and unpublished—and that just means those authors who haven't put their books on paper yet. The show provides a platform for authors to have a global reach with their message. Teresa Talks is produced by Wordy Nerds Media Inc., of which Cundiff is the CEO.

Cundiff is also a freelance proofreader with the tagline, "I know where the commas go!" Teresa makes her clients work shine with her knowledge of grammar, punctuation, and sentence structure.

Teresa is a five-time international #1 best-selling contributing author of *1 Habit for Entrepreneurial Success, 1 Habit to Thrive in a Post-COVID World, The Art of Connection: 365 Days of Networking Quotes, The Art of Connection: 365 Days of Inspirational Quotes, and The Art of Connection: 365 Days of Transformational Quotes.* The latter three are in the Library of Congress. She is a 12-time #1 best-selling contributing author to *The 13 Steps to Riches Series.*

Author's Website: *www.TeresaTalksTV.co*

Book Series Website: *www.TheBookOfInfluence.com*

THOMAS MALAGISI

LIKE-ABILITY

First, you have to like yourself. Like yourself you say? Yes, how are you groomed? That is usually the first indication that you're taking care of yourself. If you like yourself, you'll take care of yourself via your grooming. Do you spend your waking hours dragging or full of energy? So, here we're not speaking of ego and "look at me" type of ego, just well-centered, energetic, and groomed. You see, you have to like yourself before others will like you.

It comes from the inside to the outside. Your external expressions will show fear, upset emotions, or love. If you extend love to those you come into contact with, they'll most likely have good feelings about you.

Taking a special interest, in what the OTHER person has an interest, in is a sure way to say I'm interested in you. Starting a conversation with a sincere compliment helps. Once you're past the intro of your conversation, many will then wain in their interest. That's insincere. This is quickly received by the person you're engaged with and will allow him/her to think you're just another average person. So, if you desire to show interest, keep that interest throughout the conversation. Heck, you may learn and really like what you hear.

Doing a kind deed for someone that might take a bit of your time and focus, without requiring it to be reciprocated, is a nice thing to prompt that "likability" that we all strive for. Who doesn't want to be liked? We all do. Accepted, liked, a part of something or some group.

Have you ever seen people gathering around someone who is always frowning or a person who is always complaining? Probably not. If your desire is to be liked you should probably smile a lot, laugh some, fill your day with direction, and make it fun. Who doesn't want to be around a person like that, right?

Making contributions towards someone's growth. Ahhhh who doesn't want some help from someone who is willing to give something? It may be a gesture, it may be a kind word, it may be a small something that lets the person know that you were thinking of them. You've made a deposit into their emotional bank account.

Within this group that is putting forth this book, we have a saying. It goes by the name of NDSO. That stands for **N**o **D**rama, **S**erve **O**thers. This I find to be very authentic from the folks we surround ourselves with. As I have looked into this expression for some time and have seen it put into action, it surely prompts likability. We serve others in various ways. It's not the same for all that we come into contact with.

Control. Lots of people believe that they need to control others. Some may do this through direct communications. Others may do things 'behind the scenes' unnoticed by the person they're attempting to control. Either way, no one likes to be controlled. People like to be free. Free to choose. Free to make their own mistakes. Free to learn. So, if you desire to be liked, let others be themselves. If they seek guidance from you, you may do so. Maybe you guide them through a story you know. Stories have been good as it removes both parties from feeling emotion towards one another. Storytelling is a gift that we all think we have, but it does take practice. You'll want to leave the person with something to think about. What if you're around someone who is headed nowhere and you want to help? Maybe a loved one. I suppose you limit your association with that person or cut it off entirely. That will be left to you to decide.

Helping others may be good and godly, in some cases. It depends. If you're a person who wants to give and can keep yourself on track, that is great. If you're a person who wants to give to another and gets pulled down through your giving, then you might want to rethink if your generosity is really helping the other person. People typically like to help. Those that are on the receiving end, typically like the help you've put forth. So, why not? It depends if both the giver and receiver are uplifted through the action. If so, then I suppose a good deal of likability is transferred. If not, then the total opposite will happen, and those bad emotions may last for a lifetime.

A good way to increase your likability might be to constantly learn something. Learn something as opposed to merely knowing about it. Everyone has opinions and you know that those are worthless. So, when I say learn something; I mean to have an intelligent conversation on that topic. It could be something simple or very complex. Learn something and hone that skill. That will bring you intelligence to believe in and perhaps share. You'll be amazed at how others will soon come to like you. You see when you do so, you're telling the world that you are not like everyone else. No, you're not a sloth, just meandering through life. You are telling the world that you have something that you like so much that you learned it well. I remember someone once told an audience that I was in, that if you read three books on some topic, you'll be classed as an expert in that field. Maybe so, maybe not. But I think you get the point. DO Something and go do it well.

Once upon a time, I saw a person that was older than I play solitaire on a tablet. I knew this person fairly well. I asked if she could do it in under 3 minutes per session. You know, I never saw her do it again. I hope that I didn't squelch the desire to pass the time that way, but I always thought; did she achieve that status or just quit? The old saying; nobody likes a quitter. As you navigate your next few days and view people, maybe a few or maybe many, ask yourself if they are the majority that quit at the first issue encountered. I think you'll be able to tell if they are or are not, just from their external appearance.

So, going back to the beginning of this writing, do you like yourself? How do you carry yourself? Are you a slumber of a person or a person of controlled energy? Do you always have a moment for that one person? Are you just to busy to care, wrapped up in yourself and your things?

Likability is really through giving. Giving a kind word. Giving a smile or a nod. Your reservoir of what you have to offer has limitations.

Limitations of time. Limitations of your knowledge resources. Due to these limitations, and many others, you'll need to pick and choose in how you give. Some may get a bit; others may get much more. Giving of your time and investing in those that <u>appreciate</u> your gift of time, can form spectacular relations.

THOMAS MALAGISI

About Thomas Malagisi: Thomas Malagisi, BSME, MBA, has over 30+ years of Manufacturing and Business experience. Thomas enjoys working with teams in many capacities. He thrives on accomplishing that which previously was thought of as something that couldn't be done. He celebrates the achievements of those types of goals. Thomas loves building upon group and individual strength through leaders and teamwork. Thomas utilizes Development-of-Management skills when leading groups and teams. He is also focused on employee retention for companies as well as the growth of individuals. Thomas holds his standards to world-class business skills.

Thomas is a 3x Bestselling Author in the new hit series, *The Principles of David & Goliath.*

Book Series Website: *www.TheBookOfInfluence.com*

TYLER ERICKSON

THE PARADOX OF POPULARITY: A LESSON IN UNCOMFORTABLE HONESTY & GENEROSITY

THIS CHAPTER IS DEDICATED TO MY LATE FATHER, PETER CHARLES ERICKSON,
JUNE 23, 1941 - DECEMBER 11, 2022.
THANKS FOR EVERYTHING, DAD. I WISH I COULD STILL RING YOU TO CHAT AND I'M SO GRATEFUL WE GOT TO SPEND SO MUCH TIME TOGETHER.

Growing up my father guided me. Though he was also my mate, he always emphasized the virtue of facing the consequences of our actions head-on. He used to say, "Uncomfortable honesty for a moment could create trust for a lifetime and prevent a lie from running away and controlling your life. When it comes down to it, you have to like yourself first." It's a principle that has been etched deep into my soul, shaping my understanding of relationships and the concept of likability.

In this chapter, I hope to share this wisdom with you, shedding light on the potential pitfalls of striving for universal popularity (AKA people pleasing). I offer you a counterintuitive proposition: In our quest to be universally liked, we risk losing the genuine connections that lead to sincere likability. Let's explore this paradox together.

The Illusion of Universal Likability: We live in a world that often measures success by popularity and approval from others. However, the pursuit of universal likability is fraught with challenges. Why? Because people are incredibly diverse, with different tastes, interests, and perspectives. What appeals to one may repel another. Striving for universal likability can lead to the dilution of your authenticity. In an attempt to please everyone, you run the risk of becoming a chameleon, changing your colors to match your environment, and reflecting on what others want to see rather than being true to who you are.

Psychologically, people have an innate ability to sense authenticity. We're drawn to those who are genuine, who remain steadfast in their principles even when it goes against the crowd. Authentic people are not afraid to show their vulnerabilities, their passions, and their individuality. This raw, unfiltered honesty is compelling, drawing people in and fostering stronger, more meaningful connections. Conversely, a lack of authenticity can lead to superficial relationships, built on shaky foundations of insincere interactions and fleeting approval.

The Value of Uncomfortable Honesty

The concept of uncomfortable honesty brings me back to my father's wise words: "Face the music." This is about owning up to our mistakes and taking responsibility. In a world where people often deflect blame, individuals who exhibit this trait stand out. It's not an easy road; admitting our errors can be a deeply uncomfortable process. It involves swallowing our pride, acknowledging our shortcomings, and exposing our vulnerabilities.

I remember being 15 years old and I was working at my first full time job as a carpenter. I had made a mistake that could have cost the company a lot of money if I didn't fess up. I was nervous and I could have left it as there were several men working on the job and anyone could have been responsible. Something arose inside me and I knew this was my time to show the boss who I was. I told him what I'd done, with a cracked voice and a tremor in my lip—though I looked him in the eye and apologized.

He stared at me for a few moments and said, "You are going to go a long way in life, boy." And then he helped me fix the problem. It was exactly as it had been explained to me: People actually want you to engage with them, no matter the circumstances. From that day on, I always approached life this way. I have had people try to get me to do things differently and it's never crossed my mind.

The psychological payoff is immense. When we take responsibility for our mistakes, it communicates to others that we value integrity. This trait is highly valued in interpersonal relationships. It shows that we are not afraid of being seen in a less-than-perfect light, that we value truth over facade, growth over comfort. It may be momentarily uncomfortable, but it's a small price to pay for a lifetime of trust.

The Power of Genuine Generosity

Generosity, when genuine and devoid of hidden agendas, is a potent tool for bridging gaps and fostering connections. It is not just about material generosity—giving gifts or lending money—but rather, a generosity of spirit. This involves being generous with our time, understanding, patience, and kindness. This kind of generosity can eliminate unnecessary separation and judgement, as it's an expression of empathy and understanding.

When we offer our time and energy without expecting anything in return, we demonstrate that we value the person and the relationship. We show that we're willing to invest in them, to be present with them, and to support them. This leads to a deeper sense of connection, of feeling seen and appreciated. It's a pathway to genuine presence and connection with others, a key factor in being truly liked.

Actionable Steps: Applying Uncomfortable Honesty and Generosity

Practice Self-Awareness: It's crucial to understand your feelings, values, and desires. By being self-aware, you can communicate your thoughts and emotions honestly and directly. This might mean expressing when you're uncomfortable, admitting when you're wrong, or sharing your feelings even when it's challenging.

You can do this by creating a list of the ways you would like people to be honest with and communicate with you and in any situation. Treat people how you would like to be treated if you crossed a line (i.e. face the music).

Own Your Mistakes: When you make a mistake, don't shy away from it. Instead, embrace it as an opportunity to learn and grow. Apologize sincerely, make amends where necessary, and commit to avoiding the same mistake in the future.

If you make a mistake or a transgression or even disagree with someone, practice telling them as soon as possible. A good practice: If you have a time in your life that is on your mind while reading this, reach out to the person and apologize with sincerity, and remember that forgiveness is an inside job.

Be Consistent: Authenticity and honesty are not one-time acts but habits to cultivate over time. Be consistent in your actions and words. This consistency helps build trust and shows others that you're reliable and true to your word. A good practice for this is to ask yourself, every day, "Was I consistent today?" If the answer is ever no, create a plan on how you can do better tomorrow. If there is ever someone affected by your in consistency, next time you see them, simply say, "Recently, I have been out of character with my actions and I would like to apologize and let you know you can expect better from me in the future, as I'm learning and growing."

Cultivate Empathy: Try to understand others' perspectives and feelings. This empathy can help you communicate more effectively, understand where others are coming from, and respond in a way that respects their feelings and experiences.

I often get asked how to cultivate empathy. There is only one step: Ask questions and listen when it's your turn to respond; ask another question about the person when someone is finished sharing—you will know because they will ask you a question. If you refrain from sharing your point of view or story until asked, you will learn more about someone in 10 minutes than you could even imagine.

Practice Generosity without Expectation: Be generous with your time, resources, and emotional support. However, ensure that your generosity is genuine and not a means to an end. Do not expect anything in return, as true generosity comes from a place of wanting to enrich others' lives, not to gain something for yourself.

Be the Secret Generosity Assassin: Start by leaving a note in a book you are reading for the next person to find. Park further away from the front of a shop in the car park so someone else gets the better spot. These simple things will completely change someone's day and they will never even know someone is looking out for them. This will create a kindness in your heart that is contagious.

Foster Open Communication: Encourage open and honest communication in your relationships. This involves actively listening to others, expressing your thoughts and feelings honestly, and creating a safe space for others to do the same.

If this is something new to you, create a time and a space to do this: Explain to your friend, colleague, or partner what you are learning and ask them to communicate honestly with you. The best way to stay on track is to choose what the outcome of the conversation will be; for example, learn about each other's interests or find out how you can support each other better.

By embracing these practices, we can foster a culture of uncomfortable honesty and genuine generosity, creating deeper, more meaningful relationships. Remember, it's not about being universally liked, but about forming authentic connections with those around us.

In conclusion, the pursuit of universal likability can lead to a watered-down version of ourselves. Instead, by embracing the lessons of uncomfortable honesty and genuine generosity that my father instilled in me, we can foster genuine connections that are built on trust and mutual respect—a true path to sincere likability.

TYLER ERICKSON

About Tyler Erickson: Meet Tyler Erickson, the Managing Director at The Erickson Coaching Company, a business coaching and consulting firm that has a mission to impact ten thousand businesses in the next 5 years. With a diverse background in mining and resources, hospitality management, and frail-aged nursing, Tyler brings unique experience and that help business owners and their teams thrive.

Thanks to his successful work in various industries, world travel, and solid country upbringing, Tyler is equipped to help businesses solve complex problems and tackle challenges head-on.

At Erickson Coaching Company, applying expertise to empower businesses helping them reach their goals and achieve their full potential. As an accomplished business coach, Tyler has logged over 4000+ hours of coaching clients and facilitating sessions. He has helped entrepreneurs and small business owners develop meaningful strategies and implement growth plans, resulting in more successful and fulfilling businesses. His expertise is further reinforced by his studies in business pursuing an MBA.

In addition to being an accomplished business coach, Tyler is also an author, sharing his knowledge and expertise on leadership, entrepreneurship, and business strategy. He is keenly aware of the challenges that business owners face, and his writings offer valuable insights and practical

Author's Website: *www.EricksonTraining.com.au*

Book Series Website: *www.TheBookOfInfluence.com*

WILLIAM GOOD

INTENTION FOR ATTENTION

"There is one all-important law of human conduct... The law is this: Always make the other person feel important."
~ **Dale Carnegie**

This is an important topic. I mean, who doesn't want to be liked? So, let me suggest you pay attention here—because I'm a pro. You see, I've masterfully failed this lesson enough times to know what I'm talking about.

How about this, for example: In my early months as a second career pastor, I was invited to a church choir party. Held in the luxuriantly landscaped back yard of one of the choristers, it was quite the affair. There was music and candle-lit dining tables. Wine was abundant. Conversation flowed. Laughter abounded. It was a perfectly elegant evening of fellowship, all centering around several serving tables overflowing with a multitude of culinary delights.

As I moved through the crowd with my second glass of wine in hand, I stopped to survey the offerings at one of the tables—only to be confronted by a tall, statuesque, red-headed woman who I recognized as new to the church. When she looked at her pastor expectantly, I said in my finely tuned "I've known you forever" people-pleaser voice, "Well, hi! How are you this evening?"

This was met with a lengthy and uncomfortable silence accompanied by a hard stare; both broken only when she responded, "You have no idea who the heck I am, do you?" Called out in such spectacular style, I could barely stammer out the embarrassed truth, "Umm. . . Uhh. . . No. I'm sorry. I don't." At this point, she broke into raucous peals of laughter, wrapped her arms around me, and gave me a big hug; she was delighted by her ability to completely unhorse her pastor. Having been forgiven so obviously and extravagantly, I never again forgot the name of Mary Ann Fossen.

And I never forgot the uncomfortable lesson she taught me: In this age marked by superficial transactions, we all want to be *recognized;* we're all dying to be *known.* Authentic acknowledgement confers real significance—and *everybody* likes to feel significant. If we wish to be liked ourselves, we would do well to remember that.

Part Two of Dale Carnegie's famous book, *How to Win Friends and Influence People,* is ambitiously titled, "Six Ways to Make People Like You." Sounds easy enough, doesn't it? In Transformational Development circles, the buzzword is "enrollment." And the oft-repeated formula goes like this: "Life is an enrollment game. You're either enrolling someone in your life, or they're enrolling you in theirs." Simple, no? Then why are human relations so complicated?

The book was written in 1936, so predictably some of his illustrations seem a bit antiquated and unsophisticated to ears accustomed to the shrill realities of life in 2023. But one of the great truths of the human experience is that, although styles and circumstances may change, human emotional responses do not.

That's why we still find relevance in the 3,000-year-old prayers in the book of Psalms—while they may not describe a life that we know, they respond to the pain and the blessing of that life in ways that are immediately recognizable in ours.

What Carnegie says may *sound* a little old-fashioned, but what he *observes* about human desires and behavior is as true and vital today as it was in the days when the Hindenburg flew, Jesse Owens conquered the Berlin Olympics, and *Gone With the Wind* was the bestselling American novel.

So here (perhaps for your next tattoo?) are his "Six Ways to Make People Like You:"

1. Become genuinely interested in other people.
2. Smile.
3. Remember that a person's name is to that person the sweetest and most important sound in any language.
4. Be a good listener. Encourage others to talk about themselves.
5. Talk in terms of the other person's interests.
6. Make the other person feel important—and do it sincerely.

As simple and practical as these may seem, Carnegie's unpacking of them is worthwhile. The stories may be from yesterday, but the truths are for today. Together, the lit above serves as a sort of formula for creating what we are calling here, "The Likability Factor." And the last item on the list serves as the sum of the other five: Make the other person feel important.

Have you ever found yourself in the company of someone who has the gift of focusing so intently on you that—in that moment—you feel as if you're the only person in the room? Or, at least, they make you feel like only one that matters to her or him? If you have, you know what a rich experience it is. The sense of it is captured in the scene in the original *West Side Story* play where Maria and Tony's eyes first meet at the dance. The room swirls and fades, all the other dancers become a misty blur, and only the two soon-to-be lovers are in focus. It's as if they're the only ones there who matter. That's what the experience feels like.

In Phoenix, where I lived a few years back, there lived a hugely successful and well-known real estate and development magnate named Rusty Lyons. I was also in that industry at the time; but Rusty travelled in much more elevated business and social circles than I did. However, I was once introduced to him by a mutual friend at some function at which we both found ourselves.

As we shook hands, he looked me directly in the eyes and then held his gaze. I don't recall much of what we talked about other than the entire conversation of perhaps three minutes revolved around Rusty asking me questions about myself and my business. In those minutes, his attention never faltered or varied. I felt deeply acknowledged and important. And when we parted, it was as if I was left standing in some sort of vacuum. I wanted him to come back. I wanted more of him.

And I implicitly understood how he had become as successful as he had! He had mastered the fine and all-too-rare art of making others feel important!

You see, it's not what we *do* for others that creates real relationship. It's how we *are* with them. It's our way *of being*. If we do a lot of things for people, we are appreciated because we are useful. However, if we are genuinely committed to knowing others in the fullness of their human-ness, we are liked (perhaps even loved) because we are compelling.

So, as we consider our "likability factor," we are called to some critical reflection: What are our *ways of being* evoking from those with whom we interact? How are we showing up in their lives? Are we coming to them from our head or from our heart? There's a world of difference between the two. As Carnegie perceptively observes: "You can make more friends in two months by becoming interested in people than you can in two years by trying to get people interested in you."

The first and most important step in increasing your "likability factor" is setting *intention* to pay *attention*—sincerely, not strategically. Turn your people-pleaser off. It's not about you; it's about them.

This points us toward cultivating a sense of genuine interest in others. Greet the people you meet with humble curiosity and listen to them attentively. Welcome them with a smile on your lips and warmth in your voice when you're introduced. Focus on remembering their names—our names set us apart, and it's a fact of our human-ness that theirs is the only one they really care about, anyway. Then—and, most importantly—*listen*. Listen intently to their stories. They won't ever hear yours if you haven't first shown an interest in theirs.

Observant listening is fertile ground for raising questions; this is where paying attention pays off. Ask yourself: Why are these stories important to them? And what do they reveal about them? These questions signal your recognition of them as individuals and your interest in their particularity. They provide the entry point to the path to authentic connection. They light the way to the road to being liked and creating a relationship.

Setting intention to pay attention is key to increasing your "likability factor." You see, nobody cares how much you know until they know how much you care.

Trust me in this. Mary Ann Fossen told me so.

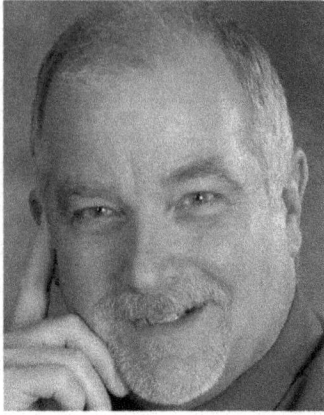

WILLIAM GOOD

About William Good: Bill is passionately committed to bringing together the message of Jesus Christ with the methods and vision of Transformational Leadership. In his life, his teaching, his coaching, and his writing, his deepest desire is to bring about world change through interpersonal reconciliation and relationship recovery.

Bill holds a Master's in Divinity degree from Fuller Theological Seminary and recently retired as Pastor at Fountain Hills Presbyterian Church. He teaches at Grand Canyon University, guiding college students to develop their own worldviews and purpose.

His online ministry features devotionals and virtual biblical and spiritual curricula, which can be found on the Uncommon Community Facebook page. He is also CEO and Senior Counselor of Path to Peace, a ministry providing conciliation services to individuals and organizations seeking to overcome trauma and find reconciliation.

Bill holds advanced certifications in Christian Reconciliation and Peacemaking from IC Peace, and is a graduate of the NextLevel Masters in Leadership program.

He is currently engaged in writing two books for publication, *Between Sundays*, a practical study of Jesus' reconciliation ministry, and *From Here to There*, a collection of autobiographical essays on spiritual development. He'd love to hear from you at: *facebook.com/uncommoncommunity419* or via email at *Uncommoncommunity@gmail.com.*

Author's Website: *www.facebook.com/UncommonCommunity419*
Book Series Website: *www.TheBookOfInfluence.com*

WILLIAM BLAKE

UNLOCK THE POWER IN LISTENING: DISCOVERY

"Sometimes it's best to stay quiet. The silence can speak volumes without ever saying a word."

~ **Unknown**

There is an irrefutable power in the world most tend not to tap into. The ability to have this is important as it's part of every sound, every vibration, and every movement we take as humans. But because people aren't thinking about it, it's not practiced. What is this power? At the peak, this is the power of listening. I know from experience it's felt like I've been looking through a keyhole my entire life, only glimpsing what understanding was out there. After learning how to listen, I unlocked the door, showing me way more than I thought possible. Communication in my relationships and businesses have multiplied in their results and resolve. I love what it's done for me, and that's why I share this with you. In the first book of this series, I talked about the first of four different skills called preparation. When it came down to it, preparation means the need to be humble. Being humble in this context isn't how Google defines it as. It is to realize each of us doesn't have all the answers and we're willing to be a life-time student. Once we are conscious of that, we can be present and begin applying the second skill in unlocking the power of listening.

Do this exercise with me. Stop reading for a moment, grab your phone and open your stopwatch app. You are going to record yourself three different times. Be ready with quick fingers as some of these times will be less than a second. For the first one, I want you to time yourself counting to five as quickly as you can. Ready, GO!

Write down that number and reset your stopwatch for the second time. Once that's done, I want you to time yourself saying the first 5 letters of the alphabet. Again, do this as fast as you can. "A, B, C, D, E." Go! Once you have that and write it down, reset for the third time. On this one, we're going to alternate back and forth between the numbers and letters. For example, you'll time yourself saying, "1A, 2B, 3C, 4D, 5E." Once you have that, write it next to the other two numbers.

Here is where the magic happens. Take both the first and second times and add them up. Now take the third time and compare it to the combined one. Which one is the faster time? If you're like most people, the combined one will be faster (unless you've practiced saying alternating pieces before, in which case, pretend your third is slower). This means the sum of two separate tasks are shorter than the third time where we alternated between them.

Gary Keller did this activity in his book, *The One Thing*, summarizing that the best way to get tasks done is to focus on one, then do the other, rather than trying to "multitask." Great concept if you want to dig deeper in his book—but how does this apply to listening? It applies a great deal as it pertains to the second skill, called *discovery*.

Ask yourself this question: "While talking with someone, how often do I think about what to say next?" If you're like most people, that's all the time! Whether wanting to impress others or share their own thoughts, people's minds will focus more on what they NEED to say next rather than taking in what's being said.

I made this mistake several years back when I met one of my favorite mentors, Evan Carmichael. He was going around to all the major cities and one of them was right next to where I lived. I grabbed tickets for my wife and I and we went to his event. Being super early, I got to talk with

Evan before the meeting started. I wanted to impress him so much and my mind was constantly thinking about what to say next. Rather than listening to him, I felt the need to have "interesting" things to say. In the end, all his experience and advice went in one ear and out the other. My intention to have him "like me" backfired with him thinking I was just another fan.

Similar with Evan, we need to dial down our inner speaker and dial into our inner listener. The ability to focus on the speaker is rare. But when done correctly, it can make the experience 100 times better. This is what the skill of discovery is about.

Discovery breaks into two parts:

1. Being Quiet
2. Observing

I'm sure all of us know what it means to be quiet and to observe someone. But let me give you an example that will show you how much deeper your understanding of this can go.

When a college student has a massive research paper for a class, where do they go to find information? The library or internet. They pick a topic beforehand and begin going through the search engine to find what they want. Loads of information comes up. As they continue, each search makes the student more precise. Their searches bring in more specific knowledge and, by the end, they have the paper they want. The paper doesn't contain everything they learned, as that wouldn't make a great paper. But because they went through so much information, they used their new perspective and condensed it down into the most crucial points.

Discovery in your conversations is like a research paper. If you want the best result, you gather as much information as possible, weed out the non-essentials, and you're left with the golden nuggets. What are those golden nuggets? They are the key words you hear from the person you're talking to. You get them from listening to what they say.

First, gather all the information you can. Second, brush off the fluff to get closer to the root. And third, which most people miss, read in-between the lines (which I'll talk more about in a bit). Those three together can help you discover more about an individual.

It makes sense how being quiet helps in this. When we're quiet, the other person has an opportunity to share what they have. It gives them the chance to get an emotional breath. Just like how we breathe for our mind and heart to get oxygen, we also need emotional breaths. And sometimes, with the stresses, anxieties, and challenges, we don't get the breath we desire.

Being quiet lets the other take that emotional breath. I can't tell you how many times I've stood there listening to someone, not saying a word, and let the person talk for 45 minutes straight where afterwards they thanked me for just "listening." When looking to fix someone's problem, sometimes silence is the best healer. And when it comes to the possibility of them liking you more, silence can increase the result.

What if being quiet isn't enough? What if they need something more? That is where observing can come in. Observing takes listening to new levels. There are three levels you can use to go past normal observations that'll help with mastering listening. First, listen with your ears. What we've gone over so far expresses this. Second, listen with your eyes. This is watching what they say, how they say it, and their body language.

A study was done where they found how much information was taken in based on a few factors. It shares that 7% of what people take in is from our words, 38% is from our tone of voice, and 55% is from our body language. Imagine—most people only listen to 45% of what's being said from your voice and words. That's less than half. Think how much more you can discover by also reading their body language. People lie all the time through their words, but it's difficult to lie through your body language.

The third level is listening through your mind. This is where your "gut" feelings and intuition come into play. Most would call this "reading in-between the lines." These are the unspoken words. The words that could be said but, because of judgement, being scared, or not knowing it themselves, these words remain unsaid. The way to reach this level is through experience. As you adapt yourself to listening and gain more experience in multiple encounters, you'll begin to have an intuitive mind that'll lead you to hidden information.

Observing is powerful. The ability to stay quiet and observe is one skill set everyone needs in their arsenal. Remember to treat conversations like a research paper: Take in as much information you can. Listen past the fluff and get to the core. Listening isn't only for solving problems. If you want more people to like you, try being quiet and observing. Without saying a word, you can impact someone's life.

We've gone through two of the four skills now: preparation and discovery. The third skill needed to unlock the power of listening is what I call "illuminate." This is where you take what you learned and refine it through the mastery of questioning. I can't wait so I'll see you over in the next chapter in volume three of "The Book of Influence" series.

WILLIAM BLAKE

About William Blake: William is a speaker and motivator. He focuses on the skill sets of learning, listening, and observing to help people access new avenues of success and solutions. What might seem like regular everyday skills that most overlook, William teaches people how to find creative ways of accessing those skills.

William Blake is a stalwart professional in the world of organization, strategy, and methods. Being diagnosed with Dyslexia at a young age and struggling with reading and speaking, William is an example that through perseverance, any challenge can become a superpower.

William spearheads a dynamic coaching and speaking venture, empowering dyslexics to harness their unique strengths and embrace a world of boundless possibilities. He is also one of the chapter team leaders and corporate associates at Champion Circle Networking Association founded by Speaker Jon Kovach Jr.

From speaking to youth to being a camp counselor at Idaho Diabetes Youth Programs, William loves volunteering and helping children and teens believe in themselves and their unlimited potential. And of most importance to William is his love for his family. With his wife, he is dedicated to raising his daughters in a world of greatness, happiness, and unlimited belief.

Author's website: *www.WilliamBlakeLight.com*

Book Series Website: *www.TheBookOfInfluence.com*

GRAB YOUR COPY OF DALE CARNEGIE'S
CLASSIC FROM 1936 HOW TO WIN FRIENDS AND
INFLUENCE PEOPLE!

HABITUDE WARRIOR & INTEGRITY PUBLISHING EDITORIAL TEAM

Habitude Warrior International and Integrity Publishing take great pride in our editorial team who put their sweat, tears, and heart into each and every project and national bestseller! Thank you team!

JON KOVACH JR.
Team Manager

Jon Kovach Jr. strives to assist every author and every team member in the process of self-development for ultimate success.

PAT MINTON
VP of Operations

Pat Minton has been with the Habitude Warrior International team for over 20 years getting her start with Brian Tracy & Erik Swanson.

JILLIAN KOVACH
Editorial Manager

Jillian is a vital team member of Habitude Warrior & Integrity Publishing bringing her expertise managing our Editorial Department.

FATIMA HURD
Editorial Team & Photographer

Fatima is our Professional Photographer for Habitude Warrior as well as one of our members on the Proofing Department team.

LAUREN COBB
Editorial Team Member

Lauren Cobb is part of our Proofing Department for Habitude Warrior & Integrity Publishing as well as one of our authors.

To inquire about joining our team please send us an email to Team@HabitudeWarrior.com

THE BOOK OF INFLUENCE